C0-ATN-581

MASSACRE

A Da Capo Press Reprint Series

CIVIL LIBERTIES IN AMERICAN HISTORY

GENERAL EDITOR: LEONARD W. LEVY

Claremont Graduate School

MASSACRE

A Survey of Today's American Indian

By Robert Gessner

DA CAPO PRESS • NEW YORK • 1972

Library of Congress Cataloging in Publication Data

Gessner, Robert, 1907-1968.
  Massacre; a survey of today's American Indian.

  (Civil liberties in American history)
  1. Indians, Treatment of—U.S. 2. Indians of
North America—Government relations—1869-1934.
I. Title. II. Series.
E93.G39   1972   970.5   72-38831
  ISBN 0-306-70445-5

This Da Capo Press edition of *Massacre* is an unabridged
republication of the first edition published in New York
in 1931. It is reprinted by special arrangement with
Holt, Rinehart and Winston, Inc.

Copyright, 1931, by Robert Gessner; copyright renewed, 1959,
by Robert Gessner

Published by Da Capo Press, Inc.
A Subsidiary of Plenum Publishing Corporation
227 West 17th Street, New York, N.Y. 10011

All Rights Reserved

Manufactured in the United States of America

MASSACRE

DECORATIONS BY LOIS HARTZELL

JONATHAN CAPE AND HARRISON SMITH, INCORPORATED,
139 EAST 46th STREET, NEW YORK, N. Y. AND 91 WELLINGTON
STREET, WEST, TORONTO, CANADA; JONATHAN CAPE, LTD.,
30 BEDFORD SQUARE, LONDON, W. C. 1, ENGLAND

A CHIPPEWA AND HIS PERMANENT HOME

MASSACRE

A SURVEY OF TODAY'S AMERICAN INDIAN

BY

ROBERT GESSNER

NEW YORK

JONATHAN CAPE AND HARRISON SMITH

0751902   99750

COPYRIGHT, 1931, BY
ROBERT GESSNER

FIRST PUBLISHED, 1931

PRINTED IN THE UNITED STATES OF AMERICA

DEDICATED

To the first Congress that will eradicate
what Lincoln seventy years ago called
"an accursed system."

"Look upon your hands! They are stained
with the blood of your relations."

BENJAMIN FRANKLIN

CONTENTS

The Case of the Sioux

I	INJUNS!	3
II	BLACK HILLS — BAD LANDS	11
III	THE LIVING SIOUX	17
IV	BRANDED	24
V	THE CASE OF THE SIOUX	29
VI	THE PINE RIDGE RODEO	44

Propaganda

VII	LO! THE WEALTHY INDIAN	63
VIII	VANISHING AMERICANS	77
IX	"GOD'S IN HIS HEAVEN —"	85

Schools

X	FLOGGING CHILDREN	105
XI	WHY SUCH TALES CAN BE TOLD	130
XII	TRUTH IS FACT	139
XIII	KIDNAPPING CHILDREN FOR EPIDEMICS	159
XIV	CHILD LABOR	175
XV	ENVOY: BIRD'S–EYE PICTURES	187

Health

XVI	YOU KILL US FOR YOUR SPORT	197
XVII	"HEAP BIG WIND — NO RAIN"	217

0751902   99750

XVIII "HEALTH THAT SNUFFS THE MORNING AIR—"   231
XIX MIDWIVES, MOTHERS, AND PROSTITUTES   241
XX THE SILENT TOMAHAWK   255

Property

XXI THEY ROB US YET   265
XXII CHARGE IT TO THE INDIANS   279
XXIII THE PUEBLOS HOLD THE BAG   289
XXIV CHEATING INDIANS AND THE PUBLIC   309
XXV MEN OF BENEFICENT SEED   324
XXVI THE KLAMATH DISGRACE   339

Claims

XXVII YOU REMEMBER US NOT   351
XXVIII STILL FORGOTTEN   364
XXIX SCRAPS OF PAPER   374
XXX ROBBING THE ROBBED   385
XXXI PASSING THE BUCK   391

Conclusion

XXXII WHAT IS THE SOLUTION?   405
XXXIII MASSACRE   414

ILLUSTRATIONS

A CHIPPEWA AND HIS PERMANENT HOME *Frontispiece*

BLACK HILLS *Facing Page* 12

BAD LANDS 12

HORSE MEAT DRYING IN THE SUN 68

WAITING THEIR TURN 68

JOHN SITTING BULL 202

BLACK FROM EATING HORSE MEAT 202

DIRT FLOOR, DIRT ROOF, NO WINDOWS 286

AN INTERIOR — ABOVE THE AVERAGE 286

A TRACHOMA AFFLICTED SCHOOL BOY 388

FARM LAND BOUGHT BY A BENEVOLENT
GUARDIAN 388

I
THE CASE OF THE SIOUX

I

INJUNS!

1

WHEN Spring comes to Ann Arbor there is little you can do other than confess her presence and find yourself captivated.

The warm night air, coming through open windows, bore the odors of innumerable buds. I stirred restlessly as I sat reading in the Michigan Union. It was examination time in the University, and the thought came to me that hundreds of students were squirming nervously in their chairs, while reading romantic poets like Chrétien de Troyes, Schiller, or Tennyson. The spring air played with the fancy, and I imagined thousands of students in the schools and colleges spread throughout America, throughout France and Germany, throughout all the civilized countries of the earth, were reading Tennyson, Chrétien de Troyes, Schiller. Thousands were reading ancient stories rewoven, thread-worn mythologies vainly patched. Musty romances scented with the latest perfume.

The idea suddenly became impregnated with vitality. I sat upright in my chair. *Romances.* It was that which had saturated the evening air, and made me stir as if for something missing. But now I had it in my grasp; I knew what was wanted: Fresh, invigorating romances. Tales that throbbed with new, stark beauty! An undiscovered literature!

I was outside, walking down streets shaded with branches that softened the twilight as it lingered. And as I walked in that Ann Arbor dusk there came to me a strange lullaby, sung in some foreign tongue. It was a low, luring melody with a rhythm of water sprays rising above seashore rocks. Then I saw an unusual sight. On the porch of a Colonial house sat an aged man, with a large slouch hat pulled down toward his nose, and his hands were crossed before him on the head of a wrinkled cane. He was Dr. Hinsdale, the Indian ethnologist at the University Museum. He sat quietly in his chair, listening. To his left, and standing serenely above him, was his wife. She stood with her arms severely crossed beneath her breast, and as she sang she swayed from side to side in rhythm with the lullaby. For many minutes I stood motionless, a witness to that eerie spectacle. I turned away for fear if I stayed longer the spell would fade. As I walked softly along the shaded sidewalk my heels made a faint staccato obligato to the lullaby.

I had never heard that song before and yet I knew

instinctively it was an Indian lullaby. There lay my un-
written romances — my well of literature, undiscovered,
undefiled.

2

During the following week I acquainted myself with the
few books of Indian mythology, which I rightly surmised
had drawn but a few bucketfuls from the well. I began to
visualize the landscape which needed reclaiming. The
Indians' bible was composed of verbal scriptures, unwrit-
ten; they have been passed from the lips of fathers for centuries. Those beautiful legends, which have flowered in
the living minds of countless Indians, were now being
drowned in oblivion; the old brave, the last of the raw,
full-blooded Indian, was dying fast and the young buck
was too Americanized to listen to his father's wandering
tattles.

Greece had a fable of her own, Rome her history, and
the Norse their tales; but the Indian had all of these. All
— yet he was being Caucasianized. He was sinking into
darkness, and his history was being lost to the world forever. With the passing of the living, full-blooded Indian
there was passing the esthetic, spirit Indian who lived only
in the myths, histories, dances, and customs of his ancestors.

A comparable case would arise if suddenly a hundred
million warriors from Mars landed on our planet, and
with the use of poisonous gases wiped out all human life
in a brief hour. If our literatures, histories, and religions
were only verbal, then would be lost forever our beautiful
stories of Moses and his faithful flock wandering through

the deserts in search of the Promised Land. Lost forever
would be our stories of Christ and his band of faith-
fuls; lost would be the stories of Socrates and his sym-
posiums; of our Alexanders, of our Charlemagnes, of our
Cromwells, of our revolutions, and of all the valor and
virtue that have thrived in this world. Lost forever.

The same was happening to the Indian, whose extermination and assimilation, however, has become painfully
longer. I realized I must lose no time in my hunting of
old Indian braves, for with the death of one of those an-
cients only his ghost would know how many beautiful
legends died with him.

I first thought of the Sioux, for they were the last in the
Northwest to crumble beneath the onrushing waves of white
emigrants. Nicolet, the French explorer, said the Sioux were
the finest type of wild man he had ever seen. Old traders
among the Sissetons said it was the boast of those Sioux that
they had never taken the life of a white man. I thought there
would be some old ones among them who still wore the
blanket in spirit if not about their shoulders.

I then read deeply of the Sioux, how they loved the
Black Hills not only as their home where their ancestral
bones have slept for centuries, but as the home of their
Great Spirit. As I read I thrilled with the romances of the
Indian Wars, with what Elizabeth Bacon Custer, Long
Hair's wife, said of the chiefs' determination to fight for
their deeply cherished Black Hills, which had been guaranteed them in the Treaty of 1868. The great Indian fighter
told his wife "the Government must keep its promises to
the Indians." Years later she wrote: "There was a time

after the battle of the Little Big Horn when I could not
have said this, but as the years have passed I have become
convinced that the Indians were deeply wronged."

I read in John Neihardt's *Song of the Indian Wars* how
the wildfire rumors of free gold in plenty " from the grass-
roots down " sent white men scurrying into the sacred
Black Hills:

> . . . loud Cheyenne
> Became a tail-race running mules and men
> Hell-bent for Eldorado. Yankton vied
> With Sidney in the combing of the tide
> For costly wreckage. Giddily it swirled
> Where Custer City shouted to the world
> And Deadwood was a howl, and Nigger Hill
> A cry from Pisgah.
> . . . and the Sioux would hold
> A little paper, dirtied with a lie . . .

I also read histories in my eagerness to know the Sioux,
before setting out to interview them in the field. I read how
the Sioux, being wards of the Nation and consequently
under the guardianship of the Indian Bureau, were five
times promised land " as long as water runs and grass
grows." Each time they were ordered to " move on." There
was no place for them to go; no place where the white man
wanted them except the Bad Lands, where they could go
and rot and be forgotten. One chief calmly said: " I have
been moved five times. Why don't you put the Indians on
wheels so you can run them around more easily? " I read
how many fled to Canada, where their women had " time to
raise their children."

Custer, the hero of every boy, told a New York *Herald*

reporter that " the Indians have a strong attachment for the lands containing the bones of their ancestors and dislike to leave it. Love of country is almost a religion with them. It is not the value of the land they consider, but there is a strong local attachment that the white man does not feel and consequently does not respect."

I read how the Indians helplessly starved, as their buffalo disappeared like summer clouds. In three years white men had mercilessly slaughtered five million buffalo in defiance of treaties, which stipulated Whites were not allowed in Indian territory without permission of the Indians.

How I read over and over those battles in which they took their " last stand " for the land they loved, the snow-capped Big Horn Range. They had been pushed back — pushed from their precious Black Hills; there had been the eternal crowding of Whites. They had been hunted as villainous outlaws. Frenzied, desperate — faced with the doom of their vanishing race — they fought with courage, for they were strong in death. Through clouds of dust and heavy rolling smoke of black powder, they caught glimpses of white soldiers only to charge recklessly, senselessly into them with their bows and arrows. It was a final, brave gesture of a doomed people. If they must die they would die fighting, with their twilight falling. Thus was the Sioux's last desperate, hopeless stand, the battle of the Little Big Horn.

Broken, they were herded on reservations like droves of cattle, to live a death-in-life existence. I read the report of one commissioner: " They will run like chickens to gather the offal from the slop buckets that are carried

from the garrison kitchens; while they pass a pile of corn
and hundreds of loose cattle without touching a thing,
except when told they may gather up the grains of corn
from the ground where the rats in their depredations have
let it fall from the sacks." Such was the plight of the proud
Sioux, who, a few years back, were running down buffalo
on fleet ponies. Many had served as scouts for the Government against hostile tribes, but all were treated alike. They
had no " fixed reservations " so that their boundaries were
never clearly defined nor enforced. They virtually lived
in a prison, for none could leave the reservations without
a permit from an agent. The cattle that were offered for
meat were undersized, underfed, and many were diseased.
The flour was dark, the pork rotten. Starving, they ate
ponies, wolves, dogs, anything. I read how an Army officer
once told a chief he would try to get him a new agent, but
the chief replied: " We do not want a new agent. Agents
come here poor and get rich in a few years. If a new one
comes we will have to make him rich also." Custer, a true
friend of the red man, said of the reservations the same
as he had previously of the treaties: " The success of the
reservation system depends on the Government keeping its
promises."

It was at that time when Sitting Bull made his famous
answer: " Tell them at Washington if they have one man
who speaks the truth to send him to me, and I will listen
to what he has to say."

Betrayed by " friends " — cheated and tricked by officials and citizens alike — even massacred by Whites —
while starving most of the time — there is not a group of

human beings that have had a more piteous record than
the Sioux.

But all this was history. Nothing more than sad, dead
history. In 1890 the last flame of Indian resistance on the
plains flickered into ashes with the others. For forty years
and over Indians have ceased being a dangerous problem.
Some tribes have been under Government supervision for
almost a century. I had heard of their fabulous wealth;
one Indian had given over half a million to a missionary
cause and an equal sum to his wife. This is the day of our
Lindberghs, of our Marconis — this is the Twentieth Century, and Indians today are not a dangerous problem, so I
thought.

In the full bloom of summer I set out to hunt old Sioux
braves. Unattached, unsolicited, unsubsidized I set out —
a strict amateur in search of unrecorded beauty.

It was the sons of Sitting Bull I sought. The sons of Red
Cloud, Crazy Horse, Spotted Tail, Rain-in-the-Face, American Horse, Touch-the-Cloud, and Gall. I sought stories
from their lips, legends of their coups, of their games, of
their sacred dances. I sought the songs of their fathers,
like the song of the Sioux warrior:

> I was born a soldier.
> I have lived thus long.
> In despite of all, I have lived thus long.

I journeyed toward the Black Hills, toward the sacred,
personal home of the Great Spirit, with His well of literature, undiscovered, undefiled.

II

BLACK HILLS — BAD LANDS

1

LONGFELLOW had his Hiawatha many moons in crossing " the rushing Esconaba " — " the mighty Mississippi " — to " the Mountains of the Prairie," and yet " at each stride a mile he measured."

In journeying to the Black Hills one spends much time surveying the richness of Michigan, Wisconsin, Minnesota, and the Dakota farming lands. One is astonished at the wealth of the soil. The long plains roll on endlessly, dotted with neat farm buildings and filled with crops of wheat, corn, alfalfa, barley, rye, and vegetables — food for a million mouths. Crops that feed nations in the far corners of continents. Herds of cattle ever grazing, to be eaten in far away Finland.

Rising slowly, almost timidly, out of the prairies are the foothills of the Black Hills. They tease you for miles, play with your car as they run to the edge of the road, and then skip away. They are a tantalizing introduction to " the Mountains of the Prairie." Finally, you dodge them, round a sudden curve, and the black majesties of the Sioux lie before you.

These, then, are the Black Hills. These many dark ripples crowding one another like thick wind ruffles on a pond. Sleeping in the legends of their only lovers, in Indian lore as old as their deep ravines, lie these Black Hills. They are studded with the dark trunks of hemlock and with clusters of green pine. Silver streams sing down sharp hill-sides of rock. Sylvan lakes gather between mountains, at the foot of forests from which antelope, elk, and bison come to quench their thirst. Fish sport the streams and lakes — game for a President. Nature could not keep her freaks out of such handiwork, and so unearthed wind caves and frozen trees called petrified.

In Rapid City, the bustling, modern, key-town of that country, I found an old settler camped on a back street.

" Where are the Indians? " He slowly repeated my question, moving his tobacco-colored beard as he yawled. " There's none a-livin' in the Hills. The're down in the Bad Land country."

" I know," I answered, impatiently, " that's old history, fifty years dead. I mean today — now."

He merely spat brown juice into the dust, contemptuous of my impatience. " Times don't change," he yawled. " They're still a-livin' in the Bad Country. They weren't allowed to move back here, to land still theirs by treaty rights."

It was then that I heard of the fabulous wealth the Black Hills have been yearly producing for the Whites. Truth-

BAD LANDS

BLACK HILLS—

fully are they called the richest hundred square miles on the North American continent. They have laid $270,000,-000 worth of gold into the laps of prospectors. One mine alone has produced $200,000,000 of the purest golden fleece. The rarest minerals, over seventy of them — gold, tungsten, radium, zinc, quartz, mica, have been found there. Also virgin hardwood forests and rare game. Nothing has been wasted in the Black Hills; the Whites have taken all.

As I left the old settler his final words burned themselves into my memory.

"And the Government ain't paid them Indians yet for these Black Hills."

2

Custer described the Bad Lands as country with huge thimbles placed upon it, so frequent and ugly are the eruptions. Old timers say a jack-rabbit can't live on it, not to mention Indians.

One Government official declared that "There is at least 100,000 acres of land down there you would not take. I don't know what it is good for, and I don't believe you will find the like of it anywhere in the United States."

The road out of Hot Springs, South Dakota, for the Pine Ridge Indian Reservation winds like a buffalo trail. It is just a dirt road on some forgotten grass. No shoulders, no ditches — just a road. No fences, no telegraph poles — just forgotten grass.

There are no Indian farms on Pine Ridge worth mentioning. The dry, empty prairies are in sharp contrast to the fertile, well-tilled acres in the northern portion of the state, where white farmers prosper. The dry creek bottoms on the reservation afford no watering for cattle. The land is as empty of herds as the upper sections are filled with them.

Sad, dismal land. Longfellow's second-hand description serves well:

> Lurid seemed the sky above him,
> Lurid seemed the earth beneath him,
> Hot and close the air around him,
> Filled with smoke and fiery vapors,
> As of burning woods and prairies.

So Hiawatha also suffered.

3

" An' you want to see some old buck to tell you stories."

I nodded to the Indian trader, who repeated my question.

" Wall, up on the hill is ol' John Sitting Bull, son of the Sitting Bull who got Custer."

" Sitting Bull's son around here? " I was surprised.

" Sure, why not? Up on the hill in a tent."

I made my way along a sluggish, muddy creek littered with all sorts of rubbish — inner tubes, tin cans, and the skulls of dead horses. At the foot of a path I saw an old Indian woman scooping up the greenish looking water in a wooden bucket.

She was John Sitting Bull's woman and led me up a path to his tent. When I offered to carry her bucket she looked at me with an expression of questioning wonder. At the tent she set the bucket down, took a dipper, and drank several cupfuls, as did some ill-clothed children who were romping about the tent.

"You get sick much?" I asked. She shrugged her shoulders, more hopelessly than meaningless.

"The children either?" Another shrug. This surprised me.

"Then you're inoculated for typhoid," I stated. But she did not understand. I tried to explain simply, with illustrative gestures, but the expression on her face told me she did not understand.

Inside the tent sat John Sitting Bull. His legs were crossed in the old Indian fashion, and his long, leather fingers were fumbling in the sand before him. He did not look up as I entered, but continued to draw circles in the sand. Finally, he raised his head.

His face looked tired. As if it had borne the burden of his people's suffering. It appeared not so much worn by time, as by an inarticulate grief which furrowed the wrinkles more deeply, and stamped the face with a stolid, stoic pang.

I wetted my lips and began to speak: "In the town they told me I would find you here, and that you are John Sitting Bull. I am a teacher; I have come many miles over your monotonous prairies to see you and your people, to hear you talk about the old times. I have traveled far to come here and listen. Please tell me of your father, Chief Sitting Bull."

He made no answer. The circles in the sand curled deftly beneath his forefinger. I stirred uneasily, and tried again: "I want to know of the old faith, of what your grandmother told you about the Great Spirit living in the Black Hills."

Still he made no answer. The circles in the sand grew smaller until they finally ceased to appear. John Sitting Bull shook his head slowly, grunting as he did so.

His woman appeared in the door of the tent, and plucked my sleeve. " He no speak," she said, simply, putting her fingers to her ear and mouth. " Deaf and dumb."

I looked at the son of Sitting Bull. I looked at his ragged trousers, patched like a crazy quilt. At his thin, faded blouse. At his black, pagan hair, braided like a woman's, and at his face.

Slowly I arose and left the tent.

Outside I saw a dark red meat stretched between two poles. It apparently was drying in the sun. Long yellow strips, like yards of glue, were wound around the poles.

" Beef? " I asked the Indian woman, pointing to the meat. She shook her head and nodded toward two or three scarecrow horses grazing near-by.

" Horse meat? "

Her nod was as if she asked, " Why not? "

" But that," I insisted, pointing to the yards and yards of thin glue.

" Guts," she answered, simply. " We eat everything."

III

THE LIVING SIOUX

1

BACK in Pine Ridge I sat on a shady porch, thinking. What was this? Horse meat? Indians eating horse meat to keep alive. Creek water? Filthy, slimy-green creek water used continuously for cooking and drinking. Tents? Patched tents for a permanent residence. And John Sitting Bull. Did he not seem a symbol of his race — mute, speechless — unable to voice the plight of his people? John Sitting Bull, spokesman for the Indian, why are you enshrouded in eternal silence?

These questions along with many others kept crowding through my head. Gradually I began to surmise that there was something vastly important about the lives of these Indians of which I did not know. I had witnessed a filtering ray, and I was now eager to cast aside the cloak of obscurity and look upon the Indian in the broad daylight of his day-to-day existence.

My original idea of mythological research was not on my mind when I left the shady porch for the main street of the village. As in the pathfinder of Kipling's *Explorer*, that grand poem of adventure, there was a voice in me which persistently whispered: " Something's missing. Something's missing." So I set out to cross the mountain and see what land lay hidden there.

At the Pine Ridge Hotel I encountered Captain Ray Bonnin, a well-educated Sioux, who made his home in Washington during the winter months for the purpose of representing his people. I told him of my interview with John Sitting Bull.

" Nothing unusual," he replied. " Just another case of half a dozen women, children, and men living in one little tent on foul creek water and dried horse meat."

" But the horse meat — ? " I persisted.

" Well, they live on it. Many times they eat the unhealthy meat of horses who died of starvation or exhaustion. While driving on the reservation a few days ago I saw a crowd of people around a wagon that had stopped on the road. I got out of my car and went to investigate. A thin, yellow horse, with foam soaped over his mouth, was lying dead with the harness still strapped around him; the Indians were slicing up his carcass with their hunting knives. Diseased or not they couldn't afford to let meat go to carrion."

" But isn't there anything else they eat?"

" Yes," he replied, " dog meat, but it is a luxury."

With Captain Bonnin was his wife, Gertrude Bonnin, also known by her Sioux name, Zitkala-Sa. I found her one of the most cultivated of women, in addition to being the President of the National Council of American Indians and a descendant of Sitting Bull.

"Last summer," she said, " I happened to see some Indians bathing the corpse of a man who had starved to death. The body of the dead did not have a bit of flesh on it. It was just skin and bones. He had had no food and no proper medical care. The bathers cried aloud so hopelessly that I wept with them."

She paused, and I watched her keenly. She seemed a fine, sturdy specimen of Indian womanhood.

"I visited many reservations," she continued, " and everywhere I went I saw hungry Indians."

"But don't they get rations? " I asked.

" Only those they term disabled, the old, feeble Indians who are expected to live on seventy-three cents' worth of rations a month per person. The Government gives them a couple of shovelfuls of foul tasting flour and enough yellow bacon to last one day."

" But here, don't take our word for it," interrupted Captain Bonnin, taking my arm and leading me down the street. " We may be prejudiced," he added, with a smile. " I want you to meet Philip Romero, the Pine Ridge President of the National Council, who lives here the year around and knows conditions thoroughly."

I was introduced to a stocky Indian, whose face bore an undeniable mark of intelligence. His quick eyes gathered in the drift of our previous discussion, as Captain Bonnin explained my curiosity.

" Yes," he confirmed, " if not for our ponies we all

would have been dead long ago, and we can't live on these rations. We starve. This season we lose out altogether in putting in the crops because of the drought, and the chances are that most of us will starve to death this winter. Those that get food help feed their relatives and friends, and no one gets enough. More Indians should be getting rations, according to the last treaty with the Government, made in 1889. It stated that from the day land was taken in severalty provisions would be given during a twenty-five year period, and that period for many Indians has not yet expired, but their rations have been stopped long ago.

" The Senate Investigating Committee should do something quickly, because we need help right away. But they will drag their investigation along for another year, and then there won't be many Indians left. We will have starved to death. That's the truth.

" The Committee held its investigation here over a year ago, but conditions aren't any better. At that time I said to the Senators, ' If you only come here to stay one day don't come at all. You should stay a week and go in our homes and see how we are living.' But the Senate hasn't done anything. They are too slow and in the meanwhile we go hungry and naked almost. Yes, naked. If it were not for that ninety-eight cent overall on the market, we Indians would be naked."

Mr. Romero disappeared into his tent. So there has been a Senate investigation, I thought, which surely means there must be fire if they were looking for smoke.

My informant reappeared and presented me with Part Seven of the hearings of the Senate Investigating Commit-

tee, composed of Senators Frazier, chairman, La Follette, Pine,[1] Wheeler, and Thomas. Their purpose, the booklet explained, has been "to make a general survey of the condition of the Indians of the United States." I sat in Mr. Romero's tent, and read that on July 15, 1929, a hearing was held at Pine Ridge. The first witness was Charles Yellow Dog, who testified that considerable sickness, trachoma, and tuberculosis among the old and young could be attributed to the eating of many horses. "We got to eat horses or starve; we got nothing else," he stated, adding that about 2,000 horses were killed for meat last year. "We have not got any cattle now and no money to buy them with," he concluded.

Skipping through the pages I came upon the testimony of Charlie Black Horse, who made the following statement to the Senators:

On this reservation the conditions are in very bad shape; we are starving and most of these people here all look black; they get that way from eating too much horsemeat, and we are in very bad condition, and you people come to see about this and we hope when you get back to Washington you will do what you can to help us. I am eating horses, and I have only four or five left, and when I eat them up there will be no more food and I can not go anywhere. I eat so much horsemeat I hear the horses neigh-neigh-neigh-neigh in my sleep. The rations that we get here are not fit to eat, the bacon is yellow and the flour has an awful bad taste, and you people can go over there and see it yourself. We do not get enough to eat. We get about that much rations (indicated a small package). When we get it I count the grains of green coffee and it was 600 grains and we are supposed to live on that for two weeks.

[1] Failed to be reëlected in November, 1930.

I stopped reading. I handed the document to Mr. Romero and took leave of his company for the time being, promising him I would return for another discussion.

I sought out Frank Goings, who had been described to me as another responsible Indian by Captain Bonnin, before he returned to his quarters during the course of my conversation with Romero. Frank Goings for twenty-eight years had been chief of police on the reservation, and I found him likewise intelligent.

He invited me into his one-room home, built of rough logs, for an informal chat on the present life of the Sioux. I discovered his cabin was better than the average, for it did not have a dirt roof or a dirt floor. But the air within was greatly vitiated; no window was open and the flies were in black clusters on the plaster.

" I can't understand," he declared emphatically, " how Congress keeps on cutting our rations every year, while they pass appropriations for new buildings. Recently they constructed three cottages for employees, costing $9,500. That money, if used for rations, would keep many a grave from being dug."

At the agency headquarters for the Pine Ridge Reservation, where I called next, I found that $44,000 was the minimum asked by the local officers for rations which were distinctly needed. It was cut to $32,000. To begin with, the $44,000 was the minimum and not adequate; yet it was cut $12,000 in a drought year, when their toughest winter (1930–31) was facing the Sioux, when their meager crops had failed, when " something must be done quickly because we need help right away else we will starve to death. That's the truth."

I left the agency and walked slowly to my lodgings. I opened a suitcase and thoughtfully fingered a loose-leaf notebook, bearing an elaborate title page done in India ink. The words read: "Notes for an Anthology of Indian Legends and Folklore." I let the pages slip quietly out of my hand. They lay as dead upon the floor.

IV

BRANDED

1

THE white man has syphilized the Indian.
Primitive peoples have been found free from this curse of their Caucasian conquerors.

During the four days that followed my meeting Captain Bonnin I unearthed a pathological well of information unrefined. The Sioux, however, has had no authorship in this lurid phase of his neglect and mismanagement. The primitive Indian was not immoral, for no aborigine had a higher sense of right and wrong than he; adultery and incest were unknown to him. But his guardians, in their rapid, chaotic attempt to make him a white man, have stamped his people not with education, not with economic security, not with even a higher culture, but with their foul social diseases. The Sioux's physical undoing has been wholly the work of beneficent whites.

Dr. M. E. Burgess, for six years a Government physician

at Pine Ridge, made the following statements to me in reply to my inquiry. " Until the last two years," he stated, " the Sioux Indian has had very little venereal diseases. But now they are distinctly increasing, owing to the prominence of white neighbors."

" Venereal diseases are growing," confirmed Chief Clerk Detwiler, while temporarily in charge of the Pine Ridge Agency, the second largest in the Indian Service.

" The Indian boys meet bad white girls in the surrounding towns and thus become afflicted," stated Rev. Neville Joyner, of twenty-two years' experience as an Episcopal missionary to the Pine Ridge Indians. " They return to the reservation with their conflagration. In addition, white boys drive in here for the purpose of seducing Indian girls."

The Indian is exceptionally silent concerning his sexual ailments. New to the disease and uneducated as to its destructiveness, he does not go immediately to a doctor, with the result that comparatively few cases are recorded; yet social diseases are considered rampant through the Indian population.

According to the cases Dr. Burgess has recorded, only two diseased women are living on the reservation and only ten males. The number is estimated, however, by the Indians themselves to be many-fold higher. To present the situation more clearly and in light of their guardian's negligence: Twelve have had their cases recorded by a Government physician; 800, or ten per cent, is the statistical minimum of those who are afflicted.

2

As bashful and backward as the Indian is with regard
to examination for venereal diseases, so much more so is
the Indian woman regarding her confinement. But in vindi-
cation of her let it be said that the resorting to primitive
methods has been more of an urgent necessity than the
result of an educated choice in the matter. The lack of
education concerning maternity is as colossal as in the
venereal situation, and the results of the neglect in both
instances are substantiation within themselves.

When a Government doctor flatly refuses to attend an
Indian woman during her confinement she has but little
choice. That doctor, incidentally, receives a salary from
the Indian Bureau, the guardian of the Indian, in payment
for supposedly attending to the medical needs of that ward.
In many cases his salary is derived from the tribal fund
of his neglected patients.

Mrs. Frank Sherman, testifying " to the truth, the whole
truth, and nothing but the truth," before the Senate Investigating Committee, swore that Doctor Richardson of Pine
Ridge refused to take care of Mary Two Cows when she
went to him in the final stage of her condition:

She come home from church and she was sick and she went to
his office and asked him to come with her to the house, and he
said you go home and get along the best way you can. I don't
want to go with any Indian girl, and the girl was sick when she
got home, and my daughter-in-law live near there and she call
the doctor and he come and he said you do that job, I don't
want to do it. He said I don't work on things like this, so I have

to stay there and she gave birth to two little girls, and he would not do nothing. He said you go ahead and do the work and if the child live I buy clothing for him, and the next morning he buy two sets of clothing for the twins, and I told him I would report him and I did, but it did not do no good. It is just things like this is why we should have something done for our people and send us doctors that will take care of us.

Dr. Burgess, Dr. Richardson's colleague, unwittingly confirmed the above case, by declaring to me in his office that " we doctors have never made special trips to see confined cases. In fact, they hardly ever call us.

"It is a wonder," he continued, " that in their dirty homes with their dirty bedding and dirty floor, and with the women taking care of themselves, that there are so few cases of infection. The Indian is almost immune to diseases."

In this laissez faire attitude he continued, " The prospective Indian mother, married or unmarried, wants her baby even though she be penniless and is compelled to clothe her child in rags. She is not ashamed of the birth, although she has little choice — living in one room with half a dozen others. The birth is held right before the eyes of the children, who know all along their mother is going to have a child."

Otto Chief Eagle testified to the Senate Committee that women put in the reservation jail sometimes give birth to babies while imprisoned. " Yes, that is right," he stated. "That was Anna Horse. She was mixed up with another man and they put her in jail."

Summarizing the doctor-maternity situation Samuel

Rock made a statement: "I wish to say if we had about three good doctors some of the children would go living along."

His own daughter died last winter from tuberculosis. "The doctor was over several times, but all he gave her was some pills and that did not do no good."

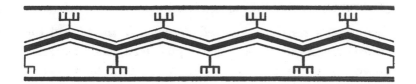

V

THE CASE OF THE SIOUX

1

PHILIP ROMERO. Proud, full-blooded Sioux. Descendant of Chief Red Cloud, president of the local tribal council. Well-educated Philip Romero speaks his mind freely.

" ' You hold council with Indians too much,' they tell me. ' You too much of a kicker.' Some others are afraid to talk, for fear the superintendent put them in jail."

He straightened his massive shoulders. " But as long as man is right," he said firmly, " I won't be bluffed or put in jail. Man has a right to defend himself."

His eyes narrowed in concentration. " The superintendent here favors his employees in flat defiance to law and order. I say every white man and Indian should be treated alike. But there is the case of Minnie-Chase-in-Sight. Here, read the testimony yourself."

He handed me Part Seven of the Senate Investigating

0751902

Committee's hearings, opened to page 2848. I read the sworn statement of a young girl who had been seduced by a Government officer, a married man with a large family, while rooming in his house during the school year.

" I made a statement to the effect [she swore] that the district farmer down the creek here, Jacob White Cow Killer is his name, I got from him, a illegitimate baby that belongs to him and when I brought the matter up to the superintendent he said I should not make such complaint against the farmer."

The superintendent claimed, according to Romero, that there was no truth in her statement and that she was trying to ruin the farmer's reputation. She showed him the two-year-old child, but he insisted on throwing the case out. Having no home, as her mother was dead, she was only asking for money to raise the baby. Her plea for assistance was repeated to the Senators, who inquired into the salary of the Government farmer. It was $108 a month — a prince's stipend in the eyes of hungry Indians. But nothing was done.

" Our local council," continued Romero, " has time and again asked the superintendent to fire Jacob White Cow Killer. At least he should be sent to the penitentiary like anybody else. But nothing was done. We asked him to fire Dr. Burgess and Dr. Richardson and all the Government farmers including Cottier, Alonzo Red Feather, and Little Hawk. Those farmers are alleged to go around looking for hooch, instead of teaching us farming. But none of them has been fired."

His eyes still narrowed, he continued, " Another inci-
dent of the Government employees sticking together is in
the case of a certain young, dissipated clerk. About three
weeks ago this clerk was dead drunk — laid out cold —
and the chief of police picked him up, carried him home,
and packed him, into bed. They tried to cover the case up,
but we heard about it. So the superintendent sent in a report
to Washington, excusing him and the chief of police, and
suggesting the case be dropped. He sent his report in by
air-mail and told our council that ' if you can beat me
go ahead and do it, but my letter is going by airplane
from Omaha.' We wired that night to Indian Commissioner Rhoads, stating that judgment on the superintendent's statements defending drunken employees should be
withheld until our affidavits arrived in Washington. But
the local notaries refused to take our testimony for fear
of getting in bad with the superintendent. So nothing has
been done."

During those four days Philip Romero told me of the
inefficiencies, abuses, and even prejudices of the Indian
Bureau officers. It is too long and discouraging a tale to
repeat in full. I can only hope to touch upon the most
typical and grievous cases, and in so doing give an accurate
panorama of the Sioux landscape.

" These ten dollar Indian judges, selected wholly by the
superintendent," said Romero, " is one of the chief maladministrations. Judge Noah Bad-Wound has had little
education; he is not broad minded and gives his decisions
out of spite and malice. The other three, Thomas Henry,
Cain Whiteshield, and John Ghost-Bear, are also unedu-

cated. Selected for their jobs by the superintendent, their decisions are thought to be one sided."

Anger came rapidly into his face. He talked with great restraint. "This has been going on long enough. We can't stand this much longer. We should have educated judges, like white people."

He continued, "Another thing that is wrong is the starving of Indian parents who are compelled by affections and family ties, to remain in the neighborhood of the day schools, which their children attend. For the noon-day lunch the children get a little coffee and bread. I know for a fact that this is all they have to live on, because they get no supper or breakfast from the family. Their parents, you see, can't move around hustling up a living. They must stay at home where the children are going to school. I went to the superintendent asking for additional rations for the parents, but he said he couldn't and wouldn't ask Congress for additional appropriations. He just let them starve. He did not understand how they suffer while trying to keep the wolf from the door. I know that if whites were hard up they would move away from the school, children and all. But the Indian parent will suffer himself to keep his child in school."

"But aren't there some who have incomes?" I asked.

"Only ten per cent," was his answer. "Only the pensioners live fairly well — the old scouts from the Indian wars, I mean. They help out the less fortunate ones, for no Indian can watch another starve, and so in the end they have nothing themselves."

"But the farming?"

" There is not as much farming now as there was before the Government organized farm clubs for the supposed purpose of stimulating and educating us. We were expected to pay high prices for seed, like $1.80 a bushel for potato seed, which was higher than the regular market price. The Government should sell us seed cheaply if they expect us to farm and join its clubs."

In the Indian Office I read reports and statistics as to the exceptional successes of the farm organizations. But these paper prosperities were constantly confronted by mental pictures of what I had seen in the field, so I delved deeper into the records.

I found that 4,157 Indians do not belong to any farm club or organization of that nature whatever; no county or state prizes have been captured by Indian farm products.

Out of 8,000 Indians 97 have remunerative jobs such as clerking, barbering, skilled and general unskilled labor. Of the other Indians — they eke out irregular incomes in the following vocations: 400 do beadwork, 133 lacework, 552 wood, 1081 " farm," and 200 " raise " stock. This leaves 5,537 Indians with no income whatever. Not even a few dollars a year earned from sewing beads on moccasins for tourists.

In startling contrast to such a pitiful situation are the figures on the value of Indian land. The undivided properties are valued at $793,026.18, the tribal at $451,829.87. Indians who eat horse flesh as a regular diet and look upon dog meat as a luxury, who are compelled to drink creek water for the want of a well, who are clothed like miserable beggars — these Indians have to their credit $1,244,856.05.

Sweet land of liberty!

There are 404 homes in Pine Ridge with dirt floors. There are 285 tents or tepees all crowded with families. The Government has built with Indian money about thirty model homes of the latest design, with deep wells adjoining — " to illustrate how it should be done." Teasers. Yet the 8,000 Indians can not draw a penny of the $1,244,-856.05 for the purpose of building permanent homes with wooden floors and a well. It is strictly " tribal " and absolutely under Indian Bureau control.

The supposed industrial five-year plan for Pine Ridge was inaugurated in 1924–5. The Government farmers set out to take a picture of every home on the reservation, besides having the occupants fill out a questionnaire. Interest ran high on this new endeavor. The superintendent and chief clerk joined the farmers to help in the interviewing. The roads became so impassable that the two officials ceased accompanying their subordinates and the superintendent remarked that he could not see how one could get in that country to take pictures. He could not see nor imagine how human beings (Indians) could exist on such land.

Months later, Superintendent E. E. Jermark, wishing to impress a body of Wabeno county and Wisconsin state officials, who neighbored the Lac du Flambeau reservation to which he had been recently transferred, stated to them with undue emphasis: " I visited every home on the 3,000,-000 acres of the Pine Ridge Agency."

Into these questionnaires and photographs I dipped rather

cursorily, but sufficiently to gather their true portrait. The five year pictures " before and after " showed no marked improvement. The majority of the 1930 negatives were identical with the 1925.

In the 1930 Annual Statistical Report I noted that half of the homes in the Wounded Knee district have dirt floors. One hundred and fifty of the Eagle Nest homes yet have sand bottoms. There are 90 dirt floors out of the 160 homes in the Kyle district in 1930. Similarly in the other districts.

Taking a typical questionnaire case — Thomas Fast Wolf of Hisle, South Dakota:

1. How many members in your family? Ans. Seven.
2. Do you live in a permanent house? Ans. No.
3. How many rooms do you live in? Ans. One.
4. Do you have suitable water supply? Ans. No.
5. What is the source of your water supply? Ans. Creek.
6. What steps have been taken to prevent contamination of your water supply? Ans. None.
7. What are the health conditions of your family? Ans. One boy is in poor health. Rest are good.
8. How many members of your family have been vaccinated recently? Ans. None.

Thomas Fast Wolf's annual income has been estimated at twenty-five dollars.

His case is not exceptional. There are many much worse. There is Iron Rope, for example. He is sixty-seven and lives along Bear Creek in a log house with a dirt roof. He drinks creek water and is in exceedingly poor health. He has no income whatever.

Bennie Scabby Face has a tuberculous wife. They drink river water and the family sleeps in one bed.

In Wallace Running Eagle's family of five only two are healthy. Living in a log house with a dirt roof and drinking river water, his family is consequently saturated with tuberculosis.

Joseph Red Bear is in poor health; his wife is tuberculous.

In Felix Slow Bear's log house one has trachoma and another tuberculosis.

The same with Joseph Red Bow, Frank Bear Nose, Reuben Bear Robe, and dozens upon dozens of others.

These facts stand out:

There is no bathroom in all the Indian homes on the reservation.

Every house lacks proper ventilation.

Almost invariably one in a family is in poor health.

Many drink no milk nor eat vegetables.

Nothing is plentiful in the home. Always one bed, one table, one cupboard, one stove, one door and many times one window — all in one room.

There are few-and-far-between outing buildings. The grasses by the creeks provide the most convenient restrooms.

" The same conditions exist all around," Edison Glenn tells me. " Every home is the same."

" It is true," Rev. Joyner confirms. " Many Indians have such poor allotments, which they can't possibly farm, that they are discouraged before they start. The Indians will soon be a homeless people, wandering about as carriers of

contagious diseases — a menace to society. They should
not sell any more of their land, but they are hungry. One
can not blame them."

Despite these heartbreaking conditions with their hopeless future, the full-blooded, raw, pagan, and untutored
Indians living in the White Clay district have made the
greatest progress, if one can consider progress as entering
in the picture. Those Indians have long lived on the air-
washed, wind-swept prairies in clean buckskin tepees, that
were moved about frequently from one blue-bottomed
creek to another.

" A certain clerk, here," Philip Romero again said
to me, " has been in the office a long time and yet he can't
pass a civil service examination. We know for a fact that
he ruins the superintendents that are sent here with his
malicious advice. He works against the Indian all the time.
We also know for a fact that he tries to ruin our reputations.
He tells the new officials, ' I know that Indian better than
his mother and he is no good. He is a drunkard, a thief,
and a kicker.' Thus he tries to ruin our reputations.
This we can prove. The whole reservation doesn't want him
here.

" Clerks and additional buildings," he concluded,
" don't help civilize the Indian. We need more field nurses
and field farmers."

2

Aside from the venereal and maternity phases already
discussed, there remains the general health of the Sioux.
I had been informed by both missionaries and Indians that

"there is an awful lot of tuberculosis." I sought official confirmation.

"Health here is no good," admitted Dr. Burgess to me. "About twenty-five per cent are tuberculous. There is no sanitation, no cleanliness, and much malnutrition. Only through doctors and field nurses can the home be improved. We have no field nurses. Three doctors attempt to serve 8,000 Indians spread over three million acres of four counties. In addition we have the two boarding schools. I recommend that we have field nurses and more and younger physicians."

Four physicians have been authorized, I discovered, but only three have been hired.

I observed that the three doctors stationed at Pine Ridge were forty-eight years and over. It is discouraging to discover that there are hardly any young physicians in the Indian Service, familiar with modern treatment and modern instruments.

I had an occasion to observe the efficiency of the dispensary, in addition to the technic of the doctors, while having a minor wound treated. I do not know which was the more deplorable — the spilt medicines and broken bottles lying about the unswept dispensary or the applying of alcohol to a raw wound with a forefinger.

"The Government does not pay enough salary to attract the right kind of doctors," testified the superintendent. "You can't expect to get the best men for $2,300 to $2,600 a year. The average country practitioner gets much more."

True, but, argues the Indian, even a $2,300 a year doctor need not be a dope fiend. He should, at least, keep case records, hold a venereal disease clinic, and go on urgent calls.

The doctor accused of being a dope fiend by the Indians has served on fourteen different assignments, according to the superintendent. But, a dope fiend doctor is better than none at all, say the Indians, yet how much deeper is our disappointment when he too will not call on the sick.

Proof lies in testimony made from their own lips to the investigating Senators and printed in Part Seven.

Senator Wheeler asks Otto Chief Eagle, " You have a hospital up there, have you? " Otto answers, " No; no hospital." The Senator's curiosity is aroused. " What do you do when you get sick, especially the children? " Otto answers simply, " Send for the doctor and he won't come; they don't use any brains; they employ anybody at all."

Romero tells of his boy, whose nervous breakdown was treated by Dr. Burgess, who instructed the boy to use five to fifteen drops of arsenic a day. Two private practitioners told Romero his son was being poisoned to death by the exceptional doses.

" These doctors we have here, one is a kind of dope fiend," he swore into the record, " and the other doctor I do not go on much, because every time I call him he does not come. I have been trying to get my daughter to the hospital, and I spoke to Mr. Jermark, and he said he would help me out, but that is all the satisfaction I got."

Luke White Hawk, who lives at Wounded Knee, was asked, " Don't the doctors up there visit the Indians when they are sick and when they are called? "

" Many times," came the answer, " they don't go when

they are asked. I don't understand why the doctor does that; my brother's child was very sick for a long time and the doctor never went to see him, and we came to the agent to get some of his money to get him to the hospital, as they had some money to their credit, but we never did get satisfactory answer."

By coincidence I met a rather slight but extremely alert man, who seemed to be enjoying life as if he never had before. He was Dr. E. F. Jones, for two years a physician in the Indian Service, and now voluntarily on an indefinite leave of absence.

" Conditions have been rotten here," he said, after carefully looking over his shoulder. " Some of the Service doctors don't speak to one another and fight like cats, and one of them is said to be crazy. The superintendent is an autocrat, and you can't ask him for anything. They had a streak of conscience here a while back and fired the school disciplinarian for whipping a child. Hell, he whipped fifty! The superintendent knew about it all the time, including the case of that child who died from a whipping."

During this monologue he had led me to the rear of his car, away from the inquisitive glances of employees who hovered about like flies. Dr. Jones was passing through Pine Ridge on his vacation trip to Yellowstone, when I luckily met him.

" There's been an underhand graft going on here for some time," he continued, safely entrenched behind his automobile. " There is a private doctor from a near-by village who comes to the reservation to do tonsillectomies.

The first month he came he made $2,000. I have known him to do sixteen tonsillectomies in one day. You see, the superintendent compelled me to sign a statement saying I was not qualified to do that work. You couldn't buck the superintendent. He could make life miserable for you. The superintendent would not okay any operation unless the patient had money to his credit deposited with him, and many an Indian with money to his credit had his tonsils out whether he needed to or not. Why would the superintendent call in a young doctor, furnish him with instruments, customers, and a glorious opportunity to learn surgery at the financial and physical expense of the poor Indians? There is but one answer to that question. A juicy split has been going on, which I know can be verified if the surgery records are investigated. He has since departed."

Later, I learned that this physician had performed thirty-five tonsillectomies in the four months previous to my arrival.

" A former well-known District Medical Superintendent," Dr. Jones went on saying, " being a countryman of this doctor — had been okaying all of his operations. The superintendent had also been loyal to his Golden Goose, who in 1926 stole some narcotics and gave the dope to his girl friend for safe keeping, but he ditched her and she spilled the dope in more ways than one. So he came out with a written confession. The superintendent, knowing about it all the time, only fined him as sort of a compromise punishment. He kept his Golden Goose still on, however, and he is operating today. All this is a matter of court record which anyone can verify. Also his colleagues know all about the case."

We had moved during the course of his discourse from Dr. Jones' car to mine. Feeling he could now converse more securely, he continued.

" The superintendent is a high liver, spending, it is said, a good deal more than his salary of $3,600 a year. They say the day-school teachers sign up for more flour or sugar than they need, but he doesn't send them any surplus. Drugs have been given away to Whites and the alcohol supply has never been accurately checked. The superintendent doesn't care, and protects others operating in liquor. Bill Lose, a trader at Kyle, is a pal of the superintendent's; and so Two Gun Heart, a policeman, was told to lay off Lose and no attempt was made to catch him."

Jim LaPoint verified Dr. Jones' statement concerning the report of operations on healthy Indians who have money to their credit. He also emphasized that another was " worthless — the poorest we ever had."

3

A tall, industrious, conscientious woman sits behind a desk heaped with papers and ledger books. She is Miss Jones. She is a clerk in the Indian Service and of great experience. A young woman approaches her with a report in her hand; she is the wife of the new Chief Clerk Detwiler. She innocently inquires of the inconsistency of two sets of figures — a Government inspector's and Miss Jones'. The corn and the wheat have been calculated on two dif-

ferent adding machines. " I don't know," Miss Jones says
somewhat befuddled. " I figure a lot of things different
from what they do."

From 8,000 throats comes one voice:

"It is the slackness of the officials in their duties that
causes us to be in want and suffer and have various
troubles."

" New equipment does not save lives. We need doctors,
not dope fiends. If Congress is going to save the Indian it
must send us good doctors and nurses else we die."

" Last summer I was sick and I sent for the doctor and
he did not come until the next morning and all he gave me
was some pills, and I think this way, since we got Mr.
Hoover we would like to have new superintendent, farmer,
teacher, and storekeeper and everything new; maybe this
reservation be run better then."

VI

PINE RIDGE RODEO

1

THIS is the three day Pine Ridge Rodeo, held every year for tourists. Many are the whites who come to see the riding, to watch the cowboys run their horses, to play the games of chance, and to watch the Indians stage their powwow.

For three days the Indians live in a Happy Hunting Ground. Such things as horse meat, creek water, diseases, and death are momentarily forgotten. It is their annual powwow, held once a year. From all corners of the four counties and from even far beyond, they come. Many drive in wagons for days, bring only enough food to reach Pine Ridge. Let the future take care of itself. They can borrow, if need be. But there is clear, pump water on the rodeo grounds — an inducement beyond calculation. They come and stand about the pumps like children before a pop-corn stand at a county fair. They stand drinking the clean water.

They store it in barrels and cart it away to their tents, where they look at the barrels and sip the water, as though it were celestial nectar. They live in rows of tents spread about the hills.

This is the three day Pine Ridge Rodeo. A city of tents — 4,000 of them dotting the dark earth. The woman next door brings me a bucketful of potatoes, saying, " I see you have none." A bucketful of potatoes for one stomach, from a woman with horse meat drying on a rope beside her tent.

This is the three day Pine Ridge Rodeo. Not a privy on the horizon for 8,000 Indians. Just the green-bottomed creek and the fields of grass. Women are seen squatting behind their tents with shawls over their heads so that none will recognize their faces. The men do not hide their faces under shawls. The babies are naked and romp about in the fields and by the green-bottomed creek. This is the three day Pine Ridge Rodeo, held every year for tourists.

I approached the large circle wherein the Indian dances were being conducted. The circle formed a complete amphitheater, with a thatched roof of pine branches protecting the spectators from the sun. In the east there was an opening in the circle, making it authentically Indian.

As I approached I heard a strange, monotonous whistling. The moment I saw the five dancers in the ring I understood the meaning of the eerie sounds. They were doing the ancient and much revered Sun Dance of the Sioux. I quickened my pace and eagerly scanned the row of spectators, looking for an advantageous position, for this was the sacred Sun Dance of the Sioux.

Beside me sat a small white man. His face was a mass of eruptions, and his bent beak and shifting eyes gave it the appearance of belonging to a special type of man who knew his way about Chicago. He kept curiously eyeing my camera as if he collected a premium on all photos taken west of Omaha. Finally, he ventured questions.

" Newspaper man? " I shook my head. " No reporter, eh? "

" No."

He instantly became garrulous. " That's okay, then, buddie. You see we don't want any publicity just now. Not till after the ceremonies are over and we're back East."

" Oh, how long does the Sun Dance last? " I naïvely asked, knowing it consumed three days.

" This Sun Dance? " He jerked a thumb contemptuously toward the jogging Indians. " Say, buddie, I don't mean this ceremony. I mean the coronation of my boss, Chief Two Moon. He's going to be made king over all these here Soo-ox."

" Really? "

" Sure. Haven't you heard of Chief Two Moon, the big medicine man from Waterbury, Connecticut? "

I acknowledged my ignorance.

" Allow me to introduce myself. I am M. J. Redican, legal adviser to Chief Two Moon Meridas. Come, I'll introduce you to the chief."

My curiosity fully aroused, I followed him to a bench quite conspicuously set among the squatted figures of aged Indians. I was introduced to a short, elegantly dressed man with a round, plump face as black as Harlem bitumen. His shining big teeth, extravagantly dotted with gold fillings, had never bitten into any horse flesh to make his skin black. His nose looked as though it had been remodeled from a pug into a Grecian cast. Nevertheless, his features were distinctly negroid. I watched his quick, dark eyes and knew he was smart, but I was anxious to hear his voice. It was soft and throaty — tropical; he spoke carefully, almost slowly, as if he had practiced its cultivation for some time.

" I swear," he said, rubbing the backs of his hands, " if I stay in this country much longer I'll soon be black as a nigger."

His eyes immediately sought mine. His attendants were laughing, and he was smiling. The introductions went around. In addition to the legal adviser I met Mr. M. E. Kidney, " my special photographer." And a small, squatty white woman with enormous breasts and a blank face — " Mrs. Two Moon Meridas, my wife."

I looked into the circle. The dancers held their right palms in the air, as though they were saluting the sun. For generations they have been sun worshipers. They were now in the midst of a sacred ceremony, expressing their ancient reverence. Such dances have always been held privately, away from tourists and their cameras; as much so as the interior of a cathedral.

" You can take pictures of the dance," Two Moon Meridas was saying. " I give you permission."

" Is the Chief a Sioux? " I asked Redican, before loading my camera.

" Well," he pondered, "not exactly. His mother was a Blackfoot."

I managed to suppress my laughter.

"His father was called Big Tom of the Pee-eb-blows," he added.

I made a mental note of the fact that the Pueblos live in the southern part of the United States, by Mexico, while the Blackfeet are 3,000 miles north, by the Canadian border. He might have read my thought, for he handed me a printed sheet of green paper, stating it to be the chief's "horoscope."

It was the " Filius Terreus " of Chief Two Moon Meridas, as recorded on February 20, 1930, by " The Heraldic Historical and Biographical Library of Guido Pitoni." Inclosed by fancy borders and imitation seals were many interesting statements. The first being that Two Moon was born August 29, 1888, at Devil's Lake, North Dakota. Later, when I had the opportunity, I referred to Bulletin 23 (1929) of the Department of the Interior and found that Devil's Lake is on the Fort Totten Agency, which is composed of the Assiniboin, Cuthead, Santee, Sisseton, Yankton, and Wahpeton Sioux. The Blackfeet resided on the Blackfeet Agency in Montana; the Pueblos in New Mexico.

In the agency office Chief Clerk Detwiler showed me two telegrams he had received requesting courtesies for Meridas. The first was from the " Foreign Language Newspaper Bureau " of Washington, which can be immediately discredited. However, Ernest K. Hill, secretary to Senator Kean of New Jersey, wired the following in a prepaid day letter from Washington on July 31, 1930: " Will appreciate any courtesies extended to my friend Chief Two Moons

Meridas of Waterbury, Connecticut, who is spending a few days at your reservation."

Far reaching are the tentacles of respectability.

Fully curious as to the intention of Two Moon's " coronation " I interviewed Gus Fonner, a veteran showman, who was staging the rodeo with his horses and cowboys.

" Gus, what is the low down on Two Moon Meridas? " I asked.

" Out in this country," he replied, " it is damned hard to make money. It isn't floating around in the air, get me? So when this medicine man says he is willing to pay $1,500 to be made ' King of the Soo-ox,' for the publicity of his medicine show, why I'm not going to try to raise corn in a drought."

No, you could not blame Gus. " But how did you get the Indians to consent? " I asked.

" Easy," he replied. " Two Moon bought them nine head of steer to divide among the tribe equally. A little better than horse meat, eh? "

" And Esau said, Behold I am about to die: and what profit shall the birthright do to me? " Thus Esau sold his birthright for a mess of red pottage.

" But, Gus," I was persistent with questions — " is Two Moon an Indian? "

He laughed. " You want to know too much." He started to walk away. " Figure it out," he called back over his shoulder.

Sitting apart from the spectators, and not the least interested in the dance, were a dozen or so ancient, full-blooded Sioux. They never once glanced at the fifty or seventy-five Indians doing " The Omaha " in full regalia. They preferred to live in memories, rather than watch the pretentious upstarts with their white man's store vests dotted with Indian beads, their white man's shoes with run-down heels, their green and pink circus tights, their Navajo blankets woven on a white man's machine, their sleigh bells, circus bells, Christmas tree bells, jangling from their ankles in beat with the white man's big bass drum. Mixed with this incongruity were their ancient feather *coup* sticks, handed down from father to son for generations — long used in counting *coup* on enemy, horse, and buffalo.

By themselves, in an informal circle, sat genuine Sioux. Kills Enemy, Bird Necklace, Eagle Pipe, Otto Chief Eagle, Short Bull, White Breast, Iron Horse, Blue Horse, Flying Hawk, and John Sitting Bull. They wore no feathered helmets, no buckskin leggings, and held no imitation tomahawks in their wrinkled hands. They were as comely and natural as the sun they worshiped.

An ancient peace pipe was being solemnly passed around the group. Once again they were smoking a common pipe, as in the old days. John Sitting Bull, with the aid of the sign language, was telling his observers of his father's famous battle with Custer. The Indian version of the Battle of the Little Big Horn has never been completely recorded. The battle started at nine in the morning, lasting two hours, in which Custer's 754 men were killed in contrast to nineteen Indians; so spoke Short Bull, who witnessed the battle as a child.

Thus they lived in the past, those dozen braves — in a

dead world never to return. They quietly circulated a much-
bethumbed newspaper clipping, engraved with the long-
hidden truth of a dying man. V. T. McGillycuddy's confession: " General Sheridan under pressure of the railroads
sent Custer into the Black Hills in 1874 to hunt for gold in
violation of the Sioux-United States Treaty of 1868."
McGillycuddy called on the Federal Comptroller to be reimbursed for his part in the expedition. " All the satisfaction I received was ' Young man, I have heard of you;
now if you can show me how you have benefited the Sioux
Nation by going out there and burglarizing their reservation, I will consider your claim.' So I had to gracefully
withdraw."

A dozen braves, sons of American Horse, Red Cloud,
Crow King, Big Foot, Black Leg, Black Shield, Touch-the-
Cloud, and Gall; Crazy Horse, Spotted Tail, Man Afraid,
Rain-in-the-Face, and Sitting Bull. A dozen braves quietly
passing around a tattered clipping, engraved with a long
hidden truth of a dying man. Like their fathers, who
" would hold a little paper, dirtied with a lie " (the 1868
Treaty), they were intermittently passing the clipping and
the pipe.

Buzzing among the crowds like hungry, persistent hor-
nets were Redican and Kidney. Armed with movie and still
cameras, they were taking pictures of Indian babies in
beaded leggings, of Indian maidens in buckskin dresses, of
Indian dancers in Omaha regalia, and of anything or anybody that looked auspiciously spectacular. " These are for
illustrating Chief Two Moon's medicine show," they explained. " In the fall the Chief is going to Europe. Those

Europeans like to see real Indians, dressed up, healthy —
you know."

During the course of their exploits many unfortunates
would come to them, asking for aid. Their children were
sick and needed help; they were without clothes and needed
money to cover their bodies; they had an allotment the title
to which was muddled, or trust money that was long over-
due. They had heard that these white men came out of the
east to witness the ceremony of their boss, Two Moon, who
was to help them in Washington. So the unfortunates approached them with their troubles, and they all received
one answer:

"We no understand you. Chief Two Moon give you
$1,000 worth of beef. We no understand you."

Of the many primitive traits yet lingering among the
Sioux the most outstanding, and perhaps the most primitive, is the carrying of children on their mothers' backs.
It is true the wooden cradle has disappeared, but it is yet
a common sight to see babies held to their mothers' backs
only by a blanket wrapped about the woman's shoulders.
Later, I came across a *Wide World* newspaper photograph
showing a Negress and her child. The caption read: "In
the Congo Today, Babies Are Carried Just as the *Primitive*
Indian Squaws Carried Their Papooses Around." Who is
responsible for such backwardness still existing on the
American continent, after the white man has been in contact with the Sioux for almost a century?

2

She sat by herself, with her back against a supporting pine post, under the shade of balsam boughs lying on the trestle above her. She had not moved during the course of the dance, nor spoken, nor altered the stoic expression on her face. She wore a black shawl over her shoulders that neatly covered her head like a nun or a Turkish woman of the Orient. At intervals she would untie a red handkerchief, containing a sack of tobacco, cigarette papers, and matches. With a single twist of her wrist she would roll the paper around the tobacco, and with the same movement glide the cigarette to her lips. Her other hand quietly arose with a match, newly spitting fire from the sole of her shoe. Her movements were so quiet, so deft, almost mechanical, that an observer would hardly know whether she were a robot or a human.

3

The coronation of Chief Two Moon Meridas of Waterbury, Connecticut, erstwhile medicine man of the East, as King of All the Soo-ox, has begun. He is led into the Sacred Circle by his employee " Chief " Spotted Crow of Atlantic City, who has preceded Two Moon into the West to arrange the beef feast for his people.

Spotted Crow's women come forward and present Mrs. Meridas with a white buckskin dress, beautifully adorned with beads. They help her into the dress, and deck her head with a beaded band and a feather. Men come forward and crown the king with a flowing headdress of eagle feathers that trail on the ground. They present him with a white buckskin jacket and a richly scrolled medicine bag. Two Moon pays heavily for his regal robes. One hundred fifty dollars for a buckskin dress at the Alex Johnson in Rapid City. A dress is cheap, but beef is high.

4

A strange, tattered figure is riding hard on his horse. You can see he has been in the saddle long by the way the two come; the horse is tired and the rider slumps forward. Long has he ridden from his shack in the hills to the Pine Ridge Three Day Rodeo. He has heard that his brothers would be there — 8,000 of them — for the old-time dances done in the old-time way. He pulls up to the fence in a cloud of his horse's own making. He ties the reins mechanically and stoops under the barbed wire.

Only his shifting eyes betray his excitement. He tries to pick out familiar faces in the crowd. He goes to a pine post, supporting the circular trestle of shade-lending boughs. He folds his knotty fingers around the pole and leans heavily against it, peering at the ceremony.

He sees Spotted Crow place an eagle bonnet on the head of a strange, dark-faced man, and then whisper into his ear. He with the black face nods, takes a step toward the silent rows of Indians.

He listens to the talk. " Me no say here. Me no say here. Me do plenty for you elsewhere," the dark one says in pidgin English. The lone rider grunts to himself as a loud murmur runs through the silent rows. He sees Spotted Crow become nervous and again whisper hurriedly into the massive headdress, which turns and speaks in a strange tongue to a half-breed. He watches the half-breed turn to the Indians and say in the language of the Sioux: " He says he will protect you and help you until the Great Spirit calls him."

The lone rider hears a handful shout " Ho! Ho! " in approval, but he is silent and so are the thick rows of standing Indians.

He turns his eyes toward the center of the sacred circle. Beneath the sacred altar he sees a white man with a movie camera taking pictures of the ceremony. He sees a stray dog smelling the heels of the camera man.

" Hi-Kola," he exclaims in Sioux to a familiar face. " In old time they shoot dog with arrows till he sprouts like the porcupine, if he dare profane our Sacred Circle."

Without bidding his friend adieu he wheels suddenly and goes to his horse. He unties the reins and slowly lifts himself into the saddle. Without a backward glance he sadly turns his horse's nose into the distant hills.

5

The King of All the Soo-ox is riding with the Pine Ridge postmaster in the Pine Ridge postmaster's car. The King of All the Soo-ox is getting together his regalia for the courts of Europe.

Spotted Crow, give me your necklace of eagle claws. Do not hesitate. I want it, Spotted Crow. And I want many more pairs of beaded moccasins. Have you told those women to make me another buckskin jacket, Spotted Crow? Look! what is that silver dollar that Injun is wearing around his neck? A distinguished medal Uncle Sam gave the Soo-ox chiefs sixty-five years ago? What for, Spotted Crow? For good faith, keeping out of war? Spotted Crow, you get me that medal. I need that for my outfit. Sacred? Handed down from father to son? Spotted Crow, here is the money. You get me that medal. There, that's a nice boy, Spotted Crow. You will like Atlantic City in the winter.

The King of All the Soo-ox is riding with the Pine Ridge postmaster in the Pine Ridge postmaster's car. Four and twenty black birds baked in a pie.

Dick Whalen, postmaster, opens pension checks for Indian Scouts Charlie Black Horse and Fast Whirl Wind. He gives the checks to Henry Davis, who has the Indians print their thumb marks on the checks. Silas Yellow Boy swears to the investigating Senators: " Several Indians here draw money and he [Mr. Davis] is taking the money from the post office into his office, and when the Indians go there he has them endorse this check and sign it to him when they owe money at the store, and he takes the money out and when they deny it he takes the money out as he pleases, and I can prove it by one Indian; he was thrown out of the store."

Charlie Black Horse thinks this is wrong, to turn over his check to the storekeeper. He objects to Whalen, who writes the Post Office Department at Washington. They answer him on March 14, 1929: " You are informed that this procedure is improper, and the procedure is about the same as turning it over to claim agents." But Charlie Black

Horse swears that his scout check of May, 1929, was turned over without his consent.

The superintendent rents Charlie Black Horse's 320 acres to Henry Davis for $2.50 for six months' rent. Between the Government and a storekeeper Charlie is made penniless.

Dick Whalen tells the Senators conditions are " pretty good I think."

Fearless, honest Philip Romero says: " Dick Whalen is too much pro-Indian Bureau." Philip Romero is an uncle to Dick Whalen.

Dick Whalen is anxious to know my mission. " Are you from the Department of the Interior? " he asks. " No? " Relief bursts upon his face. " You know," he talks confidentially, " Chief Two Moon knew you were a newspaper man all the time. He's not against publicity later on, when he gets back East. But out here he's afraid the Indians might think he was commercializing. You know, he doesn't want to give them the wrong impression."

Head Chief Two Moon Meridas is a zealous ruler. He will protect his people until the Great Spirit calls him. The Great Spirit is ambitious for him. Head Chief Two Moon Meridas desires to parade about Washington with his senatorial customers, bearing his new crown of eagle feathers. " You need a representative in Washington, a representative of the Sioux nation. But representatives are expensive. I will make a donation if the right man is chosen."

6

Charlie Black Horse testifies why the Indians are afraid of the superintendent: " The old generation of Indian people said that the Indian agents in old times do not have so many guns then as our superintendent. The other evening he said he used his gun by shooting on the street here right in town at Mrs. Going's nephew. The boy's name is Oliver Nelson, and he was not doing anything that I know of. I suppose he has three or four guns, but he always carries a gun and the Indians are afraid of him, and the Indians never see no Indian agent carry a gun — only him."

Like master, like pupil. Chief Clerk Detwiler carries a pocket-sized automatic Colt. I have seen it. He also has other guns. " It makes a man feel safer," he says.

Dear days of Deadwood — 1876 — Kit Carson, Buffalo Bill — long dead, but not forgotten.

An Indian agent is a Czar unto himself and his province. His authority is complete, unlimited.

" If I think this Two Moon person or this dance hall, with all these young girls rouged and jazzed up, are not morally wholesome for the Indian population, why, I only have to give the word and pouf — they're gone." So talks Chief Detwiler to me the second evening of the Three Day Rodeo.

But no one played Houdini.

7

The Pine Ridge Three Day Rodeo comes to a close. The agency office is crowded with old Indians, inquiring about claims, about rations, about trust fees, rental fees, about pension checks. They are hungry as they are always hungry. They want the only thing the white man has for them to quell their hunger: White man's money to buy white man's food. Indian food has long been killed off; millions upon millions of buffalo senselessly slain in a few years.

But other powwows are being held throughout the tourist belt. Other Indians are gathering at agency headquarters. On August 10 the Governor of Wisconsin flies to Pittsville to become again Winnebago Chief Red Bird, Wa-nig-chu-ge-ga. Tourists from twenty-two states and over 10,000 farmers watch their governor "practice some Indian steps."

The Pine Ridge Three Day Rodeo comes to a close. The Indians slowly pull up their stakes and fold their tents. The twilight is falling, the summer is lingering; they will soon steal away, to sleep like hungry bears throughout a dead winter. They will steal away over the famous Black Hills Highway — "the shortest, most direct route to Yellowstone and the Black Hills." Thousands travel over it yearly. Yet it is naught but a backwoods road. Plain dirt, not even graded or graveled. Let a paved road be built, a macadam road, constructed with Indian labor. The only one hundred per cent Americans, hungry for work and a living, are idle while a million Mexicans are imported yearly to build roads.

Into the low-hanging twilight clouds, into the sun setting

upon the Black Hills, into the phantasmagoria of the evening sky — into all those uniquely beautiful formations, rides the Sioux Indian. The beauties of his horizon do not disappear. No white man can steal them from him. They alone are ever with him and follow him, even as he rides out of the rodeo grounds, with an empty pocket and the memory of a full belly. He rides forth bareheaded, sitting at the head of his prairie schooner, with his wife by his side and his children asleep within the wagon.

He had a beef roast. A very fine beef roast. His stomach tasted beef, and he was happy for three full days. But now he was going home, a hundred miles or so away. It had been a very fine beef roast, but it was over, and he was going home. Going home.

II
PROPAGANDA

VII

LO! THE WEALTHY INDIAN

1

THE vast majority of Americans possess the same point of view I entertained before setting out for the Black Hills. But in all fairness to us, I say we have had our romantic information predigested by the United States Indian Bureau.

My contact with the day-to-day existence of the Sioux sent me to Washington, reading reports, official statistics, and all sorts of documents. It sent me over many thousands of miles to reservations where I observed Indians at home, at labor, and in council. It sent me to Government schools where I saw the living conditions of hundreds of Indian children. It sent me conversing and corresponding with Government agents, superintendents, and officials of sundry ranks; with Indians of many tribes; with Indian benefactors, who have been fighting the Indian's battle for years. And everywhere I found a distinctly different picture from the one constantly painted by the Indian Bureau.

Very early in my reading I wrote the Indian office at Washington for information on health, education, schools, property, and on similar subjects which would assist me in studying the Indian problem of today. I received numerous neatly printed pamphlets, the product of the print shops of Chilocco, Chemawa, Phoenix, and Haskell boarding schools. There were also many mimeographed excerpts from the Bureau of American Ethnology. On the whole they were pedantic, uninteresting; some were ambiguous. Many were hopelessly useless as far as understanding the Indian of today. They were of such nature as: Bibliography of Indian Stories for Young Folks, the American Indian in the World War, Indian Wars and Local Disturbances, 1782–1898, Primitive Agriculture of the Indians, Cliff Dwelling, Mounds and Mound Builders, Indian Music, Indian Historical References, Indian Missions, Indian Religion, the Social Heritage, along with postcards showing aborigines in blankets and feathers seated before tepees. One pamphlet looked interesting: Indian Home Life, Past and Present. It contained thirteen pages; the first twelve dealt with the past. Of the present the most committing statement was that the Indians were " fast assuming the habits and customs of modern civilization and becoming good citizens in every sense of the word." Another looked inviting, entitled, " Indian Reservations," but it turned out to be an ethnological excerpt printed in 1923.

I turned to the pamphlet on the Sioux and found the latest date mentioned in their history was 1890 when Gen-

eral N. A. Miles " subdued " a Ghost Dance uprising.
Nothing of their life on the reservation. Nothing of the success or failure of their farming activities, the purpose for
which they were forcefully settled on limited territories.
But upon reading Helen Jackson's *Century of Dishonor*, an
indictment printed more than fifty years ago, I came across
this sentence: " Had the provisions of these first treaties
been fairly and promptly carried out, there would have
been living today among the citizens of Minnesota thousands of Sioux families, good and prosperous farmers and
mechanics, whose civilization would have dated back to
the treaty of Prairie du Chien [1830]." Miss Jackson, in
1880, lamented that the Sioux could have been prosperous
farmers for fifty years or more. But today, a hundred years
after the treaty of Prairie du Chien, I found no prosperous
farmers among the Sioux. Rather, a farmer who owned a
horse was eating it.

I read nothing in Government print concerning the
syphilized Sioux; but Miss Jackson recorded how, over
seventy years ago, " the Indian chiefs, in their interview
with the President in September last, begged that they
might not be sent to the Missouri River, as whisky-drinking
and other demoralization would be the consequence." Needless to say they were sent, and for almost three-quarters of
a century they have been helplessly under the influences
of " the gambler and the pimp, the coward and the fool."

This trail-covering by the Indian Bureau has been con-
tinuous and is responsible for the distorted opinions of
Indians held by the American public today. Dr. Haven
Emerson, professor of public health at Columbia Univer-

sity, as president of the American Indian Defense Association, has led that organization for many years in its fight against Bureaucratic propaganda. On May 9, 1930, he wrote the following to Dr. Ray Lyman Wilbur, Secretary of the Interior, the Department which fathers the Indian Bureau: " We are not without a keen sense of our responsibility to a considerable public which has over a term of years been met by deception, falsehood, and abuse whenever an attempt was made to learn the plans and policies of the Indian Commissioners for the most elementary rights and needs of the Indians."

2

The most effective smoke screen the Indian Bureau has used to cover its own incompetency has been the much discussed wealth of the Indian. There has been so much prolific publicity about the " rich Indian " and his constantly growing wealth that the public, unfamiliar with actual conditions, have been misled by the glittering accounts of Indian prosperity. For example, there have been such statements as the following by ex-Assistant Commissioner of Indian Affairs Edgar B. Meritt to the Oakland Forum, the Commonwealth Club of California, and the Chamber of Commerce of Los Angeles: " The per capita wealth of the American Indian is nearly twice as great as the per capita wealth of the other citizens of this country. The per capita wealth of the American Indian is approximately $4,700."

However, the opening paragraph of the report of the Institute for Government Research, the most important single document in Indian Affairs since Helen Jackson published her *Century of Dishonor* fifty years ago, calmly eradicates this favorite and most effective propaganda of the Bureau. " An overwhelming majority of the Indians are poor, even extremely poor."

This 872-page report was the result of a detailed survey accomplished at the request of former Secretary of the Interior Hubert Work, in which department the Indian Bureau functions, and was submitted to him on February 21, 1928. It is the most restrained yet heartbreaking survey of Indian health, education, and human needs. One reads it with great shock and dismay as he learns of the conditions which the Institute's scientific investigators discovered existing on reservations and in Indian boarding schools. No American with a conscience can forget its facts. Nor can the Bureau officials comfort themselves with the excuse of " exaggerations offered by reckless and irresponsible individuals."

The report, couched in the quietest of restrained official language, confesses the power of such propaganda in a paragraph on page 437:

The wealth of the Osage Indians in the oil fields of Oklahoma and of certain individual Indians of other tribes has received wide publicity. As a result some people who have made no detailed study of the subject have an impression that the Indians as a race are fairly rich. This impression is erroneous.

Chapter Ten of the report, " General Economic Conditions," adds to the field observations numerous facts out of the *Indian Bureau's own statistical tables*. The following tribes have less than one hundred dollars per capita per annum income, including individual and tribal:

Carson agency (Nevada), Havasupai, Siletz (Oregon), Bishop (California), Northern Pueblos of New Mexico, Leupp (Navajo), Western Navajo, Warm Springs (Oregon), Walker River (Nevada), Zuni Pueblo, Tulalip, Pine Ridge (Sioux), Fort Belknap (Montana), Sacramento (Northern California), Neah Bay (Washington), and Yuma (California).

The Carson agency of Nevada has the lowest per capita income with the startling amount of $15 per annum. Havasupai of Arizona is next with $18 per annum. I remember receiving from Washington, when I wrote the Bureau asking for information, a nicely printed pamphlet entitled " The Havasupai Indian Agency, Arizona."

I have it before me as I write. On the front page is the picture of a beautiful waterfall. The caption reads: " Sky Blue Water." The pages are chiefly concerned with descriptions of the "wonderful scenery and unique characteristics as a habitation for man," which are fully illustrated. Surely the Havasupai country, where Indians live on a per capita income of $18 a year, must present a different picture to the eye of even the most casual of observers.

This pamphlet was printed eight months and three days after the Secretary of the Interior had received the report of the Institute for Government Research. Evidence of whitewashing is found in obviously contradictory statements regarding the $18 per capita per annum income. The official writes of the men as earning " three to four dollars a day " and " are engaged eight or nine months

HORSE MEAT DRYING IN THE SUN

WAITING THEIR TURN

during the year." He continues: " Some earn money pack-
ing freight into the agency. The Indian policeman at the
agency who receives $40 a month and $100 a year for the
maintenance of a horse is not considered well paid by
the rest of the Indians. They can do better than he, on the
average, working at other jobs. A number of these people
make enough to keep second-hand automobiles up at the
head of the trail leading to the canyon." [1]

3

Out of the 65 jurisdictions completely under the control
of the Indian Bureau only two are found by the scientific
investigators of the Institute to have per capita annual incomes of more than $500. They are the Osages of Okla-
homa and the Klamaths of Oregon.

Let us briefly look at the supposed wealth of the Oklahoma Indians. This stronghold of Indian Bureau propaganda is being definitely blasted in the current hearings
of the Senate Investigating Committee. There are approximately 150,000 Indians in Oklahoma, of which only
3,000 are Osages. The Senate Committee has discovered
thousands suffering in dire poverty; the Chickasaw, Choctaw, Cherokee, Creek, and Seminole tribes have been found
to be " broke." Of the much advertised Osages, they are
rapidly approaching the state in which they lived before oil
was miraculously discovered on their arid soil; they are
once more facing want. The revenue-producing capital

[1] The Havasupai Indian Agency, Arizona. Printed at Haskell October 24,
1928, by the Department of the Interior, Office of Indian Affairs. P. 18.

was once above a quarter of a billion; it has since dwindled 209 millions, leaving an estimated total of only thirty millions. Where annual incomes were once $13,200 they have now shrunk to a bare $1540. The average monthly income of an Osage today is $125. " They are now riding in Fords," Senator W. B. Pine of Oklahoma told me, " and dilapidated ones at that."

What happened to $209,000,000 of the principal, not to mention the interest? By what means was one of the wealthiest groups in America stripped of wealth? This sensational squandering was accomplished solely through the Indian Bureau. It must be remembered that not one dollar of a restricted Osage was or can be spent except under the supervision of the Bureau. An Osage could not buy a $7,500 limousine or build a $50,000 mansion unless the Indian Bureau superintendent and his subordinates sanctioned the expenditure. A garage proprietor could not receive a $12,000 check for automobile repairs unless his bill was okayed by an Indian Bureau official. Nor could an undertaker for an eighteen-hundred-dollar funeral, or for a fourteen-hundred-dollar monument. A physician could not be made a health consultant of an Indian he has never seen nor has any intention of seeing, at a lordly salary, unless he were *persona grata* with the agency staff. Nor could numerous probate attorneys, supervising probate attorneys, clerks, fee clerks, and hundreds of bloodsuckers be listed on the pay roll, dispensed from the Osage tribal fund, unless the Indians' protector saw fit to put them there. Nor is it credible that whole families of white professional guardians would be appointed

to disburse moneys unless their commissions were satisfactorily split. Nor can the Indian Bureau be absolved of
all knowledge and responsibility when Indians have been
extravagantly insured, their insurance deeded to Whites,
and then found a few months later with bullets in their
heads.

The conversion of Senator Elmer Thomas of Oklahoma,
where these practices have been and still are flourishing,
from a Bureau apologist, believing former Commissioner
Burke had some competency, to a militant accuser, having
" no use whatever for Burke's successor," has been most
encouraging to his 120,000 Indian constituents. The *Daily
Oklahomian,* under a Nov. 29, 1930, date line, printed
the following:

In an interview, the Oklahoma Senator vigorously criticised the
practices, personnel, and administration of the Indian Bureau,
and announced that he thought the Senate Indian Affairs Committee should demand the resignation of Commissioner C. J.
Rhoads, head of the Bureau. Senator Thomas's viewpoint has
undergone a complete change as the result of the recent tour of
inspection made by a special Senate subcommittee, of which he
is a member.

" Rhoads refuses to do anything to remedy conditions," Thomas
said. " He even refused to accompany the Senate subcommittee on
the inspection tour to get some first hand information.

" The Indian Bureau needs to be cleaned out completely, and
placed in the hands of able business men."

Senator Lynn Frazier, chairman of the Senate subcommittee, investigating Indian affairs, issued the following statement with regard to the Oklahoma hearings, which

was printed in the December 2, 1930, issue of *Labor: A National Weekly Newspaper:*

" We found cases where wealthy Indians have been encouraged to build palatial houses with extravagant furnishings. Their diminishing oil royalties will not now support them in this grand state and they may lose every cent invested.

" Other cases were found where Indians had been induced to spend their entire income, and were charged extravagant sums for ' administration of these expenditures.' "

Senator Burton K. Wheeler of Montana, also a member of the Senate Investigating Committee and present at the Oklahoma hearings, stated in the same issue of *Labor* that " The facts disclosed to us are such as to warrant the overhauling of the Indian Bureau from top to bottom. Our findings indicate that the Indian Bureau is the most completely mismanaged and incompetent in our government."

4

Only nine out of the 65 jurisdictions have incomes as high as $300 a year. Forty-three have incomes below $200 a year. Almost 8,000 Sioux, living on the Pine Ridge Reservation, have an income of $15.94 a year, according to the Bureau's budget officer. It was only a short time back when they were running down buffalo so thick the hills looked black.

The Institute report makes it plain that the compounding of the tribal with the individual incomes causes a falsely rosy picture to be drawn, because the millions from tribal incomes are used for the support of the Indian Bureau, not for the Indians. A cruel example of this fact is provided by the San Carlos Apache reservation. On page 450 the report lists San Carlos as sixteenth from the top in the income group, and with a tribal fund fluctuating from $75,000 to $170,000 in successive years. But the San Carlos Apache children, locked up in the Rice Boarding School, were permitted by the Bureau to spend nine cents a day on food (page 327).

It has been the fluctuating appraisals of property upon which the Bureau has based its business ability to increase the Indians' wealth, rather than on any real alteration in value. For example, the total estimated wealth of the Indians in the United States in 1922, according to official figures, was given as $727,000,000. In 1926 this estimate had jumped to $1,693,844,000, or an increase of $966,-000,000 in four years. The face of such figures seems to confirm the Bureau's assertions as to the amazing prosperity of the Indian, but a closer examination of their own figures reveals an interesting light shining on the audit book.

According to the 1926 report, the estimated value of oil, gas, and other mineral resources on Indian land amounted to $1,033,947,224. If this " estimate " is subtracted from the total amount, given as the value of individual and tribal property, there remains $659,897,582. In comparing this figure with that given for 1922, when no estimates of mineral resources were included in the land values, we find there has actually been a decrease of $69,000,000 in those four years of allotted lands held in trust.

The total shrinkage in the four years has been $122,-000,000.

Indian lands were more valuable in 1922 by $122,000,-000 than they were in 1926. Yet by padding the totals with estimated mineral and oil wealth the Bureau has created an apparent increase of 119 per cent for those four years.

To bring these figures up to date: Commissioner Rhoads, in a letter sent me under the date of June 26, 1930, roughly estimated the land and mineral wealth of the American Indian at two billions of dollars. This is an approximate increase of $967,000,000 in the last four years. Thus the Indian Bureau is consistent in its fable: A 93 per cent increase of wealth since 1926, or the grand total of a 206 per cent increase in eight years!

The 119 per cent decrease is not taking into account the $31,000,000 reimbursable indebtedness placed upon Indian lands unconstitutionally. " To be ground under even a just debt is misery, but to be ground under an unjust debt, unwillingly incurred, not even knowingly incurred, is a worse misery. That is the position of the Indians." [2]

The Indian estate is shrinking rapidly. Its diminution, in four years, through 1926, was four per cent a year. This covers all tangible, measurable, known property, both tribal and individual, such as lands, houses, timber, cattle, and money. The dwindling of any estate at four per cent a year means complete annihilation in 25 years. At the Indian Bureau's present speed of mismanagement the Indians of America will be penniless by 1951. Many already have gone over to the red side of the ledger.

The National Bureau of Municipal Research made in

[2] Hearings before a Subcommittee of the Senate Committee on Indian Affairs pursuant to S. Res. 341. Pp. 38–9.

1915 one of several reports which the Indian Bureau has suppressed. The following statement, which has been buried for fifteen years, discloses present methods as existing a decade and a half previous:

> Behind the sham protection which operates largely as a blind to publicity have been at all times great wealth in the form of Indian funds to be subverted; valuable land, mines, oil fields, and other natural resources to be despoiled or appropriated to the use of the trader . . . [there is] fraud, corruption, and institutional incompetence, almost beyond the possibility of comprehension.

5

The following short table, the figures of which have been taken from the property values of the Indian Commissioner's report, proves that the increasing total wealth of the American Indian is a myth:

Agency	1922	1926	Decrease
Fort Apache	$12,894,485	$6,903,592	46%
Western Navajo	2,808,791	331,070	88%
Yakima	18,252,463	9,281,122	48%
Turtle Mountain ...	3,585,731	1,401,343	60%
Yankton	4,552,144	2,666,990	41%
Flathead	10,605,406	6,326,413	30%

The decrease in the per capita wealth is correspondingly great. For example, the per capita wealth of the Chippewas decreased $726 from 1922 to 1926. In the case of the Sioux Indians the decrease during the same period was over $1100 — an outstanding example of the " ever-increasing wealth " of the Indian. In six years their per capita earnings diminished from what was almost a white man's income, $1274, to a dung pile of $165 per annum in 1928.[3]

What can be the meaning of this? Why all the inconsistent, incompetent bookkeeping? Why all these watered estimates of wealth, when millions of dollars in land values yearly disappear? Why does the Indian Bureau advertise the per capita wealth of the Indian at the exaggerated figure of $4,700 when, in truth, it is $485.33 — an error of over $4200 per capita?

Such propaganda is a smoke screen used to hide the Bureau's own incompetence as a guardian, false to the nation's trust, the proof of which will be the task of succeeding chapters.

[3] *The Prob. of Indian Administration* by the Institute for Governmental Research. Pp. 449–50. The Institute's findings were based exclusively on the Indian Bureau's records, which discloses the contradictory, chaotic state of those records.

VIII

VANISHING AMERICANS

1

IN public speeches, in printed documents, in news re-
leases, and indirectly in many other publicity channels,
likely to be given great credence by the American
public, the Bureau of Indian Affairs is declaring that
the Indian population of the United States is steadily
increasing."

Thus speaks the *American Indian Life*, a magazine issued
by the Indian Defense Association of California. Former
Assistant Commissioner Edgar B. Meritt has been responsible for much of this publicity, the effect of which is still
in evidence today. One of his published statements reads:

The truth of the matter is that the Indians in the last twenty-
five years have been steadily increasing in population and are no
longer a vanishing race. For example, in 1900, there were 270,544
Indians in the United States, and today we have 349,876. The
Indians are increasing in population at the rate of about 1500 per

annum, which is the result of the work of the Indian Bureau along educational and health lines.

As we have already seen, the Institute of Government Research blasted the dungeon in which the public mind has been confined regarding Indian wealth. In the case of Indian population its statistics have again proved illuminating. On one jurisdiction, where the population had been long announced at 3700, it was discovered that an actual enumeration disclosed only 2200. Different members of the survey staff on separate occasions were presented by superintendents with " distinctly different figures." When the investigators requested a less fluctuating number they were given " a tabulation made from a mailing list," which was " materially lower than either of the figures previously given."

But the blasting has only begun. Many prominent senators and laymen have turned their microscopes on the remaining bit of Indian bacteria. Dr. Haven Emerson, professor of Public Health Administration in Columbia University, already mentioned here, wrote the following regarding the " increasing Indian population ": " I have the mortality tables before me, showing the deaths per thousand of Indians within the registration area. These tables show an increase of 48 per cent in the mortality rate among the Indians in the four years ending 1924, the last year for which complete data have been tabulated. In 1921 the Indian death rate per 1000 of Indian population in the registration area was 17.5. In 1922 it was 19.2 per 1000. In 1923 it was 22.5 per thousand. In 1924 it was 25.9 per 1000, or approximately twice the white death rate."

Dr. Emerson also disclosed the death rates in separate states. In Montana, a state with a large Indian population under the exclusive jurisdiction of the Indian Bureau, the rate in 1924 was 34.5 per 1000. In North Dakota it was 33 per 1000, in Washington 34.5 per 1000. In Wyoming the Bureau's Indians had a death rate of 86.1 per 1000 in 1924. " These figures presage the extermination of whole great tribes, proceeding swiftly or slowly," he concluded, and yet " the Indian Bureau, in the face of the yearly census reports, and without referring to them or challenging them, continues to announce a steadily falling Indian death rate, when the contrary is the fact."

In analyzing the Indian death rate the Columbia professor drew particular attention to the infant mortality. Such deaths in the population at large in 1924 were 70.8 per 1000. Among Negroes they were 114.1; among Indians 190.7, or two and five-sevenths times the general population rate.

Dr. Emerson was aware of the political situation when he stated " the chief action of the Indian Bureau appears to be a propaganda action designed to allay the public mind and to present the Bureau as the efficient agency working among rapidly improving conditions. The facts have long been known to the Indian Bureau."

2

The Indian death rate approximately triples the rate of the general population, as there has been an increase of

62 per cent through the five years ending 1925. The Indian tuberculosis death rate in the registration area is six times the white rate as a whole, according to the United States census, while it is seven and a half times the white tuberculosis death rate.

One of the prize tuberculosis death rates is to be found in Wisconsin, where for five years the State has fought to take over the medical services for its Indians against the successful opposition of the Bureau. Wisconsin's tuberculosis death rate for the population other than Indian is 60 per 100,000 per year. The Menominee tribe, one hundred per cent under Bureau control, has the highest tuberculosis death rate of any group of human beings: 2540 per 100,000 per year. For the Lac Du Flambeau tribes it is 1790. The Menominees, who support the Bureau from the cutting of their virgin timber, have had their tuberculosis death rate run up to over forty times the tuberculosis death rate of the state as a whole.[1]

Nevertheless the Indian Bureau for some reason or other sharply increased its population totals 6.37 per cent for Wisconsin between 1923 and 1924.

The similar procreation of the State of Washington's Indians has been nothing short of a miracle. According to the Bureau they numbered 10,906 in 1923 and 12,264 in 1924, an increase of 12.64 per cent in one year. This would mean the doubling of the Washington Indian population in seven and a half years, which obviously has not been accomplished.

In the case of California the Bureau laid its smoke screen

---

[1] *The Prob. of Indian Administration.* P. 203.

on too heavily. In one year the Indian population of California was increased by 5,367 or 41.75 per cent. At that rate they would return in a few years to their original count of 100,000, which they numbered before the Indian Bureau took complete charge of them.

Dr. Allen F. Gillihan was employed by the California State Board of Health to make a survey of the Indians. He found one doctor serving 1500 Indians in a territory extending 100 miles eastward of the hospital and 25 miles to the south and west. He reported "that the ill treatment during the past seventy years has resulted in reducing the population from over 100,000 to 17,300."

The hands of the Indian Bureau are covered with the blood of 83,000 California relatives.

The Census Bureau was unwilling to add the Indian Bureau's 41.75 per cent increase to the California Indian population, which they deemed an 84 per cent excess.

3

In 1492, say ethnological experts, there were 918,000 aborigines within the continental limits of the United States. In 1820, according to the report of Morse on Indian Affairs, there were 471,000. But in 1924 the statistics of the Indian Office listed only 162,602 full bloods, in a total of 299,761. Another set of Bureau statistics listed the 1924 Indian population as 346,902. In other words there are over 47,000 bodiless Indians living on the pages of the Bureau's statistical records. But with the United States Bureau of the Census numbering Indians at 244,437 in

1924 there appears to be 100,000 bodiless Indians living on the ink-dotted pages.

The Indian Bureau fought against Senator King's resolution for a Senate investigation of Indian Affairs. It begged that an indictment of the Indian system should be made before the Senate Indian Committee and that the Bureau be allowed to reply into the record. The indictment was made and published February 23, 1927. None reading it can question its detailed, documented information any more than its terribleness. Then the Indian Bureau elected to make no reply, for it had none.

The Secretary of the Interior followed the Bureau's silence with this statement: "The department refutes nothing, admits nothing, and denies nothing."

One week after announcing it would not reply to an indictment, made at its request so they might refute it, the Bureau broadcast a press dispatch. The newspapers throughout the country printed a bulletin which repeated the already exploded claims about increasing population and increasing wealth. The next day the Bureau again shone with even greater glory. They had released a full page feature which was run by scores of newspapers: "The civilization and education of the Indian race constitutes an everlasting monument to the Department of the Interior. Those who have private axes to grind, start outcries about the oppressed, downtrodden Indian. These accusations are without foundation. The Indian race at present is more affluent, better educated, better housed and fed, and healthier, than any body of dependents on the world's map."

4

Such propaganda, appearing in newspapers throughout the states, have helped crystallize a public mind once brought up to believe the Indian a filthy, treacherous savage of a fortunately vanishing race. As our competitive strength increased our hate and fear gradually diminished as we saw the " red devils " transformed into pathetic brown children, huddling on reservations. After our sordid victory of Wounded Knee, when a mere handful of hungry bewildered Sioux were massacred on South Dakota's Bad Lands, the " Indian problem " dropped quietly out of sight. Our impressions in the meanwhile have been based on the victories of the Carlisle grammar-school boys over the choicest of the nation's college gridiron stars.

With the American eye trained to compass the international horizons of London, Geneva, The Hague, and Paris we have failed to see our own back yard littered with an inter-planetary spectacle. Dr. Emerson, whose eyes have observed this national disgrace, has declared that the publication of these high mortality rates as " affecting any population in the United States of America other than Indians, would result in immediate action by State Boards of Health."

Why hasn't the Federal Government acted?

Seventy years ago that question was answered by Edwin M. Stanton, Secretary of War in Lincoln's cabinet. In 1862 Bishop H. B. Whipple of Minnesota went to Washington on behalf of the Sioux Indians, and upon hearing of his arrival Secretary Stanton said to General Halleck: " What

does the Bishop want? If he came here to tell us our Indian
system is a sink of iniquity, tell him we all know it. Tell
him the United States never cures a wrong, never reforms
an evil until the people demand it. Tell him that when the
hearts of the American people are reached the Indian will
be saved."

For half a century and two decades the hearts of the
American people have remained untouched.

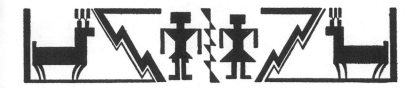

IX

" GOD'S IN HIS HEAVEN — "

1

IT is regrettable that some Christian missionaries have had their humanitarian field work tainted by an unsavory affiliation with the Indian Bureau. It is obvious that the average church-goer and minister are unaware of the discreditable monetary and political liaisons being quietly conducted in Washington. I have found the Christian missionary, as a whole, an intelligent, conscientious servant; there are those, however, whose antiquated, revivalistic, " left-wing " practices can neither be praised nor excused.

The Indian Bureau, fully aware that only Congress can review its actions, has taken means of preventing that review by a systematic, though indirect domination of institutions which control public opinion. Of those institutions the home missionary boards of the churches have proven the most valuable to the Bureau.

One observer of this phase of Indian propaganda has remarked that " The Bureau, both by direct use of its absolute authority and by indirect means, can make or ruin the work of a mission society. The recapitulation of the Bureau powers, remembering that they are not theoretical but actual powers used here and now, will give the reader his clues."

To be definite: A specific charge of " subsidization " has been directed at a national home mission agency, which, ever since 1922, has " strenuously defended the Indian Bureau system and the officials at its head." John Collier, executive secretary of the American Indian Defense Association, asserted in the January 1, 1927, issue of the *Survey Graphic* that " the Bureau of Catholic Indian Missions was receiving, in 1924, $190,000 a year from the trust funds of restricted Indians, not illegally but under rules and regulations of the Interior Department and essentially through the voluntary act of the Indian commissioner. The subsidy continues; the facts are not reported in the commissioner's annual report or in the bureau's yearly statement to the Appropriations Committee."

If this charge be true the Bureau of Catholic Indian Missions has received, during the past seven years, $1,320,-000 from the Indian Bureau, who in turn unchallengingly obtained the money from the trust funds of restricted, incompetent Indians. The proof of the validity of Mr. Collier's charge lies in the fact that the *Survey* sent an advance copy of his article, entitled *Are We Making Red Slaves?* to the accused Bureau, offering them the opportunity " to protest, comment, or present rebuttal statements " before

publication. The editor's simple enumeration of this procedure was that " the Bureau of Catholic Indian Missions
returned the manuscript without comment."

Silence may be blissful, but in the above case it apparently implies something quite different. Further, I am
informed that the subsidy has been continued. In 1928 and
1929 it was increased to approximately $230,000, all of
which is contrary to express statutes of Congress.

Besides the Catholic another national home mission
agency has arduously defended the policies of the Indian
Bureau during the past eight years. In 1923 the American
Baptist Home Mission Society was to receive immediately
the sum of $550,000 from the trust money of an old, il-
literate Creek, known as Jackson Barnett; who was described as a half-wit in the confidential reports of the Indian
Bureau, a fact later proven before the Senate Investigating
Committee. Another $550,000 was designed for the private
pocket of Barnett's " legal wife," who was described also
in the Bureau's own confidential reports as a woman who
kidnapped the aged Barnett, fed him liquor, married him
in several states, and brought him to the Indian Bureau's
office in Washington where the above enumerated fifty-
fifty split was consummated.[1]

I interviewed Senator W. B. Pine of Oklahoma, Barnett's
native state, with regard to this case. " It has been proven
and is a matter of the record," he said, " that this woman
went with nigger bell boys. In fact, the porters got her dates
with traveling men. She has been nothing but a nuisance.

---

[1] The American Baptist Home Mission Society in 1924 issued a whitewash of the Indian Bureau and an attack against all its critics.

She kidnapped Barnett and so needed a whitewash; William Atherton DuPuy was employed by her to write a whitewash story for five hundred or six hundred dollars. DuPuy is now the publicity agent for the Department of the Interior, and writes articles for Secretary Wilbur on Indian affairs for the *Saturday Evening Post,* rose-colored and well-illustrated. You know the type I mean.

" But much more important has been the procedure of the Indian Bureau in this case. The Commissioner wrote Mr. White, the Executive Secretary of the Baptists, at 23 East 26th Street, New York City, asking him to manipulate influential men, such as the Honorable Charles Evans Hughes and Senator Wadsworth of New York, and have them in turn influence the President. You see, they wanted the weight of presidential approval behind that action of taking $550,000, and their means of attempting to secure that approval shows how far-reaching are the tentacles of the Indian Bureau with the aid of a religious institution."

Picking up a news clipping from his desk, Senator Pine said, handing the paper to me, " This is the speech Dr. Weeks of Bacon College, which received the $550,000, gave before the Lions Club of Muskogee, assailing our attempts to halt Barnett's gift."

The clipping was from the Muskogee *Daily Phoenix* of Thursday morning, January 19, 1929. I read:

Why shouldn't these Indians give to institutions which help other Indians? [asked Mr. Weeks]. Few of them earned their wealth. It came to them as a golden shower, through a fortunate chance.

" Weeks' psychology," Senator Pine commented, " is
that since the Indians' wealth has been a matter of chance
or fortune, why shouldn't he take their money, for somebody else will. Weeks told the Kiwanis Club that you can
do anything to an Indian but laugh at him. He implied by
that, of course, that you can rob him and get away with it."

I continued reading the clipping:

Each year we must raise $21,000 in gifts, above our income,
to avoid a deficit. There will be none this year, as we are constantly on the lookout for gifts.

" I have been in Oklahoma since 1904 and never have
I seen grafters with a program so complete, so crafty for
collecting money," was Senator Pine's comment. " White
had fixed their ' friend ' in Washington. All Weeks had to
do was get the Indians to consent to a donation, and the
rest was taken care of. There was only one thing they had
to be certain about, and that was to get the money. They've
gotten already over $750,000 from incompetent Indians,
and in so doing have disinherited Indian heirs in favor of
the Baptists. They have taken land also; they hold 550
acres now of Indian land, and have prospects of securing
several thousand. Nothing has been left for the Indians'
children; all has gone to the Baptists."

Again looking at the paper I read:

I have never been refused by an Indian [Weeks said], unless
married to a white person.

" He means by that," said Senator Pine, " that when
Indians are married to whites they have some protection.

He can collect his gifts only from Indians who are unprotected by relatives or their guardian in Washington."

I concluded my examination of the news clipping by reading the following:

We've had enough investigating of the case, and photographing and rereading of the original papers to wear them out. As long as the senior senator from Oklahoma feels toward certain persons in the Indian department the antipathy he does, I see no hope for us.

"That," said Pine, "is the greatest compliment I have ever received while holding public office."

2

When a justice-seeking, fact-disclosing clergyman, who knows the Indian intimately, once attempted to "speak without prejudice or fear of discipline from ' higher up ' " he was severely taken to task by those higher ups for having heretically strayed from the fold.

The Rev. Irwin St. John Tucker was one such offending clergyman. His reprimanders were the members of the Council of Missionary Bishops of the Episcopal Church. His article appeared in the July 2, 1927, issue of the *Churchman*, the opening paragraph of which read:

For sheer cold-blooded long-drawn-out horror, the massacre of native Americans in government schools, as carried out by the Indian Bureau with the benevolent intention of assimilating their lands, has never been equalled since the days of Cromwell in Ireland.

The third paragraph:

But an unkind searchlight, turned upon the dealings of the Indian Bureau with our genuine hundred per centers in the course of the hearings in the recent Congress by certain pernicious enemies of law and order, disclosed a state of things which must have made the inventors of the Belgian outrages blush with shame and gnaw their finger nails in helpless jealous rage.

But the Rev. Irwin St. John Tucker did not confine his article solely to historical comparisons and rhetorical outbursts. He made specific charges based upon the testimony, affidavits and letters, and official reports which composed the printed hearings of the Senate's complete investigation of Indian affairs, proposed by Senator William King of Utah. Much of that evidence from time to time appears in this book. Nowhere in his article did Rev. Tucker misquote or misrepresent those Senate hearings, which, although preliminary to the investigations by Senator Frazier's committee, have already proven:

That the Indian race is being physically destroyed. (Pp. 54–63, Senate Hearings.)

That this decimation through death is being accelerated in recent years. (Pp. 46 et seq., Senate Hearings.)

That Indian property is being diminished at the rate of four per cent each year by the exclusive actions of the Indians' official guardian, not by the Indians themselves. (Pp. 38–40, Hearings.)

That the most elementary of the Constitutional rights are being denied Indians with an open consistency. (Pp. 24–31, 51–52.)

That the boarding schools are unnecessarily overcrowded. That in some schools the physical and moral conditions are inexcusably bad. (Pp. 24–31, 47–50).

And that in recent years the official, legalized exploitations and graftings have accelerated. (See cases throughout Hearings.)

What was the Missionary Bishops' answer to Rev. Tucker's charges? They issued a manifesto which was printed in *The Living Church* of October 8, 1927, and was signed by Bishops Howden, Remington, Mitchell, Barnwell, Beecher, Burleson, Cross, Moulton, Sanford, Seaman, Tyler, Roberts, and Casady; and Carroll W. Davis, Domestic Secretary of the National Council. It disproved nothing. The bishops merely exclaimed that they were convinced that the charges " are erroneous or distorted," and that " there is no adequate justification for the extravagant and outrageous assertions in this article."

Copies of their whitewashing opinions were sent to church papers, the *Spirit of the Missions,* and the publicity department of the National Council of Bishops, " for whatever use they might desire to make of it."

Upon the wide publication of this lame, limping negation, the Indian Defense Associations of Central and Northern California, Santa Barbara, Pasadena, Southern California, Milwaukee, and Washington placed the issue-dodging bishops on a gridiron. " You are obtaining momentarily," these associations wrote, " the result which the Indian Bureau, if not yourselves, would desire. That is the clouding of terrible and unanswerable charges, by means of a cloud of words. . . . And you, the Missionary Bishops, denying unspecifically the charges which you avoid quoting, omit to name one of those who made the charges." The associations then enumerated more than thirty for the edification of the bishops.

" You have unwittingly," declared the already quoted open letter, " lent yourselves to the Indian Bureau's campaign, now under way, to destroy the effect of the (Senate's) indictment while not explicitly disproving or denying it (for disproof or denial are impossible); to hide an unanswerable arraignment behind clouds of indignant, if unresponsive, words."

Words, said Hamlet, words.

But all clergymen can not be condemned for idle enunciation.

The Rev. Hugh D. Smith, for many years a Presbyterian missionary on the Navajo Reservation, has written under date of October 4, 1927, concerning the conditions on his reservation. To quote but a few of his assertions: " The greatest need of the Navajo is hospitalization . . . Tuberculosis and trachoma are our worst enemies . . . Taking children from the reservation to non-reservation schools over the protest of the parents and against the advice of reservation agents is a great evil . . . Taking our boys to the beet fields where they contract typhoid fever and come back scattering this disease among their people . . . Undermining the average Navajo child's health . . . Not sufficient food is furnished the average boarding school child . . . Further proof of these statements will be furnished on request."

What was the Episcopal Missionary Bishop's comment with regard to that specific reservation? The extent of their unsubstantiated declaration was that "the conditions among the Navajos are vastly better in every way."

3

There apparently has been no limitation to the means employed by the missionary departments of various churches in their zealous efforts to proselytize new customers to their faith. The Indian Bureau has been their outward, official agent in such connivency.

In 1921 the Bureau, under pressure of sundry missionary boards in Washington, accelerated the slow persecution of Indian religions, which had been going on for some time. This was accomplished through the Bureau's autocracy; for the Indian Bureau makes its own laws, known as regulations, which are as binding as court statutes, and can be overruled only by Congressional action.

Some Christian missionaries have found the Indians religiously irritating. The reason for this vexation has been the old religions of the Indians, a reason which the reader will readily understand when he reads the following sketch by one who has known Indian religions intimately:

The Indians are deeply and universally religious. Their religions are older than Christianity. These religions teach about the creation of the world and of man, the relation between man and God, the duty of man to man. They contain the moral code of the Indians, which is a code of truth-telling, honest dealing, kindness to children and the old, loyalty to the community, faithfulness in marriage, and cheerfulness in the face of sorrows.

No wonder missionaries have become discouraged and disgruntled in competition with such a religion. Instead of competing fairly in the open market those missionaries have desired to smash the Indian religions by force.

" To please these missionaries, who represent a considerable political power," wrote John Collier in the Scripps-Howard newspapers of June, 1924, " the Indian Bureau has instituted a persecution of these ' pagan ' Indian religions. It has classed the religious rites as ' Indian offenses,' punishable by imprisonment."

From the central office of the Bureau there issued, on April 26, 1921, an order to the superintendents in the field to prosecute any " so-called religious ceremony " as an Indian offense. These " Indian offenses," solely concocted by the Bureau, are not tried before the courts of the people; but before subordinates of the Bureau, thus completing the vicious circle. The reasons given for declaring the ceremonies " offenses " were that they " promoted idleness, were prolonged or excessive, caused Indians to give away their property recklessly, contained danger to health, or promoted indifference to family welfare."

A patriotic Russian can today, with some logic, condemn every Christian religious practice under one or all of the above descriptions.

Not thoroughly satisfied with the ground already gained, the missionaries saw that another order was issued embodying their specific recommendations. On February 14, 1923, that order appeared, explaining that the missionaries' recommendations " could be heartily endorsed." Some of those accepted suggestions were to the effect that no Indian younger than fifty years of age should be allowed to either witness or participate in a religious ceremony of his tribe; also that propaganda should be launched to " educate public opinion against " the religious dances and festivals. For the " Indian dance " is simply a form of Indian worship.

Finally, the Indian office, sorely pressed by the missionaries, issued its most nihilistic ultimatum on February 24, 1924, to the effect that " all Indians " were to abandon every religious ceremony within one year, or coercion would be employed to see that they did. The Pueblos, described by Commissioner Burke as " half-animals," were ordered to suspend the religious training of their young, by requiring that the boys, who had been temporarily withdrawn from school so that they might train for the Pueblo priesthood, be immediately returned to their respective schools. This meant the absolute destruction of the Pueblo religion, for their ten-thousand-year-old Bible is not written, but passed on from the old priests to the young by a painstaking instruction. The Taos Pueblo retorted by all its members announcing that they would go to jail before they would abandon their religion.

What was the fundamental cause of this religious persecution? What offense had the Indians committed against their almighty guardian, which caused him to hurl his wrath upon them?

" The offense," Collier said in his Scripps-Howard articles, " is simply that these religions are Indian and that they stand in the way of the Christian missionaries. . . . There is no precedent in American history for this course of action by the Indian Bureau. It means a return to the Spanish Inquisition."

In this persecution the missionaries pushed the Indian Bureau an inch too far beyond the line of public indifference. Nation-wide protest was aroused against the Bureau's autocratic undertaking, which was ultimately tempered; though the Bureau still insisted that its rules and regulations, which govern the Bureau's Indian courts, should have preference over any due process of law.

No Indian today, however, is *openly* persecuted for his religious beliefs. Instead, the Indian Bureau continues its policy of indirect persecution through legislation. On April 29, 1930, the National Council of American Indians and the American Indian Defense Association jointly launched an attack upon the newest Bureau proposal:

This Bill, H. R. 11429, was drafted by the Indian Bureau and endorsed by Secretary Wilbur [they stated]. Its declared purpose is to regulate dishonest collections of money from Indians, but its practical effect would be to institute a censorship over *religious* and political expression by Indians and over their self-defense against exploiters, and to intensify the dominance of the Indian Bureau over all Indian life. . . . No more un-American measure was devised by Commissioners Burke and Meritt, predecessors of the two reform Commissioners now at the head of Indian Affairs . . . [who] apparently have forgotten that Indians are citizens living under the Constitution of the United States.

No, Indians today are not *openly* persecuted for their religious beliefs. Instead, the children are still compelled to take Christian instruction in the boarding schools, regardless of their parents' or their own desires for religious liberty. Instead, they still can not complain when fanatical, venal missionaries are allowed to settle among them, and invade the privacy of their homes and the sanctity of their religious ceremonies.

4

The soul of the Indian is today hounded in an additional manner, vastly more effective and destructive in character than the reign of absolutism, which was launched in 1921 through the religious ultimatums.

I have attended a sufficient number of fanatical religious services conducted among the Indians, and have observed the technique of a sufficient number of mercenary missionaries at work to have arrived at the conclusion that the soul of the Indian is being hounded as systematically and horribly as that of an Inquisition heretic.

To the proof: I have before me, as I write, Bulletin No. 544 of the Gospel Union Publishing Company, located at 1841 East 7th Street, Kansas City, Mo. Five hundred and forty-three publications of this type have been printed prior to this bulletin; I do not know how many hundreds have been printed after. This tract, which I have on my desk, has been written by Bishop J. C. Ryle and is entitled, " Is There A Hell? " It is a typical tract. Some of its 543 predecessors are better suited to prove my point, but this tract is typical. Doubtful readers can secure additional specimens by writing J. A. Knowles, Lock Box 429, Kansas City, Mo.

I read from " Is There A Hell? "

" Reader, I love your soul [says Bishop Ryle], and

want it to be saved. I am therefore going to speak to you
about *hell*. Do not throw down this tract when you see that
word, but read on.

" There is such a place as hell. Let no one deceive you
with vain words. What men do not like they try hard not to
believe. There is such a place as hell. . . .

" All who are found impenitent and unbelieving — all
who have clung to sin, stuck to the world, and set their
affections on things below, all such shall come to an awful
end. Whosoever is not written in the book of life shall be
' Cast into the lake of fire.' Rev. 20:15. *This* will be
HELL.

" Do you believe the Bible? Then depend upon it *hell
is real and true.* . . . Then depend upon it *hell will have
inhabitants.* The wicked shall certainly be turned into hell,
and all the nations that forget God. The same blessed
Savior who now sits on a throne of Grace will one day sit
on a throne of Judgment, and men will see there is such
a thing as ' The wrath of the Lamb.' The same lips which
now say, ' Come unto Me,' will one day say, ' Depart, ye
cursed! ' Alas! how awful the thought of being condemned
by Christ Himself, judged by the Savior, sentenced to
misery by the Lamb!

" Do you believe the Bible? Then depend upon it *hell
will be intense and unutterable woe.* It is vain to talk of
all the expressions about it being figures of speech. The pit,
the prison, the worm, the fire, the thirst, the blackness, the
darkness, the weeping, the gnashing of teeth, the second
death. . . ."

I have heard Christian missionaries shout into the ears

of superstitious, child-minded Indians these horrible descriptions " of a real and true hell." I have seen the Indians droop their heads in self-inflicted shame, believing that all their poverty and oppression, all their diseases and misfortunes, have been dealt to them by " the wrath of the Lamb " because they did not " believe." I have seen preachers point their fingers at those bowed shoulders, shouting: " Hell is real! Hell is true! Hell will have inhabitants! " I have seen Indians, their primal passions thoroughly stirred, rock and moan to themselves, until they finally accelerate their emotions to the point where they suddenly jump up, run down the aisles with hands waving like Negroes, drop themselves down with a cry at the feet of the raving preacher, and commence to sob pitifully.

I have seen such spectacles within a twenty-five minute drive from my home in northern Michigan. I have seen tuberculous Indians, doomed to die within a year, prostrate themselves before the preacher's platform and, with tears on their cheeks and limbs quivering, ask forgiveness from the Lord, who dealt them the dread disease, because they were pagans and did not " believe." I have listened to missionaries describe hell as " the pit, the prison, the worm, the fire, the thirst, the blackness, the darkness, the weeping, the gnashing of teeth, the second death " et cetera. I have observed those missionaries, completely oblivious of any real, unimaginary suffering already inflicted upon the Indians, circle among the swaying, wailing bodies and whisper the terrors of hell into their ears. I have seen thumb-sucking babies hanging to the skirts of their prostrated mothers, crying, and not knowing why.

These observations have wrapped themselves about my memory with the tenacity of the arms of an octopus. As I write I see old grandmother Antoine, her head thrown back, her hands wringing in the air. Blind grandmother Antoine, her eyes closed, her wrinkled face wet with tears. I see her open mouth, showing its one jagged tooth. I hear her shouting over and over, " O Jesus, Jesus, Jesus . . ."

Such sounds and sights I will recall as long as I have a memory.

Those Indians die and we are now told they die like Christians. I quote from the case of *Fremont and Jackson versus the United States* in the United States Court of Claims: " The California *Christian* and coast Indians perished without a struggle or a murmur, and without any expense to the Government."

Nice, convenient Indians.

Perfectly satisfactory Indians.

III
SCHOOLS

X

FLOGGING CHILDREN

1

A T the fishing camp they told me how I could reach her cabin. " She knows lots of them old songs," they said, " she's a full-blooded Chippewa."
So I left the Brule, with its thick cedar banks, with its winding water paths between jutted rocks, and took a narrow dirt road that curled like a gliding snake over hills, between lakes, and into the hearts of virgin forests. For several days I had been driving westward toward the lands of the Sioux, and upon finding myself in Chippewa country I was not averse to gathering Ojibwa songs.

I came upon her cabin in the late afternoon and found her standing in the doorway, as though she expected my coming. When I announced my mission she looked at me steadily for a naked half-minute. Slowly she folded her arms stolidly against her stomach, and commenced to sing. She was intelligent, a teacher in a township school, and she assisted me in recording the notes on a scale. In the gathering twilight she sang Ojibwa mother lyrics to an imaginary sleeping baby. All the time she sang she eyed me curiously, almost pathetically. It made me uneasy. Finally, she ceased singing. I looked up from my pencil and saw her deep brown eyes, deep like dark ponds.

" He would have been as tall as you," she said, quietly. " But they sent him home in a box."

I was puzzled, but I remained silent. I saw her brown, soft face animate, her eyes fire, as she pointed savagely to a distant hill. " My brother's boy was also sent home in a box," she said, angrily.

Then suddenly she was as calm as when she sang her lullabies. Her voice ran smoothly like a brook, but there was an undercurrent of heart-breaking grief. " We have many wrongs," she said. " We are losing our lands, our water rights, our personal freedom. We are being robbed, starved — even diseased at your hands. But we will forget all that for the present, if we be granted only one thing — better treatment for our children in the Government boarding schools."

As I listened to this passionate yet calm plea I became aware of a race that places love for its children above all worldly gains or losses.

Later, on the Sioux reservation, on the other reservations I visited — in numerous villages and hamlets, in the Capital of the Nation—in the thousands of miles I have traveled I have heard one great plea: " We are starving — yes, we are being robbed and oppressed — yes, but first save our children."

2

Hours of reading confirmed these verbal statements. I learned of children as young as six years of age being taken forcibly from their mothers' arms and sent to distant boarding schools until they were eighteen years old, without seeing their parents during that period. I learned how they were underfed to the point of starvation, roughly treated, even beaten, and all the time made to work half a day at hard industrial labor in the fields, in the bakery, or in the laundry — child labor.

I have learned of the lives of those lonely children — frightened, flogged, exhausted children — ever hungry children. I have seen how they sleep in dormitories so crowded the beds touch each other and fill the aisles. They exist under so little protection from disease that epidemics sweep through entire schools as freely as winds. I have seen the stamp of overwork cruelly branded on their young but always tired faces. I have heard of children so underfed they snatch at plates of bread like famished animals. I have seen the jails they are thrown into after being flogged for infringement of minor rules.

The Government maintains boarding schools for approximately 25,000 Indian children. To the American citizen this sounds somewhat luxurious. The Government not only operates these boarding schools free of charge to the Indian, but also requires his children to attend. " A rather insistent benefactor," the citizen exclaims. " But the aura of luxury about that word boarding school vanished in thin air as one reads the facts," says the *Survey Graphic*.

3

Mr. H. J. Russell, construction engineer of the Indian Service at Leupp, wrote of his observations: " I have seen Indian boys chained to their beds at night for punishment. I have seen them thrown in cellars under the building, which the superintendent called a jail. I have seen their shoes taken away from them and they then forced to walk through the snow to the barn to help milk. I have seen them whipped with a hemp rope, also a water hose. Forced to do servant's work for employees and superintendent without compensation under the guise of industrial employment and education." [1]

W. Carson Ryan, Jr., formerly a professor of education at Swarthmore College, as one of the Institute's investigators, describes the jail he found on his trip to Wahpeton, North Dakota, which made him " wonder if Dakota is not the Siberia of the Indian Service.

" The superintendent showed me a dungeon in the basement previously used for girls, up to his coming two years ago. ' I never locked up any Indian child yet, and I don't intend to begin,' he said. The dungeon is 18 by 8, absolutely dark. Girls told the superintendent of two or three of them sleeping there on mattresses and rats crawling over them at night. Their food was bread and water. Brick walls showed where the girls had worked holes through and escaped." [2]

Mrs. Gertrude Bonnin, Zitkala-Sa, is a descendant of

[1] Hearings Before a Subcommittee of the Committee on Indian Affairs pursuant to S. Res. 341. P. 30.

[2] *The Problem of Indian Administration.* Chapter Nine on Education.

Sitting Bull, but more important, the president of the National Council of American Indians, the first organization to fight the cause of the Indian against the Bureau. One of the most cultivated women of her race, Mrs. Bonnin stated the following concerning the Ogallala School in South Dakota:

" Conquering Bear's two boys were in Ogallala boarding school, and they ran away to Corn Creek, about forty miles away. Policeman Jumping Eagle and the disciplinarian went after them and brought them back and gave them a severe beating. They were about twelve and fourteen years at the time. Their heads were shaven, though it was winter. One of the boys had a ball and chain locked onto his leg and was locked to the bed at night. My informant saw this herself. The boys were in the jail above her room. They were in a dirty, filthy place, with a bucket to be used as toilet.

" She said it hurt her so to see all these things, such as this little boy carrying the ball when marching to meals, that she could not eat. The boy even went to school with the ball and chain on, and it bothered the other children. Many requests were made to the principal to have the disciplinarian take the chain off, but days went by before this was actually done." [3]

Concerning the same reservation boarding school, the Ogallala on the Pine Ridge, Philip Romero, President of the Sioux Council, made the following statement to me: " They whipped Mary Rough, a young girl, and when her

[3] As stated to Vera L. Connolly. Published *Good Housekeeping Magazine*, Jan., 1929.

granddad went to see her the guard asked, ' What the hell are you going to do about it? We've got a right to give her a whipping.' "

Chief Clerk Detwiler of the Pine Ridge reservation stated to me with a bitter, intolerant nod of the head: " Three hundred and ninety-five out of the four hundred in the Ogallala school need a whipping."

Luke White Hawk, living in the Wounded Knee district of the Pine Ridge Reservation, testified to the Senate Investigating Committee of his children being hitched to a plow by a district-school teacher, still in the Indian Service:

> I have two going to school there and one of them came back sick; he was sick still in the morning, and I ask him about it, and he said the teacher had eight of the larger boys hooked up to cultivate potatoes and the teacher's boy had a punch and punch them along when they lag behind and that was the cause of his sickness. Two of the boys are right here and could tell it.[4]

There is even testimony from Bureau officials, given under oath. Patrick Kennedy was engineer at the Rice School on the San Carlos reservation before being transferred to the Fort Mohave School. He has testified about Indian girls, 11 and 12 years old, who escaped from the Rice School and were pursued and captured. Part of their punishment consisted in walking with heavy cordwood on their shoulders, around and around the school yard the whole of an afternoon. One girl stood dumb, her head and shoulders bowed, offering passive resistance. The principal

---

[4] Hearings before a Subcommittee of the Committee on Indian Affairs. 1929. Part 7. Pp. 2836–7.

" seized a club from the ground, beat the girl until she fell, and beat her on the ground. Then the girl carried the cordwood for the afternoon."

Engineer Kennedy testified these girls were chained to their beds for the night. They were compelled to sleep in chains. During the day they were marched to the dining hall for three-cent meals, held by chains fastened about their necks.

Further Bureau testimony has been produced about the Towoac boarding school for Ute and Navajo children in Colorado, where " recalcitrant " children were locked in darkness and fed on bread and water.

4

On January 10, 1929, former Commissioner of Indian Affairs Burke forbade corporal punishment in boarding schools because of brutalizations administered by disciplinarians and principals. Those brutalizations had already been established before the Senate Indian Investigating Committee, and included, for example, the beating of young Indian girls with clubs, and the scourging of Indian boys until they howled all night with pain in the school hospitals.

On March 20, 1930, Commissioner Charles J. Rhoads, appointed by President Hoover to replace Mr. Burke who had " resigned," yielded to the pressure of holdover men from the régime of Burke and Meritt by repealing the former order. Burke's prohibitive order was explicitly rescinded in the following statement: " Superintendents are authorized to adopt such emergency measures as may in their judgment be thought necessary." (Circular 2666 on Student Control.)

When President Hoover appointed Charles J. Rhoads and J. Henry Scattergood, Philadelphia Quakers and humanitarians, Commissioners of Indian Affairs, it looked like the coming of day for the Indians. The past year and a half, however, has proven those appointments to be a false dawn. The " reform administrators " have not reformed the Indian Bureau. They had an opportunity in 1929 which took years of effort to achieve. Congress, for the first time, was ready to act. The stage was set. But instead of attacking the deeper administrative problems, instead of attempting to relieve and emancipate the Indian, they became puppets under the control of Bureau chiefs, who are holdovers from the infamous régime of Albert Fall. Besides the one incontestible forward step in the appointment of Professor W. Carson Ryan, Jr. as head of Indian education, there has been no vigorous reorganization of personnel. Some notorious superintendents, such as Daniels, Estep, and Everest, have been pensioned and retired, not for their gross mismanagements but because of the sixty-five-year-age retirement law affecting all Civil Service employees; their positions have been filled by members of the " old school." Other superintendents, such as Arnold, Campbell, Mossman, Coe, and Jermark, have been protected, justified, and retained. Rhoads and Scattergood themselves have been consulting with the " resigned " Meritt, who still holds forth in the Interior Building. Although H. B. Peairs, Burke's infamous educational direc-

tor, is not an educator, he has been placed in charge of
Haskell, the largest boarding school in the Service. Not
one Indian school is an accredited institution of the standard accepted by state boards of education. The abuses and
wrongs, which fungated under Burke, are still being perpetrated by incompetent, unrelenting employees under the
widely heralded " reform administration." For example,
the sensational Klamath and Flathead abuses have been
defended and intensified; the Genoa, Nebraska, boarding-
school scandal has not been criticized; the abuses of the
Standing Rock, Yankton, Yakima, Sacramento, Winnebago, White Earth, La Pointe, and Blackfeet agencies have
not been eradicated; the Menominee timber situation has
not been altered, which is in open defiance of all expert
investigations; the irrigation abuses have been definitely
increased. In all, " a new record in the protection of abuses
has been achieved." Rhoads and Scattergood have completely discarded Secretary Wilbur's plan for reorganiz-
ing the Bureau's Irrigation and Reclamation Service; in
their contrariness to the reports of engineers and other experts they have plunged into a renewed extravagant and
to some extent unproductive spending, which has already
placed a debt of more than $30,000,000 on Indian lands.
Other maladministrations will be discussed from time to
time in the course of these chapters.

Commissioner Rhoads confesses his ignorance of the
tendency in modern education away from any use of
punishment whatsoever: " superintendents are authorized
to adopt such emergency measures as may in their judgment be thought necessary."

These last words, according to an editorial of the *New Republic*, May 7, 1930, " bode ill for the Indian children. Applying a strap to their bare backs used to be called a flogging. If it is now to be described as an ' emergency measure,' what difference does it make to the boys and girls who are flogged? And, if they are once more to be kept in solitary confinement, what do the Indian children care whether the place of punishment is called a jail or merely a ' quiet room ' ? "

The " disciplinarians," whose plenary authority has been reëstablished in the euphemistic terms, are those who are guilty of the atrocities listed in this chapter, for the personnel of the Indian Service has remained practically unchanged. R. E. L. Daniel, head of the Yankton Sioux Agency, South Dakota, recently pensioned for his good behavior, received complete protection from the new Commissioner of Indian Affairs for having " children beaten with leather straps, knocked down for sarcasm to the disciplinarian, struck with fist and hard objects until covered from face to knees with blood."

The " emergency measures " are to be administered by men who already have committed previous floggings. What goes on thousands of miles away in a " quiet room " between a czar-ruling superintendent and an " offending " Indian child few humans will ever know. The children do not possess an articulate link with their distant parents; they actually live in prison-like institutions. If the return of disciplinary action has been necessitated by the past relationship between pupil and teacher, then it is a sad reflection on the personnel of the Indian Service.

However, there are those who are unwilling to believe an order for corporal punishment actually exists. Jonathan M. Steeres, President of the Indian Rights Association, an organization of which C. J. Rhoads was both treasurer and president before he became Indian Commissioner, protested against "the statements recently published in the *Times* and elsewhere which endeavor to show that the Commissioner has thrown wide open the doors to corporal punishment in the Indian schools. As we understand the facts, nothing could be further from the truth." Mr. Steeres asserted that if floggings and brutalities have existed "and doubtlessly they have, they were . . . *prior to the present administration.* Should any superintendent presume to interpret the ruling to allow flogging and such inhumane treatment, it is our firm belief that he should be *promptly and sharply brought to account."*

In connection with this letter it is interesting to know that the Indian Rights Association, organized as a defense organization for Indians, was supplied with the facts of the Phoenix School flogging before April 15, 1930, but in that Association's denial of May 13th, no mention was made of its having seen the said information.

In order to determine the merits of this denial let us look to cases not "prior to the present administration," and wherein superintendents were not "promptly and sharply brought to account."

5

In Washington on Friday, May 23, 1930, I listened to the Senate Subcommittee on Indian Affairs discuss such cases. Those present were Senators Frazier, chairman, and Pine and Thomas of Oklahoma, all members of the Subcommittee. There were also present Senators Ashurst and Hayden of Arizona, the state wherein the brutalities under consideration had occurred. Commissioner Rhoads, Assistant Commissioner Scattergood, and John Collier, also appeared before the Subcommittee.

I heard read into the record the testimony of employees and Indian children from the Phoenix boarding school of Arizona, one of the Government " show " schools equipped with a swimming pool, spacious playgrounds, and the like. The testimony placed in the record consisted of affidavits and sworn statements of facts, known to a large number of persons outside the Indian Bureau as well as within for well over a year. The evidence was as startling as it was indisputable, charging the chief disciplinarian, Jacob Duran, and his assistant disciplinarians, including Parker, of beating a large number of children with leather straps, striking them on the head and mouth with fists, knocking them down, and kicking them with boots.

First, there was the evidence presented by Mrs. Elsie Schmidt, given under oath to Inspector Carl Moore on June 18, 1929:

Willie Bread was attempting to take a bath after " taps," which was against the rules. The night watchman, Mr. Parker, stood by the side of the bathroom door and when Willie came out he struck him across the forehead with a heavy club, knocked him down, and when he attempted to rise he struck him again and then stood over him with a gun. When Willie came to, he managed to get to the room of Major Frederick, who assisted him to the hospital where Doctor Loe took the necessary stitches in his wounds, and called Mr. Duran who informed him in the presence of the boy that the night watchman was privileged to use any form of punishment he found needful, and would be backed not only by himself, Duran, but by the superintendent, which statement he repeated to all the boys the following morning.[5]

Willie Bread, the boy who was assaulted rather than punished, also testified:

As I passed him [Parker] I smiled. I honestly didn't mean a thing when I grinned. This is the only thing that might have made him beat me up. He already had a club in his hand. It was about an inch thick and about a yard long with very sharp corners. He struck me with this club from behind four times. I ran, but he ran after me and caught me again and beat me some more, and I turned around and tried to catch the club, but he struck me on the head and knocked me unconscious. I still carry my scars on my elbow and head, and if they don't believe it they can come and see for themselves.[6]

Was Parker disciplined for his confessed assault and battery? Was he removed? Or, at least, transferred, which has been the customary procedure of the Bureau in such cases? No, he was neither disciplined, removed, or moved.

Honest, efficient employees of the Phoenix School began

[5] Hearings before a Subcommittee of the Committee on Indian Affairs United States Senate pursuant to S. Res. 79 and S. Res. 308. See Part Eight, P. 3031.
[6] *Ibid.* P. 3031.

to complain of the floggings administered the children. It is impossible to enumerate all the complaints, or even a representative number. " Many of the boys who have been beaten or whipped seem afraid to sign statements, and some employees who know of wrongs are either afraid or doubt that it will do any good," wrote one conscientious worker. However, there are enough to indicate the nature of the increased brutalities following Commissioner Rhoads' lack of decisive action in the Bread-Parker case.

One boy, Francis Makill, was beaten by the disciplinarian, when he asked him for a pair of khaki pants. The facts of this beating have been sworn into an affidavit of March 22, 1930.

Eighteen-year-old William Grey swore on March 8, 1930, that Jacob Duran slapped his face in the dining room of the Phoenix School " before all the boys and girls. The reason for such action this affiant does not know."

Two Indian boys, Haisie Clifton and Victor Cough, were locked in the guardhouse with a drunken man from the reservation, who had been caught escaping. His punishment was denying him to leave his cell to go to the toilet. That kept up for three days. The stench in the jail became so bad that the boys could neither sleep nor eat. Upon Victor Cough's release he was taken sick with typhoid fever and confined to the hospital for some time.

Ernest Somegastava of 21 years has sworn that during the past four or five years he has seen Jacob Duran " whip boys between the ages of 10 to 14 years with a leather strap, two thicknesses sewn together, giving them five or six stripes each, respectively."

Simon B. Thomas, also 21, on March 5, 1930, swore that " Jacob Duran puts this affiant in jail at the Indian School, Phoenix, Arizona, and kept him there for three days because this affiant walked from the Indian sanitarium to the street-car line with an Indian girl, said Indian girl not being in attendance at the said Indian school."

Willie Curran has given testimony to Inspector Moore that he, being a big boy, was on one occasion commanded to participate in the mass flogging of 80 Indian boys, much smaller than he. The affidavit stated the little boys made a break for a merry-go-round that was nearby the playgrounds of the Phoenix School. Disciplinarian Elario ordered the bigger boys to round up the youngsters and bring them to his office. Elario himself then flogged six or seven, and commanded the larger ones, including Curran, to flog the rest. Two harness straps sewed together was the instrument used in the flogging.

There has been no disproof of the Curran affidavit. There has been no challenge, no explanation.

The complaints that followed Commissioner Rhoads' lack of decisive action were not limited to the continued floggings and assaults of the school disciplinarians, but, in addition, uncovered past brutalizations which had been concealed by the officials, but not forgotten by the Indians. Not when one was beaten unto death.

Mr. Walter Schmidt, husband of Elsie Schmidt who testified to the beating of Willie Bread, sent Chairman Lynn Frazier of the Senate Investigating Committee six affidavits alleging the death of a Phoenix School boy. In his letter of March 11, 1930, Mr. Schmidt stated that four close relatives of the murdered boy came over 200 miles to voice their wrong, as friends in Yuma, California, their home, would not make out the affidavits for them. " I suppose that years of experience have taught these people living near reservations of the uselessness of trying to help the Indians under the Indian Service gang," he wrote. As for the relatives: " They feel deeply the injustice even after seven or eight years. They have tried in vain to have this matter investigated."

Mary Tone, an aunt of the dead boy, and who raised him from a baby, swore into an affidavit of March 8, 1930, that she saw Tsule Catahqueshamal arrive " at her home one morning about three o'clock and that he was in a very weakened condition . . . his face contained several bruises and that his back was covered with bruises from his neck to his belt."

Tsule's uncle, Cum-its-mat-ow, swore " that this affiant saw that the back of this boy was nearly covered with bruises from the neck to the waist; that the said Tsule Catahqueshamal spat blood. . . ."

Others have sworn to the death of the boy, better known as Taloole Escalanti. Arising from their calm, restrained, almost breathless testimony is the story of the life and death of Taloole Escalanti. The boy had $17.50 coming from the Phoenix School, and many times he asked for his money, but each time was refused. The answer to his latest request was a severe beating and kicking on his back and head. When he recovered consciousness he ran away from the school and managed to cover the 200 miles to his home. How he staggered along that road no one knows, nor is it best that any living person should know. One morning, at daybreak, he appeared before the cabin of his aunt. Four days later at sunset, Taloole Escalanti, an orphan boy, died from heavy contusions on his body and head. His medical certificate stated spinal meningitis with contributory injuries as the mortuary causes. Taloole was cremated according to tribal custom.

The cause of the tragedy — $17.50 — was not paid to the boy's relatives, but along with an additional $90 received for a land lease was transferred to the Indian Irrigation Service in payment of water charges, from which neither the boy nor his relatives derived any benefit.

Mr. Walter Schmidt, honest employee, wrote to Senator Frazier: " We should have an honest investigator here to look into all this in behalf of the Indian children. The disciplinarian has boasted that he expects to continue with his method of discipline and he is being supported in this action by Superintendent Brown. . . ."

Mr. and Mrs. Schmidt along with two other employees of the school — men and women with records of excellent service — furnished the above revealing evidence to Commissioner Rhoads. They knew they were risking trouble for themselves. But they believed that a reform administration, drafted by none less than the President to supplant Burke and Meritt — two men of notorious " inefficiencies," surely wanted the honest facts. And so they testified, along with various Indian pupils, to a long series of brutalities continuous at the dates of their affidavits.

6

Commissioner Rhoads ordered an inspection by H. H. Fiske, a holdover inspector from the Burke-Meritt régime. The result was not unexpected. Inspector Fiske's report was a whitewash. Concerning the case of Taloole Escalanti, whose death is an established fact, Inspector Fiske did not state whether there was a hospital record — the hospital where he was hopelessly treated — or whether the hospital was asked for a record. There were three doctors in the case, but Fiske made no report of interviewing any of them. There were many Indian witnesses, but none was mentioned by him. Commissioner Rhoads, completely supporting the decisions of Fiske, has simply dismissed the case as unproved, the dismissal being " without prejudice."

Of the more than 99 flogging cases not one was examined by Fiske. What occupied his time for ten weeks while he was residing at the Phoenix Boarding School?

As the Fiske report was a whitewash for the officials it was more so a framing of the four protesting employees.

Mrs. Walter Schmidt, tailoress of the school, had been the sharpest thorn. It was her initial charges of brutalizations, of overworking, of substituting what is called " industrial production " for " education," of the food, of the extreme regimentation of the children which destroyed their initiative and self-reliance — it was those charges which were responsible for an admirable investigation by Inspector Carl D. Moore. Following this unbiased report of Inspector Moore which sustained Mrs. Schmidt's allegations, Superintendent Brown of the Phoenix School repeatedly wrote to the Indian Commissioner urging that she be removed. But Inspector Moore, Principal Wheatley, and even Disciplinarian Duran gave her such a fine character as a superior person, exercising a great and good influence among the children, that Commissioner Rhoads could not comply with the repeated requests of Superintendent Brown. However, he warned Mrs. Schmidt to be careful and above all *discreet* in her allegations.

When H. H. Fiske arrived in Phoenix he took meals with Superintendent Brown, attended social gatherings at Brown's home and elsewhere with him, rode around in the same automobile, and conducted his two and a half months investigation at the opposite side of Brown's desk in an office room where they were by themselves. It must not be forgotten that Fiske was sent to Phoenix to investigate charges against Brown's mismanagement. The situation proceeded to develop interestingly.

Inspector Fiske gathered evidence against Mrs. Schmidt, a married woman of middle age, the mother of five children, charging her of being too affectionate with Indian boys; such as stroking the foreheads of children sick in the infirmary, of sending them flowers and food, of allowing them to come into her home and listen to the victrola or radio. All these charges were termed " insubordination." Also Fiske secured an affidavit from Disciplinarian Duran, who swears he saw Mrs. Schmidt in her garden, digging among vegetables, and that when the *Star Spangled Banner* was played she did not come to attention. From this allegation Inspector Fiske developed the existence of an elaborate plot by the Germans to overthrow the United States. Mrs.

Schmidt, he pointed out, was born in Germany. Mr. Ucker, a member of the Board of Indian Commissioners, corroborated the existence of this widely known German plot. In addition, Mrs. Schmidt, Mr. Green, another conscientious, protesting employee, and Willie Curran, the Indian boy whose affidavits had become annoying, were charged with " cancerous bolshevism."

No evidence of even a hearsay nature was presented by Inspector Fiske or Superintendent Brown supporting their charges. Commissioner Rhoads, if not by thought at least by action, agreed with the judicial conclusions of his inspector. He followed the recommendations of Mr. Fiske, and, repeating the charges enumerated above, ordered Mr. and Mrs. Schmidt to be summarily dismissed from the Indian Service.

Willie Curran, the Indian youth who testified that under orders from the disciplinarian he had flogged smaller Indian boys, received far more discouraging treatment than the Schmidts. He was demoted from major of the second battalion to adjutant, and then to captain for no reason whatever. (The Indian Schools are maintained like military institutions with battalions, companies, etc.) Industrial-Inspector Rivers confessed to Willie that he was told to " get something on him." Willie's grades were dropped by the instructors from 95 to 70 and 65, when they had repeatedly stated Willie to be their best mechanic. It was not enough to discourage and dishearten a student eager to learn a white man's trade, but Willie Curran was expelled from school, and his expulsion was approved by Commissioner Rhoads. Willie was not expelled because he had flogged younger children, whether obeying orders or not. Rather, he was charged with consorting with employees who had testified to floggings and brutalizations.

Director of Agriculture Green, who had complained against Farmer Nielson's inefficiencies, the assigning of pupils to severe duties, the condition of the chicken yard, and the most unpardonable of all — against Fiske's method of investigating, is next to appear as a victim of the Fiske-Brown tribunal — a tribunal comparable to the judgments of Robespierre and Trotsky rather than two 1930 Indian Service employees.

Mr. Green came away from one of Fiske's investigating conferences so boiling with indignation that he wrote Commissioner Rhoads. He heard Fiske severely reprimand Mr. F. David Blackhoop, Phoenix bandmaster, for having brought a nurse's attention to a neglected sick boy. No matter how urgent the matter Blackhoop had no right to tell the nurse not to let it happen again. The nurse had failed to answer the boy's call, whereupon he went to the bathroom alone and was forced to crawl back to his bed on hands and knees. The boy died two weeks later.

Mr. Green also reported Fiske as angrily telling Mrs. Schmidt " that it was none of her business about what form of punishment another employee used on the children in his charge, no matter how severe the punishment nor how it endangered the health of the children; that she had no business to speak to an employee so evidently abusing the children nor to speak to anyone regarding it." [7]

Mr. Fiske supported Brown in his right to instruct his

[7] Part Eight of Hearings. May, 1930.

"lieutenants" to watch the homes and actions of other employees. When Mr. Waters, school baker, acknowledged Brown's orders for him to watch the Schmidt home, Fiske told Waters that he was "very disloyal to the school for acknowledging the fact."

Commissioner Rhoads forwarded Green's complaining letter to Fiske for such an "answer as he may care to make."

What was Fiske's answer? Nothing other than the transmittal of evidence against Green. He produced affidavits by Nielson, whom Green had criticized for inattention to duty, testifying that he saw Green spit tobacco in the school yard. Green was also charged with having a temper and employing cuss words. Fiske did not corroborate these statements but merely asserted them, summarizing Green's offenses as "constitutional agitation."

Commissioner Rhoads wrote Green saying that his satisfactory work has saved him from dismissal, and so would be transferred to the Sherman Institute. Thus another complaining employee was hastily removed from the Phoenix School. "The criticism made and conclusions drawn by you have not been substantiated in full," the Commissioner wrote, and further warned Green that if he does not get along with "those in authority or with whom you are associated, it will be necessary to take more drastic action."

There remains the case of F. David Blackhoop, Phoenix bandmaster, which further illustrates the methods of the Indian Bureau in dealing with employees who disclose floggings and other mismanagements. When called before

Inspector Fiske, Blackhoop voluntarily stated that he had signed an unfavorable affidavit, under pressure of Brown, against Mrs. Schmidt at the time when the superintendent was " out to get " the tailoress. Fiske's retort was to produce miraculously a letter signed by Reverend G. E. E. Lindquist, a member of the Board of Indian Commissioners, stating that at a remote date Blackhoop was compelled by moral and biological reasons to marry one of two girls. No testimony beyond Lindquist's word was produced to substantiate this underhand compliment to Blackhoop's virility. Lindquist's charge was a deliberate, malicious falsehood. In addition, Fiske delved into the private life of Mrs. Blackhoop, a non-Indian-Service-employee, alleging that she had a miscarriage, or at least brought on an abortion in some unnamed year in the past. Further scandal-mongering myths were concocted: Blackhoop was charged with being publicly brutal to his family, beating his wife until she appealed to neighbors, threatening to shoot her, and tying his small daughter in her bed while he and his wife spent the evening elsewhere.

Not satisfied with this evidence, Brown's chief clerk Minor laid a plot to catch Blackhoop at night with a young training nurse. She exclaimed to the bandmaster: " Oh, boy, I heard that you will be our night nurse at the hospital. We'll have a big time. I think they'll detail me to help you." But Blackhoop did not bite.

Fiske and Brown demanded Blackhoop's scalp. So on April 19, 1930, Commissioner Rhoads wrote: " Your services are unsatisfactory, and therefore you are allowed ten days from the receipt of this letter to show cause in writing, to be transmitted through your superintendent, as to why you should not be dismissed from the service."

Now comes the most startling step which concludes this bit of factual melodrama.

Blackhoop received a letter from the Commissioner stating he was going to be dismissed unless he replied to the charges the Commissioner specified. Blackhoop made such a reply, supplemented with numerous affidavits. His wife testified he had never beaten her, never threatened her life with a gun, and never tied the baby to its bed. Neither did she cause herself to have an abortion.

Such sworn testimony was presented to the Commissioner in contrast to Brown's charges based on hearsay. Furthermore, a letter, by the chief of inspection in the Blackhoop case, to the effect that Fiske's evidence did not justify dismissal was not included in the file of the case presented to the Senate Investigating Committee. Before that Committee Chief of the Inspection Division Daiker testified that no further investigation was made following the submittal of Blackhoop's affidavits.

And so Commissioner Rhoads, ignoring the fulfilment of his own request for vindicatory statements, presented Blackhoop, an Indian, with a dishonorable discharge, placing him out of employment, and beyond the possibility of securing any.

We have thus seen what employees were " promptly and sharply brought to account."

As for Superintendent Brown, who had been charged with countenancing flogging and mismanagement, Commissioner Rhoads wrote him on March 28, 1930:

Careful consideration has been given the several reports of Field Representative Fiske covering his investigation of the various complaints filed against you and others of your school in the treatment of the pupils, and in the main, it is found that these complaints are without justification and therefore are dismissed without prejudice.

The Commissioner took another action. Flores, one of the disciplinarians who forcefully relieved a boy of his bracelet, was chided by Commissioner Rhoads for his theft. That was all.

As for the employee, Disciplinarian Duran, who should have suffered the most under the weight of undisputed accusations, the Commissioner wrote: " The reports of Mr. Fiske show several instances where Captain Duran, apparently upon the impulse of the moment, has slapped and kicked boys." The Commissioner cited cases of strappings, of blows on the mouth and on the head with fists and hard objects, of kicking. He continued: " Captain Duran should be admonished to exercise great self-control."

That was all. A second gentle admonition, nine months later, for the disciplinarian " to exercise great self-control."

XI
WHY SUCH TALES CAN BE TOLD

1

TO an American, weaned on fair play and raised on the principles of freedom in thought and speech, the existence of such conditions in the United States should be of genuine astonishment.

I have gone into detail on the Phoenix cases because they are illustrative of a great many others. By seeing how Senators, inspectors, and other officials of Washington maneuver in some instances we learn how certain affairs and attitudes have been allowed to continue. We learn how it is that anybody can write such a tale as told in the previous chapter.

On May 23, 1930, I listened to Senator Carl Hayden of Arizona, when he appeared before the Senate Investigating Committee at Washington " in order to preserve what I think are the rights of constituents of mine whose actions are here criticized." He confessed complete ignorance of the facts; he disproved nothing; he merely disagreed. Senator Hayden's defense of his constituents' characters constituted in the main an attack upon the Senate Committee " as a sounding board to broadcast to the world that evil conditions exist." The purpose of the hearing being merely to get " publicity and spread it over the United States that the Indian Service is conducted in an improper manner."

The Senator from Arizona has forgotten that the silencing of criticism has been the chief weapon of the Indian Bureau. Sane logic tells us that if something is rotten we certainly should hear about it, and if later is discovered to be wholesome, so much the better for having had it broadcasted.

The Senator did not confine his defense strategy to the Senate Investigating Committee; as for the complaining employee: " He will squawk and squeal, tell the world how terribly he is abused, and make any kind of a charge to keep the issue alive. The more trouble he can make, the longer he can hang on, sucking at the public teat."

Chairman Frazier answered the above assertion by stating that his " observation has been just the opposite; that any employee that makes complaint about anyone concerning irregularities in the department, according to my experience has been fired because he complained. In order to hold their jobs they have to keep still, and sign such resolutions as the one you have presented." (Senator Hayden had presented the Committee with a whitewash resolution signed by the Federal Employees Union of Phoenix.)

Senator Hayden's colleague, Ashurst of Arizona, presented himself before the Committee as Exhibit B in the evidence as to why reforms in the Indian Service have not been forthcoming.

He prefaced his remarks by likewise pleading dumb. " Next to yourselves," he addressed the Senate Subcommittee, which has been investigating Indian matters for over two years and has traveled many thousand miles, " I am probably as ignorant of the facts as a person could be. Therefore it seems to be unreasonable and outrageous that upon somebody's hearsay, somebody's character is to be impugned or destroyed." Waving his hand in the general direction of Arizona, he shouted: " If the charges are that the superintendent is discharging men and women who have been making complaints, then on the evening train as it tonight speeds west should be members of this committee to investigate that charge."

The Senator, attired in white from shoes to hair, had dramatically brought his statement to a close. His speeches along with Senator Hayden's had consumed much of the morning. The audience and the Senators had listened patiently, but there was a noticeable tension in the air. Those present seemed to be smarting from the counter-accusations aimed at the Committee. An unintroduced official, who had been squirming in his seat, leaned toward my ear. " He may talk all he wants about the high caliber of the Arizona people — about them being just as good as anybody in the Indian Service — but with all their intelligence they won't give the Indian a vote."

In that hushed Senate room, with its walls lined with interested white faces intermittingly sprinkled with the leather countenances of Indians, there arose the slight figure of a modest man. He stood in a room decorated with the portraits and feathers of dead chieftains who fought for the lives of their tribes — a room in the Senate Office Building for investigating Indian affairs, where fights are still carried on for the lives of Indians. He moved toward the long mahogany table in the center of the room, where the Senate Committee was seated. He stood before them, with shoulders slightly stooped and his thin lips drawn into a slender line. But his eyes glistened with all the spark of a fighter.

" Mr. Chairman," he said, in a small voice that poured forth rapidly, " I ask to be sworn."

After swearing he stated his name and position. " John Collier; executive secretary, American Indian Defense Association."

Without altering his modulation he went on to state that the evidence now objected to by the Senators from Arizona was none other than that on which Commissioner Rhoads discharged three employees from the service, transferred another, and expelled a boy from school. As for the " fair play that still exists in this country," as Senator Ashurst declared — and as for the destruction of human character — Commissioner Rhoads discharged the employees without further investigation when he had requested the submittal of vindicatory statements during the ten-day acquittal period.

However, such error-erasing was largely wasted, as Senator Hayden had left the room immediately after his statement, and Senator Ashurst followed his colleague after listening a few minutes to the evidence. They had delivered their speeches, fulfilling their duty by their constituents, and nothing further was demanded of them. So they moved on to greener pastures.

2

Aside from senatorial opposition to reformatory action many individuals may be found in the Indian Bureau's central office, who have successfully perpetuated their careers with prejudiced decisions on reports, complaints, and àll forms of protesting evidence. This detailed treatment of the Phoenix case has its reward for the reader, by indicating to him that somebody in Washington, in constant contact with the work of the inspectors in the field, has been viciously determined to hide the truth.

Who that somebody is I am not concerned. There are many more besides him. It is not the purpose of this book, nor should it be of any individual, to sink civilian fingers into the slime to pull out one or two vermin. Let the Senate Investigating Committee, which has governmental weight, eradicate such men. But — let us see the slime!

The Phoenix case is not an isolated case. It illustrates how Mr. Fiske carries on his investigations, which are acted upon in preference to other reports. Fiske is still in the field carrying on further inspections and further terrorizing employees as he did the Phoenix people. Honest employees, who give testimony not wanted by him, must know that everything in their past lives will be inquired into, whether or not it affects their services. Employees must know that the maternal irregularities of their wives will be dragged in against them.

3

Besides the flogging of boarding school children, full grown adults, living on reservations, have been subjected to severe physical punishment by superintendents still employed in the Indian Service, or who have been recently pensioned for their splendid careers. In Wisconsin and Montana Indians have been jailed with the aid of a ball and chain between their legs. An Indian woman was recently put into a one room jail with three men. Mrs. Gertrude Bonnin, President of the National Council of American Indians, wrote to the editor of the *New York Telegram* in a letter of May 19, 1930: " Among the most triumphant superintendents must be he who brags how he armed his employees with hickory wagon spokes and caused them to knock down, cold and insensible, a number of Indians who refused to be thrown into a vat of sheep dip, thus intimidating the tribe into submission. No ordinary prudent stockman would knock his sheep down senseless to dip them in his vat."

Assistant Commissioner Scattergood replied by saying that " we have had an investigation in this case, and from the facts submitted we find no basis for criticizing the superintendent."

However, the National Council of American Indians, the organization which submitted the complaints, was neither notified nor given an opportunity to be heard in the purported investigation. Mrs. Bonnin continued: "It was a bureau 'white-wash' — such as we had not expected from these two new commissioners who came widely heralded for their humanitarianism. Mutely crying to Heaven for justice are the countless graves of little Indian boys and girls, and with them helpless old men and women whose untimely deaths were caused by slow starvation and fatal beatings under cruel superintendents on Indian reservations."

When an Indian delegate recently complained against the maladministration of their affairs he was answered by a letter from Mr. Scattergood stating that " we feel that you are mistaken in your belief that there is inefficiency . . . and a lack of sympathy on the part of those in charge with the advancement of the welfare of the Indians."

Again the Bureau had based its letters and actions upon the reports of the very officials of whom the complaints were made. Thus the Commissioner and his assistant daily extend their approval with signatory authority to the actions of men whose pasts were already blotted with the blood of relations.

In a recent conversation at his office, Assistant Commissioner Scattergood mentioned a particular class of juvenile incorrigibles who had forced the reëstablishment of corporal punishment upon the Indian Bureau. Those children, he said, were girls who, homesick and unhappy, ran away from school. Those girls are now made happy and forgetful of their homes by a severe flogging, an account of which is ordered to be posted on the school bulletin board for the edification of their classmates.

The opinion that new actions are needed, actions distinct from those of the past, is not one confined to the close students of the Indian problem. A general feeling of disappointment exists, as expressed in the following editorial from the *Arizona Labor Journal* of April 5, 1930:

When President Hoover appointed as Commissioner of Indian Affairs Mr. C. J. Rhoads, there was general approval from all classes of people. . . . The situation in Phoenix and the developments of the past few weeks would indicate that these hopes have been too sanguine; that even yet there is not at the head of the bureau a man who stands ready to compel humane treatment of the pupils, justice for subordinates in the service, and the spirit which is supposed to pervade the Government's pretended efforts at educating the Indian.

4

On May 27, 1930, the second day of the Senate Investigating Committee hearing on the Phoenix floggings, Chairman Frazier addressed the Commissioner of Indian Affairs confessing his ignorance as to " how you can expect to build up an effective working organization on any reservation " if certain discharge awaits " any employee who apparently has the courage of his convictions to tell the truth about the situation at a school or at an agency." Chairman Frazier went on to state that he had received a letter that morning from a lady he knew and had every reason to believe, saying that her daughter-in-law is a teacher in an Indian school where conditions are bad, but that the daughter-in-law did not wish to make any complaint for fear she would lose her position. Such statements, he concluded, have been "made over and over again by employees from various reservations."

Senator Pine of Oklahoma, a fighter of equal caliber with his fellow committeeman, also told of receiving a letter that morning from an Oklahoma agent, saying he would be glad to furnish the Senator information of the rotten condition of that agency provided it was kept a secret. The agent wanted to know if it were possible to bring the information to the attention of the Committee without naming himself, as he was afraid of losing his job. Senator Pine likewise concluded that "it is my opinion, after visiting seven or eight states as a member of this committee, that the employee who reveals the facts is transferred or ultimately discharged." In his opinion the Phoenix case, with its three dismissals and one transfer of complaining employees, was in no way different from the usual.

Senator Wheeler of the Committee, also a veteran warrior for the Indian, stated similar cases that have come to his attention. "On most of the reservations that we visited, some man would come to me and say, 'Senator, this is the fact, but I do not dare to testify to it,' and they would simply say that they were afraid of the superintendent."

Turning to the Commissioner of Indian Affairs, seated at the far end of the long mahogany table, Senator Wheeler asked: "Do you get many criticisms from employees?"

"I hate to exaggerate," Commissioner Rhoads answered, "but I would say we get a great many."

There are some that are fearless, but more that are fearful. And many that are not heard from again.

XII

TRUTH IS FACT

1

I SAW him half a mile ahead, shuffling his feet in the dust of the sandy road. He walked stooped forward as if he bore a weighty burden on his shoulders, but his back was bare except for a thin, blue cotton shirt. I stopped the car beside him, but he did not cease his painful shuffle. " Bo-zhoo! " I greeted. He slowly turned his brown, wrinkled face with its few shreds of grey whiskers, and nodded respectfully. " Can I give you a lift? " I asked. He looked at me a moment without answering, as if my question made little difference. I had been talking with many Indians but this one's stoicism was puzzling. " I'll take you to town." I insisted. He gave a slight gesture with his shoulders and lifted himself into the seat beside me.

We rode several miles in silence. I kept glancing at him, but he sat as he walked — stooped forward with his invisible burden — and rigid as rock.

I ventured a question. " Where you go, ah-cue-wan-zee? "

His eyes brightened as he turned his head. " You know 'Jibway? " I nodded. He looked at me hard, and said slowly: " Me go on agent, me. Me tell-um plenty 'bout that letter I got. Pete Joe, that grandson, write how hungry and cold he is at that In-zhun school. Me tell that Mister Agent plenty . . ."

Again that singular plea. A hundred thousand voices through one great throat pleading: " First our children. They are beaten, starved, half-naked. First their wrongs — ours can wait."

2

Throughout America voices are murmuring:

Alvino Lujan sits in a desert pueblo house telling Vera Connelly of a visit to the Santa Fe School. Miss Connelly writes the following words of Lujan's for the *Good Housekeeping Magazine:*

" I sat down to supper with the little boys and when the bread arrived the boys grabbed all of it, yet they were still hungry. No more was served them. I asked for some bread for myself and was given two thin slices. But when it came the little boy beside me kept staring so at my bread — he was so pitiful — I turned my head away. When I looked around again the bread was gone.

" At breakfast the same thing happened. The boys snatched the bread as though half-starved. I went to San Ildefonso pueblo and asked some bread from the Indians and took it to the hungry boys at the school. All this is

wrong! Those children work very hard! The night I slept
there one boy was awakened at midnight to go out and
work on some machinery."

Mrs. Charles W. Welfelt, the cook at the Towoac boarding school for Ute and Navajo children in Colorado, swears
that the dried fruit at that school is filled with worms. She
protests, but the children are fed the worm-filled fruit. She
also swears the meat is full of maggots, and likewise protests. The principal answers: " Dead maggots are not
poisonous." Under orders she serves the maggot-infested
meat.

Others from Towoac swear the flour for bread is kept in
a cellar where the dirty water from the floors above drips
onto it. Mice nest in the flour. Portions of dead mice are
cooked in the flour. Mrs. Welfelt protests. " Nonsense,"
answers the principal, thrusting his hand into a sack and
bringing out a handful of small mice, newly born. He
orders the flour taken away, to be issued as rations to the
aged and infirm Utes. The superintendent, the principal,
matrons, and other employees, of course, maintain their
own table with their own food.

Mrs. Nellie M. Weigal, State Chairman of the Federated
Women's Clubs of Colorado, inspects the Navajo Shiprock
boarding school:

Everything was covered with flies. I never saw so many in my
life. While I was in the kitchen the newly baked bread was brought
in, loaf after loaf, and placed on long tables; as soon as it was
cool enough it was immediately covered, completely covered,
with flies.

I watched the little tots coming from religious instruction, and

I never saw such dirty, ragged dresses on a human being in my life; every one a misfit, and of all the forlorn, lonesome, heart-hungry beggars, they were that.

Dr. S. S. Warren of the Leupp boarding school reports the result of his daily health inspection:

Teachers report that children complain of not getting enough to eat; and that some are eating from the swill barrels; coffee being served to children for breakfast. Bakeshop full of flies and dirty. Boys still committing nuisances in rear of bakery.

Another conscientious Indian Bureau physician, Dr. B. O. Thrasher, writes of the Fort Apache Indian School that the children were fed "no fresh milk, no butter, no eggs, no fresh fruits nor fresh vegetables."

"Does this school (San Carlos Apache Reservation School) exemplify a condition general to the 29,000 in Indian boarding schools?" asks the *Literary Digest* of January 26, 1929.

"Yes," answers John Collier, Executive Secretary of the American Indian Defense Association, "with inconsequential shiftings of detail, the school exemplifies a general condition which the Indian Bureau knowingly maintains."

Throughout America Indians and Indian-minded Whites are testifying to a similar diet.

Mrs. Tettie E. Robertson, formerly assistant matron at the Yuma Indian School, testifies before the Senate Investigating Committee as to the food fed the children:

Every morning for breakfast they had bread and gravy and coffee; there was never any change; and every day for lunch it was boiled beef, beans, and bread, sometimes cake — but you would have to be told it was cake; it was just a kind of sweet bread — every day, never any change, Thanksgiving, Christmas, and all, the same. The evening meal was more or less the noon meal; was just warmed over — and the beans were often weevily, and so was the flour weevily; and if there was fruit or anything like that, it just stood around until it was not fit to be eaten, and finally thrown out. . . .

Gravy was the butter — that is, called butter — in the Indian Service.

Mrs. Robertson testified before the Senate Investigating Committee that " on the school campus a familiar sight was mothers sitting with their children and feeding them." She was asked: " Would you say that the children whose parents did not bring them food would not be as well off? "

Mrs. Robertson answered: " Yes; you could notice it."

3

As a summary to the above testimony the Institute for Government Research in its *Problem of Indian Administration* presents the picture with statistical evidence, couched as usual in reserved, scientific language, yet declaring the survey staff " obliged to say frankly and unequivocally that the provisions for the care of the Indian children in boarding schools are grossly inadequate. The outstanding deficiency is in the diet furnished the Indian children, many of whom are below normal health. The diet is deficient in quantity, quality, and variety. The effort has been made to feed the children on a PER

CAPITA OF ELEVEN CENTS A DAY, plus what can be produced on the school farm, including the dairy. At a few, very few, schools, the farm and the dairy are sufficiently productive to be a highly important factor in raising the standard of the diet, but even at the best schools these sources do not fully meet the requirements for the health and development of the children. At the worst schools, THE SITUATION IS SERIOUS IN THE EXTREME." [1]

One of these extreme schools spent NINE CENTS A DAY PER CAPITA FOR FOOD. The survey staff examined the dietary at this, the Rice School, for three successive days and obviously discovered the children were being starved. " Malnutrition was evident. They were indolent and when they had the chance to play, they merely sat about on the ground, showing no exuberance of healthy youth." [2]

In regard to this tribe, the San Carlos Apache, an appalling paradox has existed in the fact that the Indian Bureau's activities are supported from its tribal fund, that is, the paying of agency salaries and the like, while its children have been starved.

The Sherman Institute was cited by the investigators as one of the more humane schools, with " the greatest variety and spent more for food than any other school studied." The liberal per capita expenditure of this school, which placed it far above corresponding institutions to the heights of being a model to follow, was EIGHTEEN CENTS A DAY PER CHILD. Nevertheless, the surveyors acknowl-

---

[1] *The Problem of Indian Administration.* Pp. 11–12.　　[2] *Ibid.* P. 327.

edged that the pride of the Indian Service — the Sherman
Institute — operated " a faulty dietary."

The very poorly balanced rations served at these Indian
schools undoubtedly increase the children's susceptibility
to tuberculosis. If they contract the disease they can not
look to their food for either hope or help. At the Tulalip
School, for example, the small allowance for the purchase
of food in the open market was exhausted at the end of
four months, although forty tuberculous children were in
urgent need of a better diet than that served in the dining
hall. When the children reach an advanced tuberculous
stage, and the school officials are assured of their inevitable
fate, they are shipped home to their families to die — but
more, to infect them with " the dread disease." The Institute's report corroborates this practice, citing the case of
a girl who was sent home to a small agency hospital where
lay nearby " maternity cases in constant danger of
contamination."

Some Bureau dignitaries have contended that the meager diet is sufficient because so many of the Indian children
are at or above normal weight. However, the most cur-
sory student of nutrition knows the weight of a child is
but one factor of many to be taken into consideration. I
have seen many Indian children, raised on a diet of excess
starchy foods, possessing a flabby, unhealthy fat that is
often mistaken to indicate sound health. I have also seen
many Indian children stripped, and their nudeness stood
forth as mute testimony to their malnutrition. Their fat is
nothing more than a pot-belly, with the ribs sticking out
above. Their shoulders are stooped with hunger and de-

spair, their scapulae winged. In all, they are living, modern versions of the photographs of starving Armenian children that were heralded before our sentimental eyes immediately following the War.

4

Is it possible that such conditions have existed without some investigation resulting in correction? Yes, there have been investigations, but no adequate corrections. As for the investigations: In 1924 the American Red Cross made a study of Indian boarding schools and Indian health. This report was suppressed by the Indian Bureau. It was successfully withheld from Congress until 1928, although it was repeatedly demanded by interested members of the Senate and House, until it was finally subpoenaed by the Senate Investigating Committee.

Among the schools reported by the Red Cross were the San Carlos and Rice Schools. The Bureau did not need to heed the Red Cross report, if it did not care to, but there was the annual report of one of its own Superintendents. James B. Ketch, a Bureau employee, wrote, " I find the health conditions [in the Rice School] alarming. I have [previously] reported to your office." Superintendent Ketch of the San Carlos School also protested against the continued requirement of heavy child labor from children both starved and tuberculous. Were these reports given to Congress, or to the Indian committees, or the Appropriation committees of Congress? No, like the Red Cross report it was hidden under lock and key. Instead the Bureau beguiled from the House Appropriation committee *a reduction in per child appropriations for the Rice School.*

Did the report of the Institute for Government Research alter the dark horizon? The report entered the hands of the men who sealed the fate of the Red Cross and superintendent reports. The facts of the Institute's research were known as early as 1927, especially the per capita allowances for food. On February 21, 1928, the report was officially presented to the Secretary of the Interior. It asked for a million dollars for immediate famine relief in the boarding schools. The report, with this urgent request, went unheeded. It was withheld from Congress for a year.

The Bureau was aware of conditions as early as 1914 by the report of the United States Public Health Service, again in 1915 by the National Bureau of Municipal Research, again in 1924 by the Red Cross, and continually through the reports of some of its own conscientious superintendents. All the previous evidence of the mental torturing, poisoning, and killing of the 21,000 boarding-school children were substantiated in the powerful Education section of the Institute's report. But all this went again unheeded. The hundred million dollar deficiency bill carried not a cent for famine relief. The Institute's million dollar recommendation was withheld from Congress until adjournment and in the next Congress no heed was paid to it by the Interior Department. For another long year thousands of school children had to starve. Many were compelled to die. It was a ruthless, unnecessary sacrifice of innocent, virgin children to the hideous god of the Indian Bureau's pride. The Bureau could not acknowledge the million dollar urgency recommendation without acknowledging its own negligence and mismanagement.

5

But pride goeth before a fall. Burke and Meritt were replaced by Hoover with two humanitarians drafted from private life. The President asked Congress to approve the Institute's recommendation of a million dollars for famine relief among school children. On December 5, 1929, President Hoover submitted his request for additional funds. He asked for an emergency appropriation of $1,500,000 to be used between the date of appropriation and June 30, 1930; $1,100,000 of this sum to be used for the improvement of the diet in the boarding schools and giving other emergency aid, and $400,000 for immediate medical and health service.

Newspapers blazed with the news. At last — relief to Indians. The public, satisfied the nation was finally taking care of its wards, promptly forgot the issue.

But let us draw away the Congressional curtain and see what happened to the President's request.

First, Commissioner Rhoads appeared before the Subcommittee on Interior Department Appropriations of the House, of which Louis C. Cramton of Michigan is chairman and practically sole member — a Congressman who by cutting appropriations has hurt the Indian more than any other American. The printed hearings of this subcommittee are incomplete. There are gaps in the text where essential remarks were held " off the record." But this much we know: Commissioner Rhoads told Cramton's committee the heartbreaking facts. During 1929, in 22 sample schools, the children's ration averaged fourteen cents a day. The school gardens and farms produced another six cents, making a total of twenty cents for children in their teens doing severe physical labor in addition to consuming mental energy. Rhoads pleaded for clothing. During 1929 only $22.29 per pupil was spent for clothes. " Many of the schools are located in northern climates," he said, " where heavy clothing is essential to personal comfort and to health." The Flandreau School, located in a cold climate, he pointed out, spent $16.30 per pupil for clothing. At Haskell $7.27 was allowed for 1929. " It is not possible (unless the President's request be granted)," Rhoads continued, " to provide overshoes, heavy sweaters, overcoats, and gloves. The undue exposure takes its toll in illness. Garments worn are so patched that they present a very untidy appearance. Shoes . . . are inadequate to properly protect health." In the northern climates, the Dakotas, Montana, Minnesota, and Wisconsin, the pupils were compelled to go out doors in the dead of winter, in all sorts of inclement weather without overshoes, heavy sweaters, overcoats, and gloves. The result had been a heavy toll in illness and a consequent absence from class studies.

Not only did Rhoads plead for the health of children forced to endure snowdrifts and blizzards while scantily clad, but he pleaded for " a minimum standard of decency."

As a final crushing blow of evidence there were the comparisons of what was spent in 1929 and in 1914, allowing, of course, for the changes in purchasing power of money. For food in 1929 the Indian Bureau spent only 61.1 per cent of the purchasing power of money in 1914, only 59.6 per cent as much for clothing, and only 85.3 per cent as much for fuel. However, because it was impossible to get people to work for less the salaries of the school employees showed a slight decline in 1929 to only a little less than 93 per cent of the 1914 standard. As Senator Pine of Oklahoma adroitly observed, " They looked after themselves better than they looked after the Indians." Thus the much vaunted American prosperity which first began as a result of cannons sounding in 1914 worked inversely for Indian children, involuntary pupils of Government boarding schools.

Such facts were presented to Cramton's committee, and his reply was to question the two most urgent items, which the President and health experts had stressed — food and clothing. Those, in his opinion, are not " permanent." The money must be spent on permanent utilities. To Cramton furniture is " permanent," as is machinery, Indian Bureau salaries, and livestock. To cap his czarship Cramton declared his intention to furnish the money, to even make it available into 1931, if " permanent " uses could be found.

A word as to Cramton's aversion to food appropriations. The allotments for food first began to drop in 1921. That was the year when Representative Cramton assumed chairmanship of the subcommittee of the House Committee on Appropriations which passes upon appropriations for the Department of the Interior. During Cramton's chairmanship the food appropriations per child have been cut from

$43.74 per year to $36.64 per year.[3] For Cramton to acknowledge in 1930 the need for immediate famine relief would be a confession to his starving thousands of children during the past nine years. Instead, he announced he would not " allow himself to be stampeded by any talk of starving Indian children." He asserted there were no starving Indian children in Government schools unless they are the ones who " have just come in from the sticks."

Additional testimony comes from the Episcopal Missionary Convocation of South Dakota, which stated in the " Spirit of Missions," October, 1929: " We wish to record here and now that no boarding school child in South Dakota is underfed." In this connection it is worth noting that in the deficiency bill there is an item appropriating $300,000 especially for the needs of the Sioux Indian schools. The Flandreau School in South Dakota clothed its pupils on $16.30 per head during 1929.

6

The result of Cramton's position was the " back-watering " of Rhoads and Scattergood. They withdrew the Hoover estimates and allocations and produced a new set drawn up entirely by the Indian Bureau. Food and clothing faded away. The " permanent " uses expanded. Furniture, machinery, equipment, and household articles loomed to $692,000. Generous increases of salaries and personnel were indicated. As an explanation of the reversal of their former position Commissioners Rhoads and Scattergood

[3] Printed hearings, Appropriation Bill for 1931. P. 411 *et seq.*

frankly stated their intention to " keep faith with the committee." With Cramton.

But the Commissioners did not keep faith with the American Indian Defense Association, while that organization was working night and day for the welfare of Indian children. John Collier discloses the betrayal: " While persuading us into silence lest the food and clothing appropriation be sabotaged by Congressman Cramton, Commissioners Rhoads and Scattergood actually were agreeing with Cramton that it should be sabotaged and they consented to its sabotage. Nor did they inform us of their action until it had been taken. We saw them daily, sometimes all day; but we were uninformed and misinformed."

Of what did the sabotage consist? The request of the Budget Bureau, acting under instructions from President Hoover and with much accompanying publicity, called specifically for an appropriation for the year 1931 of $595,000 for food and $252,000 for clothing. Also there was to be $189,000 for additional personnel and $63,000 for equipment. Cramton decreased the clothing appropriation by 88 per cent, while he increased the equipment allotment by 89 per cent. He decreased food 68.9 per cent while he increased the personnel appropriation by 37 per cent.

The request of President Hoover, approved by the Budget Director and the department itself, was almost completely reversed by the single stroke of one man. The request, in order of priorities, called first for food, then clothing, and later other items. However, Congressman

Cramton placed equipment and salaries first, because they are " permanent."

Hoover's request would have raised the food allowance per child per day from 20 cents to 37.8 cents. It was a request made in December of 1929 to relieve the slow starvation of children during the year 1930. Cramton's bill was leisurely passed by the end of March, 1930, allowing 26 cents per day. When children are dying of slow starvation there should be no leisurely passing of an urgent bill. The reason for the delay? For the atrocity of postponing even for a week? When only two months had gone from the year Cramton insisted " that 1930 was flowing away."

Of the 1931 request, in which Hoover again demanded 37.8 cents a day for food, Cramton likewise sliced the figures by a third. The answer to Hoover's demand was 28.3 cents per day.[4]

When the printed record became available and the above facts became known the American Indian Defense Association decided that an appeal to the Senate had to be made. For the situation had become serious. Cramton not only had rebuffed President Hoover and the Budget Bureau but he had coerced the Indian Bureau into acquiescence. The starving of the children had continued even following a demand for relief by the President. They had been shivering in humiliating rags and they were to continue their shivering.

John Collier drew up such an appeal to the Senate, however, avoiding all criticism of Rhoads and Scattergood but

[4] Hearings before the Committee on Indian Affairs United States Senate. Feb. 27, 1930. P. 30.

dealing in plain language with Cramton. He took that document in advance to both Rhoads and Scattergood. Rhoads's answer was that if the Association acted in the food and clothing matter, it would be construed as " an unfriendly act and a parting of the ways." Scattergood emphasized the ultimatum.

7

Collier withheld his appeal, pending a Senate hearing at which the Commissioners themselves might ask for a restoration of the food and clothing grant. He obtained that hearing in the teeth of an intense lobbying on the part of Rhoads and Scattergood, who plotted to prevent any hearing whatever. At that hearing, on February 27, 1930, Scattergood begged the Senate not to disturb the Cramton allocations, which, in truth, meant not to grant the Hoover food and clothing request.

Senator W. H. McMaster, from South Dakota, a member of the Senate Committee on Indian Affairs, asked the Assistant Commissioner whether he thought he could feed an Indian child on 12 cents a meal.

Mr. Scattergood answered: " Yes. I think if we had that we would be very happy."

Senator McMaster: " You think that could be done? "

Mr. Scattergood: " Yes. That is what this committee recommends. We are not experts when it comes to the dietary and calories, and all the rest of it."

Senator McMaster: " Is there any man in this room that can feed his children on 12 cents a meal at home? "

Senator Burton K. Wheeler of Montana spoke up to say that a comparison of what a Senator feeds his children and what the Government feeds its Indian wards would not be a fair comparison.

Senator McMaster: " I agree with that; but, Senator, suppose you try it. Would you put yourself to the test of trying that thing? "

Senator Wheeler: " You could not do it in your home."

Senator McMaster: " You could not begin to do it."

Senator Wheeler: " You could not begin to do it."

Senator Elmer Thomas of Oklahoma, then pro-Bureau, attempted to provide a loophole for Scattergood by asking " how does this figure you have given us compare with the costs in the Army — favorably? "

Mr. Scattergood answered that " Of course, the Army ration is for a full-grown man, who requires something different from a child of 14 years. The Army ration for 1929 was 51 cents per man per day. The Navy ration, not counting losses, was 52.9 cents per day; with losses, 53.5 cents per day."

Senator McMaster: " That is a 50 per cent increase over what the children get."

It is a question whether a full-grown man eats 50 per cent more than a growing child of 14. Dr. Haven Emerson of Columbia University says a growing child consumes as much food as an adult. Growing children do and should eat more than adults. But Indian children, no different from others in their desire for games and play, are only allowed 50 per cent of an adult diet.

The Visiting Housekeeping Association of Detroit estimated that 40 cents a day is the rock bottom minimum for keeping a child alive with any reasonable hope of resisting disease. Yet Indian children are known to have existed on 9 cents a day, as they did in the Rice School. The average have subsisted on 11 cents a day. What a tribute to Indian vitality! But at what a sacrifice. In order for the Government to establish this all-time international endurance record the child wards of the nation were maintained on a food basis 80 PER CENT LOWER THAN THE ARMY AND NAVY STANDARD.

8

During and following the Committee on Indian Affairs hearing of February 27, 1930, Commissioner Scattergood consistently misrepresented the facts for the purpose of diminishing the more than obvious need of the children for additional appropriations for food, the original appropriations having been side-tracked for " permanent " uses. Also, it was successfully devised that the American Indian Defense Association should be denied a hearing before the Senate Appropriations Committee.

However, through the work of friendly Senators the Association was able to secure a nearly adequate appropriation in the deficiency bill through Senate action, which was later knocked out by Cramton in the House.

The bill then went into a conference committee consisting of both branches of Congress, which resulted in a poor compromise. The conference committee was composed of Senators Wesley L. Jones of Washington, Frederick Hale of Maine, Carter Glass of Virginia, Less S. Overman of North Carolina, and Lawrence C. Phipps of Colorado — the very Phipps who said in the Senate-committee hearings that Indian children need not be taught beyond the sixth grade. The Representatives were Cramton of Michigan, William Wood of Indiana, Edward Wason of New Hampshire, Joseph Byrns of Tennessee, and James Buchanan of Texas.

After about forty-five minutes of discussion, these gentlemen agreed to cut entirely the $270,000 increase granted by the Senate. Both Houses agreed to this committee's report without any discussion of the Indian question. Senator McMaster was later jockeyed out of his motion to reconsider these items.

This allotment provides $360,156 less than President Hoover requested for food, but $100,000 more than Representative Cramton first allowed. It allows three and one-half times as much as the President requested for day-school lunches. The allotment for additional personnel is $11,000 more than he asked, but $100,000 less than Representative Cramton first allowed. The allowance for equipment, furniture, and livestock is $20,000 less than Representative Crampton first insisted upon, but $502,000 more than President Hoover asked for these " permanent " utilities which are so precious to Representative Cramton.

Translating the above allotment into the terms of the food allowance, Indian Bureau officials say the layout will allow an expenditure of between 35 and 36 cents per day per child. This will allow the Indian child to get more to eat than he has ever had before, but yet his rations will be five cents a day lower than the minimum health subsistence standard set up by the Detroit Visiting Housekeeping Association. Further, Collier has estimated that the allocations made by the conference committee would allow only 32.78 cents per child, while even taking the most optimistic view of the money available for food. That is more than seven cents a day below the *minimum* health standard. This much is certain: The Indian Bureau has never yet achieved the most necessary diet drawn up by the Interior Department's own home economics staff as the standard requirement for the growing Indian child.

XIII

KIDNAPPING CHILDREN FOR EPIDEMICS

1

THE sun rises and sets on the Navajo plateau with a biased beauty that disregards the sensibilities of the rest of the world. The so honored are a race of humans, the least scathed by the white man's civilization of any group living in America. They have afforded a well of material undefiled to the poet, novelist, and painter. The children are as wild and as sturdy as their parents. Since babyhood they have coped with the rigors of the elements about them. The Navajos have ever breathed the immense, wind-blown air of their godly plateau. They have ever spoken a language which was music to their ears, which daily aligned their lives with the mystical, poetical world in which they lived. They carried on the dances and songs of their ancestors, their magical practices, their fire rituals, and their dawn and moon ceremonies. They lived as pure and wholesome a pantheistic existence as Coleridge and Southey dreamed of, and as Sir Thomas More visioned.

Suddenly there would appear among them Government officers who would snatch away their children and ship them hundreds of miles to live in heartbreaking prisons. After the frightened offspring were corralled they were herded to hot places, several thousand feet below their accustomed sea level, to the changed heat of Phoenix and Riverside where the sun burned their bodies, and their spirits drooped, and they shriveled and died in the schools.

These distant concentrated institutions are the vast non-reservation boarding schools, which are some of the most conspicuous show places the Government operates. The theory for erecting these institutions has been the belief that by separating the children from the tribe, and from the tribal customs, they would be alienated from their parents and thus started on the high road toward a white man's civilization.

This policy has been most vigorously carried out. On some reservations in the Southwest practically all the Indian children have been taken from their parents and sent to the concentrated schools hundreds of miles away, where they do not see their families for years at a time. It is the plan of the Indian Bureau that the day schools and reservation boarding schools will eventually be abandoned and all Indian children will be shipped to the distant non-reservation schools.

Congressman James A. Frear has made a statement concerning these conditions:

Children as young as six years are now taken away from their parents and in the aggregate thousands of Indian children under existing law have been kidnapped and taken from their parents. Sometimes these children die far away from their people. I was given instances where a number of children had contracted tuberculosis at Phoenix and were returned to their reservation over 200 miles distant, there to die with the tribe. But the civilization by kidnapping like former Christianizing of Indians by killing, goes on under the present Indian Bureau's management.[1]

Former Assistant Commissioner Meritt let the cat from the bag with regard to child kidnapping, when he told a House committee: " Due to a *determined enforcement* of the policy of requiring every healthy Indian child between the age of 6 and 18 to be in some school." [2]

The kidnapping is usually peaceful if the parents helplessly submit, but it is quite forcible when they refuse. The local agents on the reservations oftentimes exhibit documents purporting to contain the thumb mark of parents, for the purpose of proving that the kidnapping was not violent. However, I have talked to Indian parents who have not seen their children for years, although they have repeatedly requested the return of their offspring. I have also talked with white people who have observed conditions on reservations and they likewise testify that the local agents carry out the Indian Bureau's orders without discretion.

Today there are thousands of Indian children, big and little, who are being taken to distant schools. They are

[1] Hearings before a Subcommittee of the Committee on Indian Affairs United States Senate. Feb. 23, 1927. P. 24.
[2] House Appropriations Hearings. 1926. P. 324.

taken away from parents who possess the same affectionate love for their children as white people. Yet it is the whites who are perpetrating and countenancing this unnatural separation under the thin disguise of a civilizing policy.

The Hon. Mr. Frear proposed to the Senate Committee that we might as well rightfully and humanely take the children of the two Indian Commissioners and the Secretary of the Interior and separate them from their parents for three years or more. " Such a proposition," he continued, " would meet forcible opposition, with deadly weapons if necessary. The Indian parent is locked up when he protests, even in my own State of Wisconsin where ball-and-chain treatment is popular with the bureau and with its agents, as I have just disclosed by affidavits and correspondence. I repeat the statement made at the offset of these remarks: Inhuman treatment of American Indians is worse than ever before." [3]

The kidnapping of Indian children is expressly forbidden by statutes; further, it has been outlawed by the Federal Constitution. But it continues. Last fall hundreds were kidnapped for the winter term. This fall, again.

In their quiet way, the Institute investigators had much to say concerning the development of the family under this system:

The long continued policy of removing Indian children from the home and placing them for years in boarding schools largely disintegrates the family and interferes with developing normal family life.[4]

[3] House Appropriations Hearings, 1926. P. 25.
[4] *The Problem of Indian Administration.* P. 15.

Is this kidnapping worth while? Do the children gain anything in this ruthless disintegration of the family? Let us see, for example, if their compulsory enrollment teaches them good health habits. In many schools I have seen elaborate charts exhorting the health advantages of drinking milk and eating vegetables, when on the tables of those schools I could not find. milk or vegetables in a quantity resembling adequacy. These children regularly hear health talks on the values of wholesome and varied tastes in foods for the purpose of educating them to be intelligent husbands and wives, when in the meanwhile food is unattractively served that is sorely lacking in quantity and balance. In one school the children are told once a month in a health lecture to eat slowly, when the time allowed them at their tables is fifteen minutes a meal. Further, the hot foods served are seldom eaten when hot, because of the dishes being placed on the tables long before the pupils march into the dining halls.

In many schools the Institute discovered that the children "must maintain a pathetic degree of quietness. In fact, several matrons and disciplinarians said that they do not allow the children to talk."

One can go on at great length answering this question as to whether the kidnapping is worth while. I could enumerate, for example, cases wherein children suffering from eye trouble have not been given glasses because they become broken and hence should not be worn; or I could tell of children without handkerchiefs, children clothed in garments several sizes too large and using segments of automobile tubes for garters; or I could mention the crusted sores on their faces, the nits and lice in their heads. I could enumerate these and many more instances of the children being criminally neglected.

To conclude, however, even from an educational point of view the kidnapping is not worth while. Out of the 211 Indian schools at the present time only a few — the 18 non-reservation schools — carry instruction into the junior high school grades. Carlisle, it must be remembered, was only a grammar school before it was relinquished to the War Department. This educational fact is obvious: In spite of the Government's numerous schools little has been done to help the Indian solve the economic, sociological, and political problems which he has continuously presented. THE UNITED STATES GOVERNMENT HAS DONE FAR MORE FOR NEGROES IN 60 YEARS, FOR FILIPINOS AND HAWAIIANS IN 30 YEARS, THAN HAS BEEN DONE FOR INDIANS IN A CENTURY AND A HALF.

2

In what environment do the children starve?

" The survey staff (of the Institute) finds itself obliged to say frankly and unequivocally that the provisions for the care of the Indian children in the boarding schools are grossly inadequate." [5]

Next to the dietary deficiency the staff considered the overcrowding of dormitories the most pertinent problem. On page 192 they reported:

The boarding schools are generally crowded beyond their capacity, so that the individual child does not have sufficient light

[5] *The Problem of Indian Administration.* P. 12.

and air. . . . Contagious diseases under these conditions have almost free scope.

Health experts say the desirable cubage per child in dormitory construction is at least 600 cubic feet. Indian schools not only fall far below that figure, but the percentage of window space to wall space is so low that, in addition, ventilation is most unsatisfactory. Computations made by a northwest district officer of the United States Public Health Service have substantiated the findings of the survey staff. The average has been about half of the minimum standard. At the Fort Apache Indian School it was 310 cubic feet of air space for each cot. In many prominent instances the already stagnant air is aggravated by the practice of nailing down windows in girls' dormitories, lest the inmates might run away. The only sections of the dormitories which are assured of adequate ventilation are the porches, but these are far from ideal. They shut off light and air from inside rooms which are filled with beds beyond their capacity.

The Leupp Boarding School, on the Navajo Reservation, has a capacity of about 319, according to Chief Medical Inspector Newborne and Construction Engineer Russell. Into the rest and recreation rooms were crowded 63 more beds, making a total capacity of 382. The Indian Bureau has announced the enrollment at 402. Dr. S. S. Warren, the agency and school doctor, reported to the Indian Commissioner:

As conditions are now the beds are in such close proximity that the health of the children is not only seriously menaced, but in the event of a fire a large number of them would lose their lives.

The boys' dormitory at the Santa Fe school has been condemned for some time because of serious cracks in the main walls, but regardless of this fact the number of children housed in the dormitory has been increased. In addition, the steam boilers at this school are buckled, making it unsafe to carry a head of steam sufficient to heat the radiators, not alone the rooms. Only recently, however, was a new dormitory built at Santa Fe.

Yet at Santa Fe, $25,000 was spent in equipping a gymnasium.

At the Carson School the porch economy idea prevailed over the protest of the superintendent. The building at the Carson School was in such a sad state of repair and so poorly arranged that the real economy would have been achieved by replacing the building entirely. In sharp contrast to this dormitory are the very modern horse and dairy barns, but such contrasts are not uncommon in the Indian Service. It is not unusual to see farm buildings of the most recent design and construction placed beside dormitory buildings about to sigh their last and collapse.

Overcrowding dormitories with beds, so close together that from a distance they seem to be one huge bed, is not the only problem. In many cases two children sleep in one bed, not because they prefer to keep warm during the cold nights, but because no room is available to place additional beds. The Institute's investigators declared a single instance of such might have been excusable, " but in one case as many as thirty children were accommodated two in a bed."

Before the hearings on the King Resolution it was established that " The Indian boarding schools are at present crowded by enrollment to 38.8 per cent beyond their physical capacity, as stated by the Bureau."

3

In the dormitory buildings the main sanitary sections are usually located in the basement, making it necessary for the pupil to go down from one to three flights of stairs. Not only is he compelled to do this at night, but during the day, as these facilities on the upper floors are generally locked.

Of the main sanitary sections in the basements they are as a rule poorly lighted, poorly ventilated, and insufficiently heated. The cement floors are not laid so as to insure quick drainage. The sanitary equipment found in many of the schools is old and rarely in working order. The survey staff found leaky faucets and water closets very common. In one case " only two water closets were found in order for eighty girls. All other equipment was clogged and in some instances overflowing onto the floors. The explanation was that the engineer was also the athletic coach and the team activities were always given preference. . . . The flushing device in the boys' building at Haskell could only be operated by the use of some strength, a fact which probably explains the conditions found there." [6]

Haskell is prominent in the Central West for its football teams, which have given that institution much favorable

[6] *The Problem of Indian Administration.* Pp. 317-8.

publicity. Its athletic field is the most pretentious of the non-reservation boarding schools. The Institute has observed Haskell's tremendous concrete stadium and has declared " a vast amount of money was put into it, so that it presents a marked contrast with the living and working quarters provided for the children. A far more splendid memorial and contribution could have been made to this school if the same amount of money had been used to reconstruct the living quarters." [7]

Dr. D. O. Thrasher has told a Senate committee how, at the Fort Apache School for Navajos, a child's face is but 18 inches from an obsolete, clogged toilet bowl whenever he stoops to drink from a water fountain. Dr. Thrasher reported these highly unsanitary conditions to the superintendent. Some time later he again inspected the building, " and found the door to the toilet fastened with wire. Asked one of the older boys if the toilet had been cleaned up and repaired. Answered he did not know. Asked him if the boys did not use the toilet. Answered no, that they went to the river."

The above enumerated conditions are not out of the ordinary. The Institute found that " in practically all dormitories one or more toilets were out of order. . . . About half of the sections visited were without toilet paper."

The facilities for the children to wash their faces and hands are generally the perforated pipe method, which the survey staff found quite unsatisfactory. In the cases where the hot and cold water faucets alternate, the chil-

[7] *The Problem of Indian Administration.* P. 326.

dren, in order to obtain a satisfactory mixture, would plug up the waste pipe and then all wash together in the same trough, despite the prevalence of trachoma and impetigo.

4

Drinking water and sewage play an important rôle in the health and sanitary conditions of the boarding school child. At the Orphans' Training School at Tahlequah, Oklahoma, the water is taken from a shallow well much lower than the point of discharge for the sewage of the disposal plant. An analysis of this water supply has repeatedly shown B. coli. Money for a new well was appropriated in one of the urgent deficiency bills which, however, failed in a recent session of Congress.

In many cases the effluence from the disposal plants is emptied directly into streams. At Chemawa it is emptied wholesale on the surface.

5

Tuberculosis and trachoma are the major diseases of Indian children as well as adults. Health specialists agree that tuberculosis unquestionably can be best combated by a diet adequate to insure vigorous growth, good nutrition, a sturdy bodily resistance, and sanitary living conditions. The same is true of trachoma. However, in the previous pages we have seen the status of the diet and living conditions, and the results are consequently to be expected. Although the Indian Service has established a quart of milk

a day per pupil as the standard this good intention has
never been thoroughly achieved. Not even at a special
school for children suffering from trachoma — Fort Defiance, Arizona — is milk a part of the normal diet.

What, then, of the child who becomes sick?

" The medical service rendered the boarding school children is not up to a reasonable standard. Physical examinations are often superficial and enough provision is not made
for the correction of remediable defects." [8]

As for the health examinations, they are held on the
routine plan and rushed through so rapidly that careful
diagnoses are impossible. The Institute recommended that
the rate of examination by the physician should not average
more than six to eight an hour. Yet the inspectors tell of
a day school where the physician examined the entire enrollment of 90 in two hours. " He never used a stethoscope
or counted a pulse or took a temperature. The records of
these examinations reveal a charting of pulse, a recording
of temperature, and a check indicating that the lungs had
been auscultated and palpated. A method seen time and
again of examining a chest was to place the stethoscope
twice anteriorly and twice posteriorly without leaving
it long enough for a complete inhalation or exhalation
to be heard, and without requiring the child to cough
to elicit rales. One physician in examining for trachoma
repeatedly examined the left eye, never reverting the
right lid." [9]

When a child is acutely ill, frequently from physical

---

[8] *The Problem of Indian Administration.* Pp. 12–13.
[9] *Ibid.* Pp. 333–334.

defects overlooked during his entrance examination, he is
sent to the school hospital. Undoubtedly he has been labor-
ing long under a remediable handicap, but instead of finding complete cure in the hospital he is " discharged before
improvement in his condition warrants. . . . He may not
remain until convalescence is complete, and in the case of
tuberculosis, the child is frequently sent home, even though
the conditions in the home may be the worst possible for
the child." [10]

An outstanding example of the officials' intelligence in
handling medical cases is the treatment administered
children suffering from bed-wetting. They are punished.
They are whipped for an affliction which is no fault
of theirs. Instead of being supplied with rubber sheets,
clean linen, and made as comfortable as possible the
children so ailing are compelled to remain in their
soiled beds.

The Institute's staff recommended that " enuresis should
be recognized by all workers as a medical problem to be
handled by the physician himself or under his orders. All
punishment should be immediately discontinued."

Let us hesitate long enough to cite one of the numerous
cases wherein a child suffering from enuresis was punished.
Mrs. Rose Ecoffey was once a temporary matron in a boarding school. Untutored in the atrocities of the Service she
naturally became indignant and testified to the Senate Investigating Committee that she asked Inspector Carter's
advice concerning a six-year-old boy, " and he said maybe
the boy was doing that on purpose and to take him over and

[10] *Ibid.* Pp. 333–334.

give him a whipping, and I said I would not whip the boy for anything he could not help."

Concerning a serious epidemic in the Fort Apache School, Dr. Thrasher has written:

Upon my arrival at the school, the latter part of October, I found an epidemic of measles which had been on since September. . . . On November 21 the epidemic had again increased and the hospital overcrowded. . . . The epidemic increased among the girls at about the same time, and we had to use a residence building as a temporary hospital for them.[11]

The superintendent refused to coöperate with Dr. Thrasher in securing additional hospital quarters for the boys who were seriously ill.

Another instance of a superintendent's lack of coöperation during an epidemic is the case of Dr. Warren, an Indian Bureau physician. To quote from his official report, wherein he repeatedly notified the superintendent:

We have approximately 100 cases of measles, 7 cases of pneumonia. Having just gone through an epidemic of influenza our nursing force of teachers and two practical nurses are worn out and almost unfit for duty.

This notification followed an S. O. S. call to the agency superintendent, stating among other things:

Our measles cases are of a virulent type, some of whom have only recently had influenza.

Dr. Warren was in daily communication with his agency, pleading for medical and nursing assistance to fight an

[11] Hearings before a Subcommittee of the Committee on Indian Affairs. Feb. 23, 1927. Pp. 26–7.

extremely venomous disease which was proving deadly to children already weakened from influenza.

But he received no assistance.

In desperation he appealed to the highest power in the Indian Service, and in so appealing incriminated that authority into the circle of a woeful yet deliberate neglect in a life and death emergency. Dr. Warren telegraphed the Indian Commissioner at Washington, as follows:

We have had epidemics of influenza and measles since March 18. Four deaths; one typhus suspect in hospital now. Dormitories and hospitals are foul with contagion, etc.

These conditions were the result of an inadequate medical service, that is, the lack of reserve doctors and nurses which could be rushed to a school where an epidemic had broken out, especially an overcrowded boarding school. These conditions were aggravated by the lack of coöperation on the part of Indian superintendents. To climax this tragic drama of events, Commissioner Burke answered Dr. Warren six and a half months later in a letter:

In the Indian Service all matters of importance should be carried out through the superintendent as administrative officer. If you will inform the superintendent in writing as to what you believe should be done for the protection of the health of the population in the school and reservation, your responsibility ceases. All such matters are checked up sooner or later and should the superintendent fail in his duty, he must take the consequences of such failure.[12]

[12] *Ibid.* P. 41.

Pertinent epidemics " are checked up sooner or later." It took more than half a year for the Indian Commissioner to answer Dr. Warren's desperate telegram, and when he did Dr. Warren was, in addition, fired from the Service for these activities. How much longer did it take to count the dead and ailing?

XIV

CHILD LABOR

1

W E have seen the prominent parts diet and health play in preventing emaciated, run-down children from " picking up." Judging from the malnutrition and tuberculosis seen late in the school year, as late as June, many unfortunates never " pick up." The cause?

" It is an accepted fact that over-activity will not only produce a state of malnutrition, but it will counteract any attempt to correct such a condition by feeding."

So speaks the Institute's specialist in criticizing the child labor the Government legally maintains under the stamp of Federal authority — a legality which is seriously doubted:

" The labor of children (industrial, productive labor) as carried on in Indian boarding schools, would, it is believed, constitute a violation of child labor laws in most

states. . . . The amount of work to be done is almost
unlimited and the children must do it."[1]

To look at the haggard faces of mere children, at their
lean, undersized bodies, is to see the devastating effect of
this over-activity, resulting from half a day at hard labor
and half a day at school. Their day begins at 6 A.M. and
continues in some schools until 7 P.M. for the smaller
children, and until 9 or 10 P.M. for the older student-
laborers. Theoretically this work is supposedly educational, but in practice much of it is undertaken as profitable
production. For example, investigators have discovered
that at Haskell a boy, who has been detailed to the print
shop to be taught the trade, is instead made to fold papers
" under pressure to get a commercial job out on time.
Most of the industrial teachers admit that great consideration has to be given to production to the detriment of
education."

The strenuous day inflicted on the children is a heavy
one even for strong, healthy bodies. It is too much for a
child that eats an unbalanced, inefficient diet and sleeps in
an over-crowded, stuffy dormitory.

A visitor to a boarding school finds extensive provisions
for child labor. In contrast, he discovers provisions for
play almost completely lacking. When shown the " recreation rooms " of some of the " show " institutions in the
Southwest one sees gloomy, musty-smelling basement
rooms. Yet those schools are located on the desert, where
sunlight and space are the cheapest commodities. One no-
tices these " recreation rooms " to be empty. The children

[1] *The Problem of Indian Administration.* Pp. 331, 376.

neither have the time nor the vitality to play. They are virtually prisoners in institutions called schools, and yet they have committed no offense other than that of being born an Indian.

The laundries secure a good portion of the children in their tentacles of labor. Superintendents have reported that they can get much more work out of their charges if they keep large piles of laundry always before them. The old and poorly repaired equipment requires from three to four times the necessary labor, and all the while the children are compelled to stand. An observer need not be particularly astute to note that " The monotonous ironing of simple dresses and shirts for hours is frankly productive work, and is not necessary to teach the child the simple processes involved." In addition, the children are compelled to work directly under huge drive shafts and belts, which are not properly encased. Since there is no labor union protecting its workers the result is inevitable: Accidents are frequent.

The kitchen and the bakery are also means of sapping the strength of the children. The lack of clean linen, for the workers in two such vital departments as the kitchen and bakery, presents another interesting paradox, so commonly observed in the Indian Service. The children slave half a day in the laundries, completely hidden behind piles of soiled clothing, yet they and the regular employees cook and bake in dirty clothes. These same children who toil in steam-filled basement dungeons, termed laundry quarters, are compelled to use the soiled towels of some other child if they wish to dry their hands and faces.

The dairies, although possessing the most modern and well-kept buildings of the schools, are one of the worst offenders. Rarely one will see a dairy not so conspicuous, as at the very model Sherman Institute, where instead other buildings startle the eye with their pretentiousness. Nevertheless, the appearance of these buildings does not deter the labors of the children, as the bulk of this work is done by hand very early in the morning.

The official *Course of Study for Indian Schools*, the result of another authoritative investigation, frankly admits the child labor to be solely " productive work."

It is a fact that today Indian children are coming into the boarding schools much too young, much too emaciated for the child labor that is thrust upon them without their consent, without even remunerative reward. For example, at Leupp, 100 of the 191 girls are 11 years of age or under. The drudging labor, instead of being accomplished by the healthy bodies of 20-year-old youths, has to be done by very small, malnutritious children.

Much of this labor is not " necessary " institutional work. Much is done for profit. Donald E. Robertson of Sacramento, California, a Federal narcotic agent, has testified to that effect before the Senate Investigating Committee. When he was employed as a farmer in the Indian Service he observed the money-making aim of running the dairies and farms. As he understood it the officials kept the number of hogs down — " that is, as fast as the shoats got to be marketable size they were put on the market." None were slaughtered for use at the reservation. Upon being asked what became of 10 gallons of milk daily, he answered that many times he had personally seen the milk fed to the hogs, to fatten them for the market.

In looking at the testimony presented to the Senate Committee on Indian Affairs concerning the 1931 appropriation for the schools, one reads:

> The children in the Indian " schools " work half a day. " It has been practically a child labor proposition," J. Henry Scattergood, Assistant Commissioner of Indian Affairs acknowledged.
>
> It is hoped, with the introduction of labor-saving machinery, to reduce this child labor from a half-day to a quarter-day.
>
> Farms must be run to feed the children; buildings are old, equipment obsolete. Well — perhaps — nice healthy work in the open air . . .[2]

True, farms must be run to feed the children. But who runs the farms? Up to the time of writing (Fall, 1930) no labor-saving machinery has been introduced, and this administrative hope on the part of the Assistant Commissioner has remained nothing but — " Well — perhaps — nice healthy work in the open air . . ."

This slave-gang aspect of the schools along with its military atmosphere and regulations have penetrated into every phase of school life. The marching to and from classrooms, the dress parades, the filing into and out of dining rooms, along with the strict formality in classes have annihilated the children's initiative, warped their normal points of view, robbed them of beauty, and negated all family life. So military has become the routine of the schools that:

[2] *The Literary Digest.* May 24, 1930. P. 22.

The segregation by sex and age is carried out so meticulously that one table in the boys' half of the dining room contains the smallest boys in the school, and a corresponding table on the girls' side contains the smallest girls. Frequently these little ones can scarcely manage the heavy pitchers and serving dishes.[3]

One can not expect a six- or seven-year-old child to distribute food to his fellow boarders. " They struggle manfully and get through this task after a fashion." Nevertheless, the military structure must not be disturbed.

2

" But there are the vacations," the injured citizen exclaims. " Surely, there are three months of the year when the children can build and purify their bodies, and, above all, forget."

Yes, there are vacations. But not for Indian children. If the parents, the majority of whom have annual incomes of less than $200, can not afford their children's railway fare back to the reservation the children are compelled to remain in the school during the summer. Thousands of parents have not seen their offspring for as long as five years — some ten. A Western Navajo father, earning $47 a year, can not afford to pay railroad fare amounting to more than his annual income. Neither can many Chippewas buy a 900-mile ticket from Haskell Institute in Lawrence, Kansas, to northern Wisconsin and Minnesota. Thus, by unfortunate laws of circumstance, many children are compelled to live

[3] *The Problem of Indian Administration.* Pp. 329–30.

for eight or nine years of their lives only 200 or 300 miles away from their parents.

What does the Indian Service do with this unproductive energy? It is not wasted. As early as the tops of beets begin to appear through the soil, carload after carload of children are trucked many hundreds of miles to the beet fields of Colorado and Kansas. As the sun warms quickly in those climates the children are carted away as early as the fifteenth of May. They consequently are forced to lose at least two weeks of school.

The results of this labor have proven it to be neither educational nor healthful.

On September 30, 1926, the Albuquerque boarding school issued a report on 47 Pueblo boys, from 12 years up, who had been sent to the beet fields of Kansas for the summer.

Several of the boys, when examined by the (school) doctor last June, were found in unfit condition for work on a Kansas farm and were rejected. But they were so insistent on going that they were finally sent on with the others and they came back in improved physical condition.

What kind of work is this that made those boys " so insistent " ?

The official circular from the Phoenix office of the Indian Service, published March 24, 1927, describes the work in the beet fields as " light work, though tedious." The beet thinning, the circular explains, " is all done in stooping over or on the hands and knees. Small boys are very well adapted to this work and it can be done very nicely by the boy of from 13 to 14 years of age. It is preferred to take boys of only school age." (That is, no boys younger than six years.)

The children are packed into trucks and shipped hundreds of miles, sometimes over deserts, without an escort. The official circular frankly admits that employees are not satisfactory for this task, and so the boys are shipped without any care whatever. When they arrive they live in tents, like road-building gangs.

They are either in a stooping position or on their hands and knees all day long, thinning beets from endless rows that creep across the fields. In Colorado and Kansas it is hot in the mornings. Hotter in the afternoons. The sun goes through their backs like blazing arrows. Their knees become numb to the soil. Their hands, holding the weight of their bodies, also become benumbed. At night they crawl into their cots too tired to sleep.

It is the same day after day. Sometimes they hoe or spade, but always it is thinning beets. Their hands become so accustomed to the labor that they move mechanically. They become little, brown robots, grabbing a handful, shuffling over — grabbing a handful, shuffling over.

The economic results are as equally objectionable as the educational and health. Circulars are issued at regular intervals indicating that a boy can expect to earn two dollars or more a day, but no reports have ever disclosed actual earnings amounting to anything resembling that estimate.

Taking, for example, the reports of three schools among the Navajos, 29 boys from one school returned after 63 days in the beet fields with the average net earnings of $5.62, or *less than nine cents a day*. The report of another school in that region was *less than twelve cents a day*. They were told before leaving their schools that $2 a day would be the average. Such was the inducement. How then came the reductions?

The boys are charged $20 for their transportation to and from the fields in the Government Transportation Unit trucks. They have to provide the foreman with a salary. Also the cook. They rent their hoes used in thinning the beets. They have to " find " their own groceries, fuel, and clothing. They pay a dollar a month " for hospital." All these operating expenses are deducted from their wages, leaving as a remainder, in one case, nine cents a day.

What of this dollar-a-month hospitalization, when the children fall ill? In the summer of 1927 seven of the beet-field child-peons fell ill with typhoid. When they left their school they were not vaccinated for typhoid, because they were thought to be tuberculous. When they contracted typhoid they were not hospitalized at their camp in the beet fields, nor was their money for hospitalization returned. They were simply dumped into an Indian Bureau truck and driven 700 miles to the boarding schools from which they came. They were driven over rough roads in a season of violent rains. They passed through farms and villages and over the desert. How many white people became infected with typhoid as a result of this unusual journey can only be imagined.

What is known is this: Seven boys died from typhoid. The officials of the Indian Bureau have been familiar with these facts for several years, for it is their employees who collect and deliver the Indian child labor. Nevertheless, Indian children are again in the beet fields. Again, last summer. Again, this summer. Regardless of previous heart-breaking demonstrations Indian boys are sent to the fields without vaccination for typhoid.

The Indian Bureau heads solemnly declare:

" Indian children must be made to love work."

Yes, though they die they shall be made to love work. They shall be made to love work whether it be in the winter at institutions of child labor or in the vacation times upon beet fields. The tedious, monotonous, unremunerative tasks of thinning, topping, and hoeing beets will not make young, impressionable minds adore farming nor revere farm labor.

One precaution is taken by the Government. Good drivers of the transportation trucks are provided so that " if an accident occurs it will be simply a matter of regret and not of remorse."

3

I am thoroughly aware of the pitfalls into which books of criticism such as this usually fall. The relative merits of destructive and constructive criticism are not to be debated in these pages, nor is it the major purpose of this book to take up the numerous theories of reform advocated for the Indian Service. Destructive criticism is necessarily constructive criticism by virtue of its revelation of right and wrong, of good and bad. However, in these disclosures of the Bureau's treatment of Indian children, which have occupied so many pages, the reader will perhaps welcome the antidote of constructive critical theory.

In the January, 1930, issue of *American Indian Life* suggestions are made with regard to " Better Schools for Indians." " Curriculum as such is not the problem in Indian education," it declares, " except that getting rid of the uniform curriculum is an urgency. Improvement of teaching personnel, and an applied program of school-and-community-correlation, are the overshadowing needs."

Under the general title of *Vocational Training* the Institute for Government Research states that an almost complete lack of qualified vocational teachers along with the absence of necessary guidance, placement, and follow-up machinery have made the vocational program of the boarding schools exceedingly ineffective. In addition, no attempt has been made to relate the work of the school to the industrial needs of the country. That is, vanishing industries are taught such as harnessmaking, blacksmithing, etc., which afford little opportunity for the children to make a livelihood when they return to their respective reservations. The most notable of these useless professions are baking, tailoring, and laundry work. Of the training they receive under the present system none of the students become sufficiently skilled, even after a reasonable period of experience, to enable them to earn a living in competition with the well-trained white workmen. Cases of Indian graduates in the open market show they have experienced great difficulty in holding jobs resulting from bad work habits acquired in school.

Outside of the domestic service no other attempt has

been made to fit girls for a wage-earning occupation. Only a few boarding schools — in fact, only a mere half dozen out of 211 schools — give training in teaching, nursing, clerical and other work which might prove remunerative. Only Haskell Institute gives a course in stenography. Of this training that is provided none of it equips the graduates for competition with white girls from recognized schools, so the Institute's educator observed. Nor does it prepare them to enter colleges and technical schools.

To conclude this chapter on the treatment of Indian children no better statement could be quoted than the final testimony of the Indian Defense Association, which helped lead to a senatorial investigation of the boarding schools.

All of them are institutions of spiritual and emotional cruelty. Any institution concentrating children to the number of a thousand and regimenting them, and keeping them away from their homes for consecutive years, is an institution that destroys and torments. Many of the boarding schools are institutions of actual physical horror, and their overcrowding with ever-increasing numbers of child victims is one of the causes which explains the swiftly rising death and disease rates. These schools literally are culture grounds for disease subsequently to be spread in a methodical way throughout the Indian population.[4]

[4] King Resolution Hearings. Pp. 40, 50.

XV

ENVOY: BIRD'S-EYE PICTURES

1

YOU are rewarded with a winding drive along an isthmus, after passing through the depressing, dissipated-looking village of Flambeau, Wisconsin. The Indian boarding school is located on this beautiful isthmus, surrounded by green-skirted lakes. The natural beauty of the country surprises you, but at the sight of the school buildings your delight rapidly fades.

Hidden beneath a new, camouflaging coat of white and battleship-grey paint are the dilapidated buildings, some forty-odd years old. As you approach closer you can not help but notice the true conditions. The steps of several structures are worn and saggy. The windows are warped. No grass grows between the buildings. The weeds and sand patches are in sharp contrast to the green water and the greener shore beyond. Some buildings have not been painted and they stand like grim reminders of the past, when paint brushes were never employed to sweep dirt under carpets. In all, you are presented with a corpse, whose face has been vainly painted with lipstick and rouge in a feeble attempt to imitate robust health.

When I arrived at the school the children were eating their noonday lunch in a large dining hall. I was particularly anxious to observe their food, as the 1931 fiscal year had begun with its increased food appropriations.

The children were being served much meat of some obscure variety, which did not smell too savory. They could take as many helpings of this meat as they wished. A gravy was being served with the meat, but I found no abundance of health-giving vegetables. Nor any milk whatever. And this was the noonday meal; the children had a long afternoon of classes ahead of them; some boys had to work about the buildings and in the dairy barn.

There was, however, an abundance of bread. But upon examination I found it was newly and very poorly baked; its top was burnt while the inside was soft and doughy. The children were given these hot, unhealthy loaves by the basketful. Special students were detained as waiters. Their fingers did not look too clean. The boy cutting the bread had eruptions on his hands.

I turned to my guide, Mrs. Clara M. Lea, a kindly souled matron, and asked her, jokingly, if the boys' and girls' hands were inspected by the children themselves. " I think so," she replied, conscientiously.

An obsolete faucet, completely out of commission, was the paralyzed source of the children's water. Those thirsty had to wait until they were out of the dining hall before they could drink a glass of water.

The cook had no helper and relied on the children for assistance, which resulted in unsatisfactory service and the unnecessary cooling of warm foods.

Upon leaving the dining hall I recalled what Senator W. B. Pine told me in Washington, regarding increased appropriations. "The Indian problem," he said, "is not so much a question of money as it is of brains."

Brains to plan balanced meals. Brains to assist and supervise the children. Brains to spend money intelligently.

Another outstanding example of the brainless Indian Bureau is the case of the Mekusukey Academy for Seminole children, located at Wewoka, the facts of which are being brought out in the current hearings of the Senate Investigating Committee. Between three and four thousand dollars worth of foodstuffs, derived from the additional food appropriations, were delivered in August at the Academy; however, it was previously decided that the school was not to open that fall. Senator Elmer Thomas has stated the following, concerning the Subcommittee's inspection of the Mekusukey school: "We were told at Wewoka that nearly five tons of flour, two tons of beans, and 674 pounds of coffee were included in the storage at the Academy, and that rats and mice were spoiling a good part of it." Meanwhile, neighboring Seminoles were starving. Upon his return to Washington Senator Thomas continued his investigation. "I called out to the Indian Bureau today to find out what disposition was to be made of the food," he said. "It took half an hour to find anyone who

knew there was any such place as the Mekusukey Academy,
and another half hour for them to find out that the supplies
were there and no arrangements had been made for their
disposal. The whole thing comes down to this," he concluded. "The Secretary of the Interior depends on the
Assistant Secretary for his information, the Assistant Secretary depends on the Commissioner of Indian Affairs, the
Commissioner depends on the reservation superintendents,
the superintendents depend on the field agents, and our
testimony shows that the field agents are not doing anything."

Brains. Brains.

Additional appropriations have been made for food and
much pride has been assumed over that fact in Washington, but upon leaving the Flambeau dining hall I saw a
sight which dispelled all the propaganda and hallelujahs
of victory. I saw three small, undersized, beggarly clothed
Indian children, one girl and two boys, poking around a
garbage can, looking for bits of food. It was one o'clock
and they had just been fed, but they were still hungry. I
luckily snapped the picture, which I have for evidence.

In the town of Flambeau the waitress in the Wigwam
restaurant was a telephone operator from Chicago, sum-
mering among the lakes. "Gee, but it's tough around
here," confessed the girl from the gangsters' Promised
Land. "The Indians fight all the time, with guns, too.
There are street brawls almost every night and they get
terribly hurt. Last night the whole town joined in. The
fight started here at the Wigwam while they were dancing,
and it spread all over town. They take one drink and go

crazy like devils. Hardly any of them are married. They get together in a hurry and say they can't find the judge. Boy, but it's tough around here. I'm sure glad I'm leaving for Chicago next week."

Such is the environment in which the Flambeau school children are being educated.

2

A few miles across the South Dakota state line from the Flandreau school, where I saw a dead rat of prosperous size lying conspicuously outside the school kitchen besides innumerable flies and other signs of sanitary neglect, is the Pipestone Boarding school of Pipestone, Minnesota. It is undoubtedly the best school in the Indian Service and is run by undoubtedly the best superintendent in the Indian Service.

James Balmer is kind, jovial, patient, and constructive; above all, he has intelligence, a rare quality in Indian Service employees. James Balmer is a singular breeze of fresh air in a stagnant desert of disappointments.

James Balmer, in addition to running the best industrial institution in the Service, has the best-disciplined school. He has no trouble with his boys and girls, because he allows them to mix freely.

We stood on his well-kept, cheery campus. He pointed to a group of boys and girls playing ball on the grass. " This is the only school in the Service," he said, " where you will see such companionship. My disciplinarian happened to visit Haskell on his vacation, and he brought back

a list of rules and regulations a mile long, some not allowing the boys and girls to be seen together after a certain
hour and all that. I laughed and told him to put the list
in his memory book."

I recalled the promiscuousness of the older boys and
girls in the much-disciplined Frandreau school a short
distance away.

" Perhaps you have heard cases," he was saying, " where
the children have run away from school." He laughed.
" But I bet you haven't heard one of a boy running away
from home to go to an Indian school."

I confessed the unusualness of the procedure.

" Well," he continued, " Malcolm Dakota, 14, wrote us
a letter he wanted to come back to school after being home
a few weeks. I answered that the new term did not begin
until September, but he wired collect saying that he
couldn't wait till then. So I sent him a railroad ticket dated
August 1st. But on July 25th he walked into my office, after
having ridden the rods for 250 miles! "

James Balmer has been in the Service 31 years; when
he was stationed at Flambeau, Wisconsin, that school was
operating efficiently, but since his transfer many years ago
it has been run into the ground. Wherever he has gone his
magic fingers of perseverance, initiative, and industry have
constructed a new institution. He should be transferred
every three years to every Indian school in the country.
God grant him nine lives!

His employees, by the way, have profited from the example of their master to the great benefit of the Indian
children. They coöperate to a remarkable degree and

possess a unique humanitarian spirit of a rare Indian Service breed.

The Pipestone school has the best cook in the Indian Service. Her mess hall is as flyless as an Eskimo's igloo, which is again in sharp contrast to the Flandreau school. In fact, no flies can be found in even the dairy barn, nor in any building on the campus.

Besides remodeling and repainting his buildings and keeping them in the best possible condition, James Balmer has succeeded in squeezing enough supplemental appropriations out of the Indian Bureau to build dormitory additions, a new hospital, a new gymnasium, and other minor buildings. But the Indian Bureau, upon hearing of these improvements, has penalized Balmer by cutting his funds and discouraging his ideas. He has had to fight three years before he could get a new hospital; six years before the Bureau consented to a new gymnasium. He has had to actually fight for a new baking oven, also for additions to the class-room building, and the girls' and boys' dormitories.

When the brains are present the money is irritatingly, almost invariably lacking.

IV
HEALTH

XVI

YOU KILL US FOR YOUR SPORT

1

I SHALL never forget the intensity of those men. The very air in the room seemed charged with conflict. Federal and state officials were discussing Indian problems. There was much argument, much passing of the buck. The Indian situation, as characteristic of such gatherings, was being chewed, swallowed, and digested in an hour. Suddenly, the barrage thinned. The men began to pin one another down to specific points.

Indian Commissioner G. E. E. Lundquist, appointed by the President to investigate Indian affairs independently and report directly to the Secretary of the Interior, asked Congressman George Schneider of Appleton, Wisconsin, his solution of the problem.

" I'd say that the home is the key to the Indian problem," replied the Congressman, who has been active in Indian

matters. " It is the key to all civilization. The trade school
idea is good but it is not the whole thing."

" I'd say education was the least important," retorted
E. E. Jermark, newly transferred from the Pine Ridge
agency in South Dakota to the Lac du Flambeau of Wisconsin. (Another instance of the Bureau transferring its
inefficient employees, complained against by the Indians,
instead of discharging them). " And health is not the most
important issue," he continued. " Industry, in my opinion,
is first."

In a corner sat a well-built, grey-haired gentleman,
whose quiet eyes had been observing the Federal opinions
without much blinking. He was Dr. C. A. Harper, Wisconsin State Health Officer.

" More fundamental than education and industry is
health," he said positively. " Take as many whites as there
are Indians and give them as much sickness as the Indian
has been having and the whites would soon be poverty
stricken, ambitionless, and immoral. The sicker the Indian
gets the worse he lives. Health is the basis of all life. It
affects the moral as well as the physical being. I just saw
a 16-year-old girl, who was getting her third baby."

Before attending this informal meeting I snapped the
picture of a young Indian girl, barely 22, who had a baby
five years ago, has another, one year old, and a third well
on its way.

America has been horrified at the tales of the political
prisons of Russia. Our money has been sent to the Orient,
to relieve the diseases and famines of China, after our
hearts had been punctured by means of pitiful pictures

and unbelievable stories. Katherine Mayo succeeded in arousing America's sense of decency with a tale of India. But it takes an American physician, thoroughly familiar with the American scene, to recall our eyes and emotions from the Far East, the Far West, and the too Far Southeast, to the burnt and seedless grass in our own back yard.

Dr. Haven Emerson, professor of Public Health Administration at Columbia University, has written a letter, of which two paragraphs are sufficient:

As a student and teacher of public health, as former commissioner of health of New York City, etc., I have become technically familiar with the relations of poverty, dependency, and preventable disease.

Outside the boundaries of Russia, India, or China I know of no nation, race, or tribe of human beings which now exhibit such tragic neglect of the most elementary protection against sickness and death as is to be found among the American Indians.

2

Dr. George H. Reddick sits in his cozy one-story bungalow on the outskirts of Wabeno, Wisconsin, and talks fearlessly and intelligently with regard to the criminal deficiencies of the Indian Bureau's medical service.

" One night in February of 1930," he says to me, " Peter Jim called my phone at one-thirty in the morning. His wife was having a baby. I asked him why he didn't call the Government physician, Dr. E. G. Ovitz, and he told me that he had already refused to attend the woman. Well, she was suffering and as much as I hated to leave my warm bed

I went for the sake of humanity, for I knew Peter Jim
was penniless. On the way to the garage I read the ther-
mometer. It was 22 degrees below zero. The snow was
tremendous; I drove down a road the county had recently
plowed and it was like driving down a groove of snow, so
high rose the banks above the car. I parked and walked into
the country about a quarter of a mile. I found the shack.
Another couple was there, an old lady to help with the
birth, and an extra man. Peter Jim was sitting with them.
All three were drunk. I do not yet understand how Peter
Jim rode a pony in his condition through the snow to
a farmer's telephone. As a climax the fire was out.
My patient was standing up when I arrived, clad only
in a thin dress. She was shaking from head to foot
with the cold, and there was blood all over the place.
She was in intense pain and from the look on her face
I could see the agony she was in. Well, I got my gloves
off, but before I could remove my coat — the baby was
born."

"Born while she was standing?" I interrupt.

He nods quietly. "Yes, it dropped out on the floor —
dead."

There is silence in his office. Then — "I swore I'd never
take another Indian case, but I have — plenty."

"Did the mother live?" I ask.

"Yes, she was in town today. But the point is that if the
Government doctor had gone when Peter Jim called him
the baby might have been saved. I got there just too late."

"Is that an isolated case, doctor?" I ask, in fairness to
the Government physician.

"No, there are others," he replies. "Bill Towa's wife had a miscarriage in a tent where they were living. She was in terrible shape — hemorrhaged to death. Dr. Ovitz didn't see her.

"I delivered Harry Man's wife of twins in a tent.

"Frank Shepherd's 19-year-old boy had 103 fever, labored respirations, and pleurisy with effusion. I immediately told the sub-agent at Laona that the boy was in serious, serious shape and that he needed immediate attention. I told him to have the Government doctor look him up. About four days later the old man drove up on a pony. 'Isn't there something to be done for my boy?' he asked pitifully. The Government physician hadn't called and in face of the fact that a private practitioner had informed him that the case was serious. I immediately got the boy in my car and drove him to a neighboring hospital where I drained his lung. He felt so much better that the next day he took a train home. Four months later I met the father and asked him about his son. 'He died last week,' was his reply. The boy had developed TB. and the Indian Bureau doctor never went to see him.

"When Bill Bodah's full-blood wife was eight and a half months pregnant she developed diphtheria. I told Bill to have the agency doctor, as it would not cost a cent. But Dr. Ovitz refused to have anything to do with the patient. Well, infection during a delivery is the horror of every physician. That case gave me gray hair. At the height of her diphtheria I delivered the baby and it never developed the disease. You see, I gave the mother a heavy shot of anti-toxin a half hour before the birth and during the delivery I had four thicknesses of a towel held over her mouth so she could not cough on her womb.

" Jim Shepherd, a young fellow of 18, had been going with a loose white girl and he showed a plus four Wassermann. As the Laona doctor's contract does not cover V. D. cases he got a special compensation of $50 for treating the boy. That never looked right to me, especially after I took the Wassermann and discovered the boy's affliction. Dr. Ovitz's attitude distinctly shows he does not like handling Indians. In fact, he has told people as much, but he has not been eager to relinquish his position."

" But the Indians — what is their attitude? " I ask.

" I can go on reciting additional cases, but I say this: many of them won't go up there at all to see him."

" How about the general health conditions of the Pottawatomies and scattered Chippewas living around here? " I question him next.

" They live in such abject squalor that it is no wonder their resistance is low. In winter they use green wood for heating; they never have enough blankets. There is no ventilation in their homes; the windows are nailed down for the winter and the dogs stay indoors with them. In the fall they put on two or three layers of clothing and never remove them until spring. They are undernourished. They live on bread, baked by themselves and of the poorest quality. They also exist on salt pork, tea, but no milk; out of 600 Indians there are not more than one or two cows among them. Only a few raise vegetables. They a'l live out of a can in the winter.

" Sanitation? Hell, they have no sanitation. Three-

JOHN SITTING BULL

BLACK FROM EATING HORSE MEAT

fourths of them have no outhouses. They use the grass fields and the brush. Once in a while you will see a well. The majority use springs or dam up a stream."

"Where is the hospital located for Indians of this territory?" I ask next.

"There isn't any," is his reply. "On May 11, 1929, Congressman Schneider of Appleton introduced a bill, H. R. 2860, authorizing the expenditure of $125,000 for a fully equipped Indian hospital in Forest County. But the Indian Bureau recommended to the Indian Affairs Committee that the hospital not be built. Schneider believes that the Indian Bureau doesn't want to do anything for the Indian. Personally, I can see how and where they have been a failure. That bill is still pending with the House Indian Affairs Committee. It has never been passed. I can't understand it, for there certainly is a need for it. White people are taken to hospitals in ambulances and I don't see why the same shouldn't be done with Indians."

3

Henry Richie is a fine specimen of Pottawatomi. He is a descendant of the band that fled to Canada in 1835 to escape being deported from their native soil to the strange Kansas land. Richie serves in Canada with the famous Mounted Police. He returns to Wisconsin with part of the band. He is made sub-agent at the Laona station.

"It took the Toledo hospital from July until late in September before they wrote they couldn't take him," he confessed to me, concerning a case wherein a tuberculous

boy, George Venzile, died for the want of being sent to a
sanatorium.

"Is that an exceptional case?" I asked.

"No, I have another one hanging fire right now," he
replied. "Mrs. Jusie Alloway has TB. bad and it looks
as if her case is going to end the same way as the other."

4

The Indian picture is a Fox Grandeur. Four times four
is sixteen. Four times as large as the original four. From
the most eastern Government reservation in Wisconsin to
the most western in Oregon, from the Menominee to the
Klamath the Indian picture is a Fox Grandeur. . . .

Dr. Warren C. Hunt, private physician of Klamath Falls,
Oregon, testified with regard to the Government physicians
before the Senate Investigating Committee.

"As a rule," Senator Pine asked him, "does the reservation physician take an interest in the work, and does he
do all he can do?"

"While there are real shortcomings of the physicians,
as they come and go," Dr. Hunt answered, "any physician
in this county who comes in contact with them will be of
the same opinion: They have never been surgeons. They
have been medical men, but very inexperienced in surgery.
So, as I say, the surgical problems coming from the agency
are terrific."

Mrs. Ruth Kellett Roberts, an intelligent, magnanimous white woman, has told the Senators the case of Myrtle
Masten, who died in spasms at the birth of her child for

want of treatment. Her case was not investigated. She was
sent home to die with no care whatsoever. Mr. Allen, in
the Government Forest Service, attempted to secure aid
from a Dr. Johnson, an Indian Bureau employee, but to
no avail. To quote from the record:

Mr. Allen told the physician what the girl had told him and
insisted that they diagnose the case on his statement. The doctor
refused to diagnose it on his statement, not wishing to face the
situation, but the only reason that could be discovered for his
not wishing to face the situation was that he was about to receive his transfer.[1]

Mrs. Florence S. Sanford, an active clubwoman of
Berkeley, spent three weeks on the Western Navajo Reservation. Being a visitor she observed merely the conditions
"that were forced on me." While at Red Lake she went
out of courtesy to visit a hogan wherein she found two
sick Indian women. "One of them had a baby about three
days old, and she had it wrapped in a ten-pound flour sack;
and they had a cold; the woman had a heavy cold on the
lungs, and she was also — had a very heavy hemorrhage
and was very sick, and the baby was blue; and the other
woman was sick; and the baby was about three to four
weeks old; and I went out, because the odor was very
strong."

Mrs. Sanford returned to Red Lake and secured a nipple
and a bottle of canned milk, as the babies "had not been
nursing"; she also got clothes and blankets, as the women
"had no diapers on the babies."

A trader, Zoarl Styles, drove thirty miles to Tuba City

[1] Hearings Before a Subcommittee. Part 2. P. 555.

for the agency doctor, but he refused to attend the women. Mrs. Sanford asked Styles why he did not report the doctor to the agency officials at Tuba City:

The trader said he couldn't report it because they would take — the agent would take it out on him — and that was the first time that we heard about that sort of intimidation among the people by the agent.

The Indians there told me a story about a man who was operated on, and in the middle of the operation he was taken out and taken down to Flagstaff, in an automobile, and his bowels were open and he died on the way; and the Indians said "He was just an Indian."

Mrs. Sanford "was rather aghast" at the existence of these conditions, and when she saw the district nurse she asked for confirmation. The following conversation occurred between them:

"Mrs. Sanford, the things I could tell you are unspeakable."

"Why don't you tell about them?"

"I can't. It would just make conditions worse."

When Mrs. Sanford took leave of the reservation she noticed that the sick women and their babies had disappeared from the hogan. "Where are the women, have they left?" she asked the Indians.

"I don't know," came their reply, "they never die in the hogans. They never allow them to die in the hogans."[2]

With Mrs. Sanford was her husband, a member of the University of California and a gentleman whose integrity has never been questioned. Dr. Sanford, having no Federal

[2] Hearings Before a Subcommittee. Part 2. Pp. 547–8.

tape wound about his conscience, confirmed his wife's observations. Having been acquainted with Indian reservations for twenty years he spoke with authority. " In almost every State west of the Mississippi I have been, as a sportsman, on reservations," he told the Senate committee. " I know something about the Indians, and, without prejudice, I would say the conditions on this were perhaps no better, no worse than on others."

As final evidence, to convince any straggling doubters, Mrs. Ruth Kellett Roberts reappeared before the Senators, telling them of an old, blind, and penniless Indian, named Jack Woodbury. Mr. Morsel, the agent at Hoopa, would not allow a local physician to operate for cataract. So the blind man was taken to the agency to await the arrival of an eye specialist. He was held at Hoopla three years against his wishes by the agent, and no specialist appeared.

Finally, the general practitioner decided he might just as well perform the operation. So he examined him, sat on the old man to hold him down — they gave him nothing, not even a local anesthetic — and performed this operation for cataract on one of the eyes. The old man struggled so fiercely that they were doubtful whether the operation had been successful or not; but they bandaged the eyes and put him in a dark room for three days, and when they brought him out partial sight had been restored.[3]

Partial sight. Jack Woodbury's reward after being held a prisoner for three years. Old, penniless Jack Woodbury spent 36 months waiting for an operation without an anesthetic by a local doctor to restore partial sight.

[3] *Ibid.* P. 554.

5

The Indian picture is not a square picture, four sides by four. It is a huge circle containing every reservation in America. The same tales rewoven with the names of different tribes and the names of different doctors. But it is the same Indian — shallow cheeks sloping from his high cheek-bones and those same staring, starving eyes.

Ask Bennett, Chippewa on the Bad River. Joe is now dead from tuberculosis. There is no agency or contract doctor on the Bad River Reservation. Eleven hundred Indians do not need a doctor. Joe Bennett does not need a doctor; he is now dead from tuberculosis. Farmer Dohn can be a doctor for 1100 Indians; he is good enough for them.

Step into the Farmer's office. A shelf of bottles, old bottles with labels yellowed by age and sun. Iodine, boric acid, simple antiseptics, simpler disinfectants.

" Who prescribes these? " I ask the Government Farmer, indicating the shelf of bottles.

" I do," he replied. " It is simple to treat the Indians."

" What about TB., trachoma, and venereals? "

He shrugs his shoulders. " They get along by themselves, I guess."

The Methodist missionary at Odanah, the Rev. W. H. Thompson, has told a newspaper woman that " according to Government statistics over sixty per cent on this reservation have venereal diseases. Tuberculosis is rife here as well. I've been here four years, and eighty per cent of my funerals have been over tuberculosis victims. No effort is made to check these diseases. We have no doctor. We have no hospital and conditions are pitiful."

Rev. E. P. Wheeler, noted missionary and life-long friend of the Bad River Chippewa, has substantiated his Methodist colleague. "Things are seriously, horribly wrong here," he said. "The reservation seems wide open to liquor and prostitution. Venereal disease is rampant."

Mrs. Veronica Raiche has also testified that the "moral conditions are very low as compared with other communities. . . . Another thing that should be stopped is people coming from Ashland and other towns who stop the young girls in the street and sometimes go off with them, and very often bring them home in an intoxicated condition. I know of two cases like that myself, and I brought them to Mr. Dohn's attention, but he refuses to pay any attention to any complaint made at that office."

District Attorney Arthur Johnson of Ashland County, in which the Bad River Indian Reservation is located, has likewise testified to the Senate Investigating Committee: "Another thing I might mention is the situation with regard to venereal disease. I tried to get some action from the State government and they promised to make an investigation. There is a very bad situation existing so far as venereal disease is concerned; comparatively speaking I would say it was very bad. Finally they wrote to me and said they considered that a Federal problem and therefore would be unable to do anything."

The state of Wisconsin is a progressive state and as such has dealt with the Federal government before, with the result that they finally ceased waiting for the Federal problem to be solved by the Federals. In addition to this humanitarian impatience, the Wisconsin State Board of Health has been prompted by the conflicting reports of Federal and unofficial physicians, with the result that it has attempted to ascertain the physical condition of its Indian citizens. From April 22 to May 1, 1930, the Board held an Indian clinic for the Bad River and Red Cliff-Bayfield Chippewas. Out of approximately 1700 Indians (the Lac du Flambeau agency figures) only 780 were examined, or 46 per cent. The majority of the Chippewas never saw a Federal or State health examiner. Of the cases diagnosed 14 per cent were found to be tuberculous. Of the others nobody knows. This much is known: Death certificates show that the Wisconsin Indians die eight times faster from tuberculosis than a similar number of Whites; with one tribe, the Winnebagoes, the tuberculous death rate is 12 times greater than that of the Whites. In Montana the Indians die 15 to 16 times faster than the pale face citizens.

Of those examined in the 6 to 19 age group nearly one-half were underweight. Of those 20 years and up more than a third were underweight. Life invites tuberculosis before the first quarter of its Wheel has been turned.

The Indian Bureau hires a farmer to teach the Indians farming, and yet the lack of vegetable gardens has been " most noticeable."

The fact the Indian has never been educated in the most elementary factors, such as health, sanitation, etc., was proven when the clinical authorities explained the purpose of the vaccination: " The readiness with which this group accepted vaccination against smallpox sets a good example for the white citizenship of the state."

Education is known to have changed the course of streams; the instinct of self-preservation is as dominant in uneducated animals as in the schooled species.

Almost nine per cent of the 780 examined, or 56 to be exact, were either positive or doubtful venereal cases. This is approximately double the percentage one would find in a corresponding number of white people. In addition, one must keep in mind that 54 per cent of the Bad River and Red Cliff-Bayfield Chippewas never have had a Wassermann.

6

The Sisseton reservation has its agency headquarters in the town of Sisseton, South Dakota. The good reservation land has been sold by the Indians as a matter of necessity, while others have been tricked out of their allotments. The Indians live about twelve miles west of the town, on hopeless soil. Their moral conditions, consequently arising from their poor and despairing plight are bad. One woman, I was told, was stripped naked by her drunken companions and run through the streets of the town.

When the body is sick the heart is bad. The health of the Sisseton Sioux is bad, and " getting worse every day."

Clarence Anderberg, State's attorney for Robinson County, spoke to me in his law office at Sisseton concerning the health problems of his red neighbors. " Before 1928 the Indians here had no syphilis," he stated, " but in the past two years it has come upon them with a vengeance.

The county board of health gives treatments to the Indians for venereal diseases entirely at county expense, even in cases where Indians have trust properties direct or by heirship. The Indian department has a doctor here, Dr. Spears, who treats only Indians who call. There is no intelligent educational program among them and so they do not continue their treatments until they have been cleared up. As a result we have many tertiary cases in the county, and it is getting worse every day.

"We have been doing a lot of this work on county expense, while out of the 1600 population 1200 are Indians who pay no taxes. But for humanity's sake we've had to ignore that fact and help these poor devils out. The Federal government is responsible for its wards. The Federal government is supposed to be taking care of its Indians. But Dr. Spears doesn't make calls. He waits for them to come to him — a bad policy. Also, he only gives drugs and not the muscular treatment.

"There is, in addition, considerable tuberculosis and apparently no means of taking care of it. I do not blame the Indians. If you and I lived for a year under the same circumstances we would have TB., syphilis, and what not also.

"With regard to health I want to say something about the burial of the dead. The Indians here are poor and many are penniless. Their income is entirely from the rentals of their land and many don't own land and consequently have no income. In some cases the rent has been paid and spent two and three years in advance. They are so penniless that they can't buy a coffin when one of their number dies. Again the county must pay between $65 and $100 for each burial. Somebody must bury them. The Indian Bureau doesn't care, but you can't leave them lying around without a coffin."

Superintendent Willihan of the Sisseton Indian Reservation has spoken of the extremely bad health conditions on his reservation. " The white man brought gonorrhea to the Indian," he has stated. About 40 cases of syphilis a year come to his attention, but many diseased Indians go to a private physician for treatment and he never hears of their cases. Of the Indians in his jurisdiction afflicted with trachoma Willihan has estimated their number to be about 2,000 or 10 per cent; of the tuberculous Indians about 17 per cent.

7

John Collier addressed an open letter to Dr. Edgar L. Hewett, who besides being the director of the Santa Fe and San Diego museums has been an inveterate apologist for the Indian Bureau, concerning an address he had made to the American Association for the Advancement of Science in June, 1925. Mr. Collier's letter referred to the district around Albuquerque, N. M., where the treatment of syphilis was deliberately withheld, in face of the fact that 10.09 per cent of the Pueblos was infected, none hereditarily but all by *new* syphilis.

Now do you or do you not know, that following these investigations in 1924 which you summarize, whose value lay in that they establish the beginnings of clinical work for the cure and control of syphilis among these Indians; that following these investigations, *treatment of the syphilitic patients was withheld by the Indian Bureau, and is still withheld?* Do you or do you not know, that one syphilitic clinic had been established at one Pueblo through private funds; that the Indian Bureau, after there had been publicity in Congress, took over the responsibility for the management of this clinic, and then, having gotten rid of the private initiative, abandoned the clinic with not one case cured, and it is still abandoned? If you knew these facts, why did you withhold them when publicly using the statistics in an *apologia* for the Indian Bureau? Or will you publicly deny the facts here stated?

According to Collier, neither Dr. Hewett nor the Indian Bureau has denied the facts given in his open letter.

8

While on this severe problem of the Indian the statement of former Superintendent Robert E. L. Daniel of the Yankton Agency in South Dakota regarding the V. D. problem on his reservation will help complete the picture by disclosing conditions within two tribes, the Yankton Sioux and the Winnebagoes. Senator Wheeler of the Senate Investigating Committee was examining the Superintendent at Waggoner, South Dakota, on July 13, 1929:

Q. What is the condition in reference to morals? — A. Bad.

Q. Have you any venereal-disease clinics down here? — A. No, sir.

Q. What percentage of your Indians are venereal? — A. These Yankton Kids are remarkable in that respect. . . .

Q. To what do you attribute that? — A. Intercourse between Winnebagoes and our Indians.

Q. We are told that the Winnebagoes are 86 per cent syphilitic. — A. I hardly believe it is as bad as that, but just stop and think what that means.

Q. That was the statement of a doctor. — A. I know the Assistant Commissioner of Indian Affairs was out here and submitted a telegram to Washington about it. He seemed to be convinced that the situation was very bad . . . the situation is bad, worse than any other place in the West.[4]

Dr. Linn L. Culp, the trachoma specialist, was sent against his inclinations to examine the venereal cases on the Menominee Reservation. " It is worse than anywhere else in Wisconsin," he said.

The Menominees live on a closed reservation, and are completely under Federal supervision. The source of all their venereal trouble is the tough, lumberjack element living on the edge of the reservation. The saloons, speakeasies, dance halls, and bawdy houses breed nests of disease which in turn are transmitted to the Indian. These cesspools flourish outside the pale of reservation laws. They are located at Shawano, Gresham, Bowler, and the other border towns.

" It is tough closing them up," Dr. Culp explained to me. " There are so many shyster, crooked lawyers that you must kill the cat nine times before it is dead. But that is where the Indian picks up his V. D., from those dance halls."

Summarizing Dr. Culp's V. D. clinic among the Menominees, Dr. C. R. Weirich, physician for that band of Indians, compiled a document entitled: " Report of Special

[4] Hearings before a Subcommittee of the Committee on Indian Affairs. Part 7. P. 2759.

Venereal Disease clinic held by Dr. Culp, Special Physician, at Neopit. Said Report including all cases from November 22, 1928 to July 6, 1929." According to Dr. Weirich's calculations Dr. Culp and he made 270 blood tests for syphilis, out of which 92 positive cases were discovered. Which made 34 per cent syphilitic.

When I visited the Neopit hospital I personally interrogated the records and counted 93 positive cases of syphilis out of 166 cases examined. Which made 56 per cent syphilitic.

The two doctors treated 66 patients for gonorrhea out of 270 Indians examined. That made a gonorrhea percentage of 24.4.

Again I looked into the notebook employed by the physicians during the clinic and found that Dr. Culp found 53 venereal cases alone out of 182 examined for venereal diseases. That raised the gonorrhea to 29 per cent.

These figures substantiate the estimates of the Indians to former Assistant Commissioner Meritt, when he visited that reservation. They told him fifty per cent were syphilitic. Also, Dr. L. W. White, now associated in the Washington office with Dr. M. C. Guthrie, Chief Medical Director of the Bureau of Indian Affairs, declared that the Indians were not so far off in their estimates.

Information with regard to these estimates of the Indians and Dr. White was given me by Superintendent W. R. Beyer of the Menominee Reservation.

XVII

"HEAP BIG WIND — NO RAIN."

1

NOT long ago three Indian delegates from a distant Western reservation appeared in Washington. They were ushered into the warm, well-lighted offices of the Indian Bureau. They sat on leather-cushioned chairs and their feet rested on soft rugs. Neatly groomed white men busied themselves about the delegation, showing them many papers, charts, documents, and all the while talking glibly of future plans for providing the Indian with the highest type of medical care available.

The senior host of the puppets turned his fat, smiling face to his guests. "Now won't this be great for your people, won't these plans make them healthy?" he asked, jovially.

The seer of the delegation turned his face from the shining countenance of his host. He turned his eyes from the papers, charts, documents, for he had seen through the ink and paper. He looked out of the window upon the pretentious buildings of the white man. His gaze took flight and with far-seeing eyes he looked across the white man's thriving towns, across the white man's plentiful farms to where Indians were squatting on dead soil. He saw a land dotted with graves, but emptied of hospitals and doctors. Slowly he turned his head from the window, faced the beaming countenance, and said quietly: " Heap big wind. No rain."

2

Eighteen years ago, in 1912 to be exact, the Indian Bureau knew of the contagious and infectious diseases rampant among the Indians through a report by the Public Health Service, made in accordance with a Congressional enactment of August 24, 1912.

The Bureau, for example, knew that:

Trachoma is exceedingly prevalent among the Indians. . . .
Tuberculosis is very prevalent among Indians. . . .
The conviction can not be escaped that Indian boarding schools have been an important agency in the spread of trachoma.
The sanitary conditions on reservations are, on the whole, bad and require improvement in housing conditions and habits of living.[1]

Along with these findings the Public Health Service made 31 concrete recommendations for the betterment of Indian health, including economical and educational im-

[1] Public Health Service Report. Senate Document No. 1038. 1913. P. 80.

provements as well as medical. The medical recommendations were complete, and contained suggestions for increased hospitalization, better sanitation and housing,
additional medical officers, and intensive vaccination. As
early as 1912 it was recommended to the Indian Bureau
that they employ the educational advantages of moving
pictures to teach the Indians sanitation. Also:

> It is suggested that steps be taken *at once* by means of a sani-
> tary corps to sanitate some one reservation suffering from a
> high disease incidence. By this means a demonstration could be
> given of the practicability and benefits of sanitation, such as has
> been made among the natives of the Philippine Islands.[2]

But of all these suggestions the Bureau heeded only one
and that with a notable degree of success, namely, with
regard to trachoma.[3] But as for tuberculosis, syphilis,
small-pox — the Philippine Islands in the distant Pacific
are more of a health menace than germ-ridden, cess-pooled
reservations in our backyard.

How many Indians died in those eighteen years who
might be living today, if the recommendations of the Public Health Service Report were promptly heeded, only
their spirits know.

[2] *Ibid.* P. 84.
[3] Trachoma treatment is now satisfactorily accomplished wherever it
has been attempted. But in 1925–26 the Bureau launched a spectacular
"whirlwind campaign" against trachoma, performing thousands of tarsectomies which disastrously resulted in blindness. The unskilled field
doctors were ordered to perform these delicate operations; the Indians were
told that the operation created an immunity against a recurrence of the
disease. The Indians fear of Bureau doctors and hospitals still continues
after this ghastly experience.

Out, damned spot! out, I say! . . . *Yet who would have thought the old man to have had so much blood in him.* . . .

Shakespeare knew what it was to stain hands with the blood of one's relations.

3

Eleven years later, in 1923 to be exact, the Indian Bureau again had an opportunity to cleanse the " damned spot." Miss Florence Patterson, at present Director of the Visiting Nurse Service of Boston, was appointed by the American Red Cross in 1922 to make an investigation of the need for public health nurses on Indian reservations. She spent over nine months in making a thorough, detailed investigation. Her findings substantiated the 1912 Public Health Service Report and it was also couched in the quietest diction, although at times it dealt with horrifying, tragic circumstances. Her investigation was and still is a colossal, irrefutable indictment of the United States Bureau of Indian Affairs.

The year the Public Health Service Report was filed, in 1913, there were 47 deaths on the San Carlos Apache Reservation. The report was ignored by the Bureau. The year Miss Patterson began her investigation there were 114 deaths on the San Carlos Apache Reservation. On the Sells Reservation, containing Papago Indians, the deaths leaped from 119 in 1913 to 239 in 1922.

Miss Florence Patterson was in the American Red Cross service in Eastern Europe for over a year, doing relief work in homes as well as in hospitals. In view of her familiarity with health conditions of that district, Miss

Patterson's following statement is a powerful indictment not only of the Indian Bureau but of the American people, who for over seventy years have permitted these Federal brutalities and atrocities. In her report she stated:

The manifestations of malnutrition were general and acute in a large portion of the children seen by the writer. They repeatedly presented a picture similar to that of groups of children in eastern Europe whom government and voluntary agencies rushed in to feed in the war-devastated regions.

Miss Patterson's evidence is colossal. It is irrefutable. She tells of faked medical reports, of doctored death certificates. She tells how she found 50 per cent of the pupils at the Pima Boarding School infected with trachoma, at the Pima day school 75 per cent, and at the Papago day schools from 60 in some to 100 per cent in others. She tells how "the boarding school records showed that children who had developed tuberculosis in the schools were constantly being returned to their homes, to live for a time, perhaps, and to spread the disease among the other members of the family."

She tells of the case where 17 per cent of the Navajo pupils in the Phoenix school were returned to the Hopi Reservation with tuberculosis.

Specifically, at the Western Navajo Reservation Boarding School the following occurred:

Eleven children were sent home during school year out of an enrollment of about 200. The following histories of these cases were gleaned from the physician and the principal of the school.
One died on the way home, being a three days' trip to camp.
One died the day after he got home.

Two died three weeks after reaching home.

One died in three months.

One was apparently doing well at home.

Five were thought to be living, but no definite information was available.[4]

Miss Patterson tells how:

On another reservation, during the writer's visit, a girl about 16, without any warning or suspicion of tuberculosis, had a profuse pulmonary hemorrhage. She was sent to the hospital, kept in bed for 36 hours, and told that she could get up and go back to school.

Before she reached the door she had another hemorrhage, and so went back to bed. She was allowed to wait upon herself, and during the evening, while in the bathroom, had a third hemorrhage. Two days later the doctor said that she might go back to school or go home. It was decided to send her home; both the doctor and the nurse seemed to consider that their responsibility ended there.[5]

The Commonwealth Club of San Francisco held a meeting on December 1, 1926. Assistant Commissioner of Indian Affairs E. B. Meritt was present and the following conversation took place between the Commissioner and Dr. Glaser, his interrogator.

Dr. Glaser. If the California State Board of Health writes for a copy of the Grace Patterson report will it be sent to them?

Mr. Meritt. That is hardly a fair question.

Dr. Glaser. It was written for by the Executive Secretary of the California Board of Health and it was not received. Will it be sent now if we write again?

Mr. Meritt. If your Congressman wants to see the Grace Patterson report he can come down and see it but I doubt very much

[4] Hearings Before a Subcommittee of the Committee on Indian Affairs. Part 3. P. 940.   [5] *Ibid.* P. 943.

if the Commissioner of Indian Affairs would send that report out to an organization to be published throughout the country, which we believe is not a correct description of conditions existing on Indian reservations.[6]

Mr. Freses, the vice chairman of the American Red Cross, wrote Commissioner Burke on January 26, 1927, stating that the Red Cross report had been publicly declared impractical by an Indian Bureau official. This had placed the Red Cross in an embarrassing position and Mr. Freses consequently suggested that a portion of the report be published " so that it would give the Red Cross an opportunity to discuss the criticism openly." There was, however, no reply to Mr. Freses' letter. He again wrote the Commissioner on February eleventh of that year to the effect:

I think that you will agree that it is reasonable for the Red Cross to ask in what specific respects our statements are at variance with the facts as known to the Bureau. You did not reply to this point in your letter.

To Mr. Freses' second letter there was also no reply.

This is 1931, and although the Indian Bureau has increased its nurses it has not yet established a Public Health Nursing Service on reservations, which Miss Patterson so strongly recommended.

4

We have been looking at the picture of Indian health as it has existed for the past two decades. To bring our focus up to date we must glance at the latest medical examina-

[6] Hearings Before a Subcommittee of the Committee on Indian Affairs. Part 3. Pp. 949–50.

tions of Indians. They have been conducted by the various state boards of health without Federal subsidizing. In fact, the Indian Bureau itself has never held a national investigation of Indian health. It has always allowed outside energetic, humanitarian organizations do their work — the Public Health Service, the American Red Cross, the Institute for Government Research, and now the state boards of health. None of these institutions, however, have accomplished their beneficial work with the financial assistance of the Bureau.

In making their numerous, helpful recommendations the Public Health Service stated in 1912 that " whenever necessary and practicable coöperation should be had with State boards of health in putting these recommendations into effect."

This suggestion has not only been ignored in the past 18 years but still is ignored in 1930.

Dr. Chesley, State Health Officer of Minnesota, conducted a clinic among the Chippewas at Red Lake, Minnesota from September 1 to 13, 1930. Before the Minnesota State Board of Health could conduct a clinic for the wards of the Federal government, Dr. Chesley had to beg the necessary funds from philanthropic organizations with humanitarian interests. According to Dr. Zeigler of Minneapolis, the medical superintendent for the district comprising North and South Dakota, Minnesota, Wisconsin, and Michigan, Dr. Chesley " begged from the Rockefeller Foundation, the American Child Hygiene, the United States Public Health, and similar philanthropic organizations."

Dr. C. A. Harper, the State Health Officer for Wisconsin, was up against a similar problem. He could not expect a coin from Washington for conducting a clinic among Federal wards and for their sole benefit. The Wisconsin legislature, being one of the most progressive bodies of its kind in America, appropriated an additional $15,000 to the State Board of Health, thus enabling Dr. Harper to carry on his noble work on behalf of a red brother in whom he had centered much interest.

The energies of the Indian Bureau, in the meanwhile, have been spent on nationwide distribution of such articles as "The Indian Service Doctor Replaces the Medicine Man," which was printed and reprinted a year after the Red Cross report was suppressed.

5

It was on the afternoon of August 26, 1930, when that informal meeting took place. It was not an exceptional gathering: Dozens of similar conferences have already occurred in states possessing Indian citizens, and dozens more are doubtlessly scheduled. It was, in other words, a new but very old story.

Forest County of Wisconsin was confronted with a distasteful problem. The Federal government was neglecting to provide education for its wards, and those children were being thrown upon the county. The Government boarding school at Lac du Flambeau was overcrowded and the surplus children were told to attend the county schools. The Government had informed the county authorities they would reimburse the county for the cost of educating the Indian children, " dollar for dollar."

The impromptu meeting held in the principal's office of the Wabeno High School was for the purpose of asking the Federal officials present for the " dollar for dollar " refund, amounting to $4,890 which the county of Wabeno paid out for two and a half years free education to Federal wards.

" We figured the agents of the Government were honest," said Mr. A. P. Euler, Principal of the Wabeno Schools. " When Inspector Carter of Minneapolis came to us concerning the matter he said the Government would pay dollar for dollar. We took his word for it and opened up a new district school especially for the Indian children and hired a bus and a driver to cart them back and forth and we went through a lot of other expenses, but Commissioner Rhoads would not consider paying the full cost. The Government allowed us between 50 and 60 per cent of our costs. Now we aren't going to take any Indian children this Fall because the county can't afford to pay for them. Forest County is in a bad way. We are almost a bankrupt county with only 8,000 population. In the last three years our property assets dropped $600,000 and in another five years the timber will be gone and then what? "

Indian Commissioner Lundquist made an illuminating observation. " There has been almost a drive," he confessed, " to rid the overcrowding at Lac du Flambeau and other boarding schools, and to get the children in the county schools."

" But practically all the Indians live in non-taxable Government homes," replied Principal Euler. " The county can collect no taxes from the Indians and yet the Federal government passes the financial buck to us, while these children are all wards of the Government."

" That's what gets my goat," interrupted Dr. C. A. Harper. " The Government is responsible for the Indian and should educate its wards. These Pottawatomies were driven from Pennsylvania into Wisconsin by the Federal government; they were here before Wisconsin was a state or Forest County a county. The Government must not only educate their wards but care for their health as well. In Sawyer County on the Lac Court d'Oreielles Reservation 32 Indians died without medical attention."

6

By far the most interesting woman connected with Dr. Harper's clinic was a British war nurse, Mrs. Alice Jennings Eckard. She walked 12 miles from her station at Laona to Crandon, where the clinic was held the first day, and found herself " somewhat worn for wear."

The field nurses in the Indian Service can not be commended too highly for the work they are doing. The field work is in a class by itself, not only in its humanitarian phase, but in its uniqueness as well. Mrs. Eckard has written a most interesting letter to the Wisconsin State Board of Health, in which she disclosed one of her numerous experiences as a Government nurse in the field, bequeathing health and comfort to unfortunate Indians. The Service should have many additional field nurses.

" Found an old woman today," Mrs. Eckard wrote, " face swollen as from erysipelas. Found abscess on gums, lanced with pointed forceps. Wanted hot saline. No water, no salt, no fire, no wood.

" Walked mile through woods to waterhole (or mud-hole). Snakes swimming. Got one pail; looked clean. Then dog fell into waterhole backwards. Second pail good scrub-water. Overtaken by thirsty pony. Gave him dirty bucket. Chopped wood, made fire and hot soda bicarb water. No food in house. Went to town. Charged $5.00 to U. S. A. Swelling gone on return with food. All in a day's march."

Dr. R. L. Frisbie, Deputy State Health Officer, located at Rhinelander, Wisconsin, was likewise at the clinic as one of three men doing general examinations to the Indians upon their entrance to the clinic. He, consequently, spoke for one-third of the patients, but by the law of averages and observations the remaining two-thirds were similar. " Tuberculosis here is high," Dr. Frisbie said. " The indications thus far show it running very high. I would estimate about 40 per cent. The general physical condition seems to be very poor."

As an interested three-day spectator at the clinic I noticed a pitiful case in the infant's section. A small, under-nourished baby, not much larger than a medium-sized doll, was lying on a table.

" How old is it? " I asked the nurse.

" The mother says it just turned 2 years and one month," she replied.

" And its weight? "

" Thirteen pounds. It measures 26 inches."

The infant looked its height and weight. It lay on the table without wiggling. The only sign of life was its eyes. Like the pictures in newspaper ads, soliciting subscriptions for starving Chinese orphans, the thing lay on the table.

" It creeps, crawls, but doesn't walk," she was saying. " It mumbles, but does not speak."

Another case of malnutrition.

I found Dr. Harper. He had just discovered a boy, possessed with active tuberculosis, who was about to leave for a Government school.

" We are getting a cross-section of the actual health conditions of the Wisconsin Indians," he explained, " for the purpose of presenting the facts to Washington showing the necessity for medical relief and assistance."

" Somewhere there has been a stone wall, and I believe it has been because we haven't had the facts," confirmed Congressman George Schneider. " Why does the Indian child have more TB. than the white? The facts concerning their day to day existence should answer that question. With six, eight, and ten Indians housed throughout the winter months in one room, it is all bosh to talk about curing TB. It comes on faster than you can stop it. You can't halt the Indians' diseases unless he be started fresh in life. They need new bedding, different clothes, and better food."

He paused, and facing Dr. Harper, said: " Unless the facts of this clinic are presented to the Bureau of Indian Affairs and they in turn heed these facts and allow in their budget specific funds for the betterment of these Indians

—unless such action be taken there is no hope for the Indian."

"It is a thankless job, this Indian work," Dr. Harper replied. "But I shall, nevertheless, report the facts to Washington. Yet — " he mused — " you might as well send a letter to the Dead Letter Office as to the Indian Department."

XVIII

"HEALTH THAT SNUFFS THE MORNING AIR —"

1

NO discussion of Indian health today would be comprehensive without the antidote of history.

Anatole France, in speaking of the Gascony peasants, whom he loved dearly, once remarked: " Being simple they did not go far wrong; they beheld truths which our intelligence hides from us."

Centuries before their contact with Europeans the Indians administered to their medical needs. Those living in the Mission River region in the Southwest made their own syringes — " an animal bladder being used for the bulk and a hollow cylindrical bone, as the leg bones of a prairie chicken, turkey, or goose, or other birds, was used for the tube. The bulk was attached to the tube by sinew wrappings." Such a syringe was employed in rectal injection for obstinate cases of constipation.

Philosophy and biology were combined in the wisdom

of the Zuni, who called the sun " Yatokia," the giver of life and warmth. Through the supreme bisexual power, " A'wonawil'ona," the sun had become the giver of life.

Contrary to the popular belief the Indian of old was an ardent exertionist. He did not sit on his rump for centuries, wrapped in eternal indolence and grunting. Through his hunts, dances, walks, games, and fights exercise had become a primal factor in his life. The idea of " the body beautiful " was strictly American in origin. The Indian of old knew his next meal depended upon his bow and arrow, and he hustled. In the old days there was no storehouse to squat beside, waiting for the doling of rations.

In his food as well as in his personal habits the Indian practiced self-restraint. His diet was as simple as his pleasures. Today, however, his indulgences are widely known.

Dr. Charles Alexander Eastman, called by his Sioux brothers " Ohiyesa," is a graduate physician and an alumnus of Dartmouth College. In his book *The Indian Today* he has written of the Indian's past and present modes of life.

The Indians of old were long accustomed to pure air and pure water. Clean, wild wind seemed a part of their lean, healthy limbs. The clean air seemed to run constantly through their bodies, purifying any stray diseases that happened to linger there. The tepee was only a covering to shelter them from bad weather, and they pitched it every few days on fresh ground. Their clothing was loose and simple. They had air baths and sun baths, and baths with water and steam. They had oils that kept their skins healthy. Their food was always fresh, mostly meat and fish, along with wild and sometimes planted fruit and grain.

Instead of that vigorous, non-tuberculous life the Indians today live in one-room, mud-clinked log shacks, twelve by twenty. Dr. Eastman tells how their cooking is done on the tops of box-stoves which also serve to warm the cabins. Some bedding on the hard dirt floor completes the furniture.

An old man complains:

If I had a floor in my house I could see better. The dust from the dirt floor gets in my eyes and keeps me blind. I get dust in my mouth and nose and ears.

Some cabins even have dirt roofs. In winter almost all of them are always overheated, and the air becomes vitiated and remains so throughout the winter. In the winter whole families sit around their stoves, drinking cup after cup of strong, black coffee. In most cabins the pot boils all day long. Everybody drinks coffee, even the youngest child.

The scientific investigators of the Institute for Government Research have substantiated much of Dr. Eastman's beliefs as well as other pioneer students of Indian health. Early in its report, on the fourth page, admission has been made that " From the standpoint of health it is probably true that the contemporary, primitive dwellings that were not fairly air-tight and were frequently abandoned were more sanitary than the permanent homes that have replaced them." In these " civilized " homes " the use of modern cook stoves and utensils is far more general than the use of beds, and the use of beds in turn is far more common than the use of any kind of easily washable bed covering."

The housing conditions are found conducive to bad health because of the great overcrowding, " so that all members of the family are exposed to any disease that develops, and it is virtually impossible in any way even partially to isolate a person suffering from a communicable disease."

Dr. Eastman has told how the ration system completed the demoralization as well as the disintegration of their health. The crowding of the Indians onto reservations was strictly a war measure. The War Department wanted the Indians where they could look at them, and so the tribes were herded into pens and made prisoners. Today, Secretary Wilbur has admitted that the reservations are practically jails for the Indians.

They were fed like prisoners, and many still are today. Once a year they were given shoddy blankets and clothes. They were made into beggars, like so many chipmunks. With the ration-giving the Indian was robbed of his self-respect, his ambition, and his initiative. They were made strangers in their own land.

The Indians had no time to learn gardening nor had they the time to spend that gardening demands. Many had to ride fifty miles and more once a week to the agency warehouse to report his presence and be given rations. Then they had to trek fifty miles and more back home again, as some still do. Many had nothing else to occupy themselves with but this incessant traveling all the rest of their lives between the cabin and the agency warehouse. All that time they brooded over their loss of freedom, over the loss of their country rich in game and with its many pleasures of the wild life.

But the food — that was something else again.

At first, as Dr. Eastman observed, they could not eat the foul bacon. On ration days one could see these strips of stenchy fat lying on the sides of the trail, where they had been cast on the return trip. On the Sioux and Menominee Reservations today the Indians still complain of being rationed with yellow, foul-smelling bacon.

But starvation has forced them to swallow the foul fat, the badly prepared bread, fried in grease. The result has not been uncommon: dysentery is dissolving their guts. But the Indian Commissioners in Washington and the meat-packers in Chicago are not troubled with dysentery. They should be taken into the Indian territory and shown those yellow faces, those thin, miserable faces, and those bent, wasted bodies, from which the pressing pains have wrung out the blood. They should be taken into the woods behind their cabins, those well-fed Arbuckles, and shown the Indians where they sit across a log all day, with lips trembling and hands quivering. Perhaps the bears and the bulls would not notice them grinning at one another as they quivered, saying with all the humor of the Indian: " Ah zhe, brother, ah zhe — what for should I go back to the cabin again — "

2

Major-General Hugh L. Scott, now retired from the
United States Army, is the honorary president of the Indian Rights Association of Philadelphia. As a keen student of the Indian problem General Scott has made many
noteworthy observations. Following in the same line of
thought as Congressman Schneider, he has said: " It is
inconceivable to me that Congress would allow such conditions to continue if the facts were fully impressed upon
it, and I recommend that the Honorable Secretary of the
Interior make a special effort to secure the funds he con-
siders necessary to stamp out trachoma in one year, and
to provide sufficient sanatoria to cover the Indian country.
The present conditions are a reproach to our Government,
and should no longer be allowed to continue."

Concerning the curse of rations:

The people who are on my mind are the superannuated, the
lame, the blind, who are unable to learn anything. . . . They have
had a very insufficient ration given them at many agencies that
keeps them undernourished and makes them the prey of every
passing disease. I believe that many have died prematurely in the
past from these causes. I note that this ration is being made adequate by the issue of horse meat at the Fort Belknap Agency.

Another kindly soul who has made many visits to about
forty Government schools and reservations throughout the
country is Miss C. A. Lyford, a demonstration teacher of
home economics, employed by the Indian Bureau.

" I have found out," she told me, " why the Indians

raise so many dogs and always have some around the
house. They raise them to eat."

As an interesting sidelight on the above deplorable conditions, it is discouraging to note that during a four-year
period, ending 1924, the Indian Bureau's expenditure on
medical supplies in relation to the Bureau's total expenditure was .71 per cent. In other words, more money was
spent on forage for the animals maintained by the Bureau
in California than on the medical supplies for the entire
Indian population. Using another standard of comparison,
the expenditure for salaries has been approximately 48
times greater than the total expenditure for medical necessities. These figures were gleaned from the records of the
Indian office in Washington.

3

As a whole, Dr. Herbert R. Edwards' chapter on the
present medical and health service of the Indian Bureau
completely annihilated that service. In fact, Dr. Edwards,
who is now in charge of the tuberculosis division of the
New Haven, Connecticut, Department of Health, has stated
that " for some years it has been customary to speak of the
Indian medical service as being organized for public
health. Yet the fundamentals of sound public health work
are still lacking."

To be exact, every year since 1925 the Interior Department has broadcast advertisements to the effect that the
Indian medical service has been reorganized. Official posters were sent to all parts of the nation contrasting con-

ditions "before and after." Such propaganda has been successful in appeasing public curiosity.

The Institute's report contains the ammunitions to blast that appeasement. Unfortunately, the facts of the survey have not been as widely advertised as the "then and now" posters. The public mind is still appeased.

Let a very few quotations indicate the nature of the disclosure:

> No sanitarium in the Indian service meets the minimum requirements of the American Sanitarium Association. Not a single institution maintains a complete case record of its patients. (Page 287.)
>
> At the present time no hospital has an X-ray unit. In some few cases one may find a microscope, but ordinarily their appearance indicates infrequent use. This observation is further substantiated by the universal lack of records of such work on the meager clinical sheets. (Page 282.)

Of these case records, individual or family, only on one reservation and on one alone did the Indian Bureau claim the maintenance of complete tabulations. However, "the physician who had maintained such records had been transferred to another field, and these records were not available for examination." (Page 235.)

Yet it is widely known from one end of the medical world to the other that vital statistics are the very breath of preventive medicine. A competent physician must know the number, frequency, and development of a disease in order to cope successfully with it. However, the physicians in the Indian medical service are of a radically different school in their theories of dealing with communicable diseases:

On all reservations visited (and Dr. Edwards visited 55 reservations) the Indians were observed coming to the doctor's office and asking for medicine either for themselves or for friends or members of their families. The Indian, almost without exception, is given the particular drug he requests or a substitute of some sort without being asked more details about the malady present. Physical examinations are almost never made in these cases. (Page 234.)

The above observation was recorded fully three years after the Interior Department announced the Indian medical service had been " completely reorganized and placed on a public health basis."

The drug supplies on the shelves of practically all reservation dispensaries and hospitals are of a doubtful character and are far in excess of the present needs. Much of the stock is of a perishable nature, long since deteriorated, and of uncommon drugs seldom if ever used. At Zuni, for example, ten pints of fluid extract of ergot were found, enough to supply the entire Indian service. (Page 251.)

The general summary of its findings is included in the first chapter of the Institute's report, where they set at naught all the misinformed beliefs of Indian health. Typical of these " up-front " revelations is the statement that:

The preventive work in combating the two important diseases of tuberculosis and trachoma can only be characterized as weak. The same word must be applied to the efforts toward preventing infant mortality and the diseases of children. (Page 10.)

Thus, the simple conclusion:

" When all these factors are taken into consideration it is not surprising to find low incomes, low standards of living, and poor health."

4

There have been many investigations of Indian health, many reports on his death rate, and so forth. But little action has resulted from these investigations. It is one thing to look continually at a sick man, shaking your head with pity, and it is quite another to roll up your sleeves and attempt to make him well. To clinch this point I quote from a letter Dr. C. A. Harper wrote me on August 18, 1930, with regard to his clinical investigations:

The older Indians when we visit them say, " Well, what is it now? " We explain our purpose. " Well," they say, " we have been surveyed for the last fifty years and nothing has ever come of it or been done," and from the state of the Indians as we find them he probably is correct in his contentions.

XIX

MIDWIVES, MOTHERS, AND PROSTITUTES

1

GOVERNMENT officials have loudly condemned "the crude, unsanitary, and at times, even brutal primitive practices" of Indian childbirth. These unsanitary childbirths have not been by choice. Of the Indian midwives I have known, I have found them to be more intelligent than the average Indian woman. Their medical diplomas were earned in the university of experience. Their professors have been their predecessors in the field, usually their own mothers.

On Sugar Island, off Sault Saint Marie, Michigan, lives a kind old Indian woman. She is a widow and resides alone in a two-room, lumber-constructed house, which is one of the most immaculate Indian homes I have ever visited. The floors are scrubbed as clean as the kitchen table. The dishes in the cupboard shine and the surface of the stove is polished.

She is the younger sister of Mrs. Oller, the grand old queen of the island. She is the sole midwife for twenty Indian families, unallotted and entirely without Government supervision, drifting discursively between poverty and death. The private practitioners living in the city on the mainland will deliver babies at a reasonable enough rate, but at an impossible fee for the poverty-stricken Chippewas on Sugar Island. As for a Government physician, the closest is more than three hundred miles distant, a contract doctor located at Laona, Wisconsin, who has already refused to go ten miles to see a patient, not to mention three hundred.

And so a bronze-faced woman with an eternal stoical expression quietly goes about her business. She is dexterous with her fingers, as she weaves delicate baskets out of obstinate reeds between the occasional cases.

" Have you ever had a casualty? " I asked her.

She shook her head. " No, many have now grown up to be big boys and girls."

" What do you do when it is hard? " I asked.

" Get the doctor from the Soo," she replied without hesitation.

" And your instruments? "

She shrugged her shoulders and disclosed the palms of her hands. They were sensitive yet rugged hands.

" But for the umbilical cord," I persisted.

She went to her sewing basket and produced a pair of scissors from a heaped collection of spools, needles, and thimbles. The scissors were old and one blade was rusted.

Whatever her ignorance of sterilization or her disregard for sanitation might have been, this Indian midwife has

had no casualties of either mothers or babies. She likewise
has had no cases of septicemia. No savior figure of a
Government physician looms between the blue and the
landscape. But babies must be born.

Parallel with the lack of a sufficient number of physicians
is the more paramount deficiency in medical education
among the tribes. According to the Institute's investigators,
" It is commonly said in the Indian field that the practice
of obstetrics is difficult if not impossible among Indians,
especially full bloods."

A dislike for the presence of white physicians and nurses
during their confinement is only natural among the full-
bloods and less advanced tribes, because no effective educational program has been launched among them. In cases,
however, wherein the Government physician performed
a noteworthy operation, saving perhaps both child and
mother, the remaining women of the tribe become more
disposed toward his services during their next confinement.
It must be taken in hand that when the Indian mother for
centuries has had her obstetrical needs adequately administered by midwives and medicine men she is naturally loath
to change her custom in a few decades, and without the
convincing presence of educational enlightenment.

Proof of the Indian's desire to better the plight of his
women is found in the following statement, made by
Dr. Herbert R. Edwards of the Institute for Government
Research:

The Indians' demands for a physician at child-birth are clearly
increasing, especially on those reservations where a definite effort
is made to induce the Indian to request such attention and the

physician remains long enough to become acquainted with his clientele. It is believed that considerably more Indian women would accept the services of physicians *if their interest were solicited and adequate facilities made available.*[1]

The fact that relatively few advances are made to Indian mothers by field nurses and physicians for the purpose of educating them in the benefits of hospitalization during their pregnancy is surely not a reflection upon Indian mothers. But rather, of the inadequacy of the Indian Bureau's medical service and the deficiency of its personnel and equipment. The Institute has elsewhere acknowledged that " relatively few are reached by the nursing service of the Indian Office." Thus it was naturally discovered that in the many localities where Government physicians are not stationed the medicine men still flourish.

Only a small proportion of the girls and young women have had lessons in the care of infants and sick while away at school. Under these circumstances Indian women could not be expected to know how to care for the health of those dependent upon them or know what precautions to take during pregnancy. . . . The result is that babies die, young children are infected unnecessarily, and the old and hopelessly ill suffer needless discomfort.[2]

Because they have not been enlightened otherwise the women do not stay at home from excursions when a baby is expected. Births, consequently, are a common occurrence at powwows and other tribal festivities. The women rarely alter their daily labors as a result of their pregnancy. They adhere closely to the daily routine not by choice, but

[1] *The Problem of Indian Administration.* P. 239.
[2] *Ibid.* Pp. 557–8.

through custom and economic necessity, with the result that many primipara unnecessarily lose their first child.

The Indians' dislike for a Bureau physician lies inherent in a reason far more meaningful than the apparent lack of both an educational program and an adequate medical service. They still recall the trachoma " whirlwind campaigns," when delicate, discredited tarsectomies were disastrously performed by unskilled field practitioners. They still recall the reign of terror that swept through the Indian country when tens of thousands were captured, brought to agencies, and brutally blinded.

2

What of the babies after they are born? Although many are needlessly lost at birth a relatively large number manage to survive for several years. What of those?

Generally speaking, the Indian child is nursed indefinitely. That is, they are not fed regularly but nursed whenever they cry. This goes on for usually a year or more, and sometimes for two or three years. There are special cases on record where this indefinite nursing has been continued for a much longer period, even to the point where a four- or five-year-old child is being nursed in addition to a newborn infant.

The physical drag of such a practice on the Indian mothers is tremendous. In many instances it has caused their premature deaths. Again the Indian suffers for the want of proper guidance from his guardian and protector, the Indian Bureau of the United States Government.

It seems that the period of weaning is the crisis in an Indian baby's life. Many die under the process. They can not weather the sudden change from their mother's milk to coarse, hard foods of all kinds and bulk. In the storm of being removed from a wholly milk diet to one completely void of milk of any kind many die, for the odds are too great against them.

Trustworthy statistics on this issue are unfortunately too slender to support any authentic verdict. However, the Institute's scientific surveyors have again made keen observations worthy of repetition:

Pueblo mothers give babies chili, beans, green fruits, or anything they ask for, especially melons in season; the Sioux, especially the full-bloods, put the children on meats and other heavy foods; Cheyenne mothers offer the child a nursing bottle filled with coffee or tea if it frets. Very few children are shifted gradually to soft foods and cow's or goat's milk. . . . It is not surprising that a great many Indian babies fail to survive long when breast-feeding ceases.[3]

3

" When the body is sick the heart is bad." So said a reverent seer who has taught the Bible to the Indian for twenty-two years.

Mrs. Marie J. Denomie, as president of the Wisconsin Bad River Reservation's League of Women Voters, wrote a letter to the Rev. Mrs. O. J. Little of Stone Lake, Wisconsin, who helped organize the Odanah branch, telling of the immoral conditions flourishing on her reservation.

[3] *The Problem of Indian Administration.* P. 558.

Mrs. Denomie declared that the women of the reservation had high hopes for a thorough investigation of the immoral conditions. However, the Senate Investigating Committee spent only a day at the Lac du Flambeau agency, a day at Madison, the State's capital, and only half-a-day at Hayward, a sub-agency. Mrs. Denomie complained that those of the Bad River Reservation had barely half-a-day to voice their complaints, which they believed was insufficient. Further, " we had high hopes of the conditions here receiving the careful attention of the new Secretary of the Interior and the new Commissioner of Indian Affairs to the end that some of the abuses would be abated."

Of the conditions which have not been sufficiently aired, Mrs. Denomie wrote the following intelligent letter of October 7, 1929, to her colleague:

The conditions under which we have lived here on this Reservation are growing worse all the time. The Indian Agent, P. S. Everest, and the Indian Farmer, A. L. Doan, make no effort to stop the abuses or improve the conditions and they, moreover, seem to actively oppose our every effort to check the evils that prevail.

The particular conditions which have been allowed to grow worse from day to day, until " we live in a sort of ' NO MAN'S LAND,' " are enumerated by Mrs. Denomie as follows:

1. The use and sale of liquor on the Reservation.
2. Open and un-checked gambling, both in pool halls, and by the operation of slot machines.
3. Open and notorious houses of ill fame have and are now being conducted in our village here.

Of the third evil she wrote:

Charlotte Bashand and her daughters continue to run their house of prostitution seemingly under the protection of the Public Officials. And this matter not only is of concern to me as a citizen and as President of the League here but it seriously concerns my two minor brothers who were attacked while in the company of these undesirable women and one Sunday, about two A.M. one of these girls came running into our house and aroused our entire family, in her drunken condition, by telling us that one of my brothers was being killed by a suitor of hers and some other fellows.

Mrs. Marie J. Denomie failed to tell of other houses of ill fame operating on the Bad River Reservation to the moral degradation of the Chippewa Indian. One institution of ill repute not mentioned is operated by a woman and her married daughter, whose husband has never unexpectedly appeared upon the scene.

Arthur Johnson, district attorney of Ashland County which contains Bad River Reservation, has testified to the Senate Investigating Committee:

There are a number of illegitimate children on the reservation but I believe that will be stopped to a large extent if the liquor traffic is curbed. One of the Indians down here said to me, " Well, you white people gave the idea to the Indians, you get tired of one woman and get another and the Indians are doing the same thing."

Mr. Earl James Lockard, Government licensed trader at Odanah, has estimated there are over a dozen bastardy cases a year on the reservation. Fully three months after the Wisconsin State Board of Health conducted their clinic for the Bad River Indians, Mr. Lockard stated that three Ashland physicians, Drs. Harrison, Andrews, and Smiles, estimated 50 per cent of the Indians to be syphilitic.

Concerning the Winnebagoes, Superintendent W. F. Dickens of Tomah, Wisconsin, stated to me that " much too many illegitimate children are being born every year. Even at the school we must watch the children. One white man came into the school's summer camp and raped a 15-year-old girl."

The Sisseton-Wapheton tribes are considered more advanced than the western Sioux, because of their longer subjugation to the civilized ways of neighboring whites. To the contrary, however, this intense proximity has resulted in the white man sexualizing the Indian.

The young, intelligent State's Attorney for Robinson County, Mr. Clarence Anderberg, knows the sex plight of his brown neighbors from first-hand observation. " There are about ten young Indian girls here who prostitute with white men," he stated to me. " These Indians are Federal wards, but Superintendent Willihan does not correct such evils. When Professor Brown for the Institute for Government Research was here Willihan did not produce the evidence on adultery and other sex cases. As the State's attorney I am willing to prosecute those cases but I get no coöperation from the Superintendent.

" The Indians are in addition promiscuous with a certain element of Whites. But Willihan says, ' Well, by God, I don't know about that. The Indians are no more primiscuous than the Whites.' Thus he attempted to cover up the truth from Brown, and minimize the immorality.

" But I know the situation. When eight and nine Indians are living in one room throughout the winter, there is nothing else on their minds.

" Prosecution is rare. The Federal authorities have time and again refused to follow up cases I have brought to their attention. For example, I recall two excellent cases which were not prosecuted: Amos White versus Lydia White, and Francis Renville versus Lillian King. Both girls are under 18 and have confessed the names of their rapers. A clear case. However, the United States District Court of South Dakota has made no prosecution."

Superintendent Willihan, in charge of the Sisseton Indian Reservation, made several statements which unwittingly, on his part, substantiate Mr. Anderberg's assertion that he is attempting to whitewash Indian immorality.

Perhaps it is fortunate that the Government does not instruct its Indian superintendents to educate their wards on matters of sex. Perhaps it is better for the Indian to blunder blindly along, creating and losing many children needlessly, than to endow some superintendents with additional authority over delicate matters.

The Sisseton Sioux first sold land in 1805 to Minnesota farmers. For over a century and a quarter they have intermingled freely with their neighbors, learning and accumulating his Caucasian diseases of the mind and body. The Sisseton Sioux hindered Little Crow and his band from attacking white settlers. The Sisseton Sioux have never fought the United States Government. Their reward for such loyal and humanitarian acts has spoken for itself: The white man repays well . . .

4

In New York State, where Indians have been in constant contact with white neighbors for over three centuries, immorality seems to be accentuated rather than diminished. Fortunately in a way, one case came to the public's attention; the newspapers in turn intimated the existence of numerous illicit relationships.

Henri Marchand, artist for the Buffalo Natural History Museum, seduced Lila [" Red Lilac "] Jimerson, 39, a Seneca Indian. Flat-chested, toothless, scraggy-haired, sallow-complexioned, a consumptive with less than two years to live, Lila was seduced while modeling for Indian pictures. Marchand continued his relations with her and she loved him.

Lila told an old woman on the reservation, Nancy Bowen, that Mrs. Marchand was a witch and was responsible for the death of Charley (" Sassafras ") Bowen, Nancy's husband. The 66-year-old Cayuga Indian from the Cattaraugus Reservation walked into Mrs. Marchand's home, and asked a question: " Are you a witch? " The artist's wife answered jestingly in the affirmative. She was beaten down with a ten-cent hammer and her throat was stuffed with chloroform-soaked paper.

One of the most interesting phases of this murder is the fact that in 1930, more than a century and a half after the Indians of the Hudson were pacified by a superior white civilization and almost two and a quarter centuries after the last witch was burned in Salem, witchcraft is still practiced by wards of the United States Government. What an indictment of our administration of Indian affairs. Not even the most eastern tribes, living in the wealthiest state in the Union, are adequately educated.

After several weeks the trial of Lila Jimerson for first-degree murder began in Buffalo. The newspapers of the country had been daily filled with accounts of the tragedy, until the public had begun to grow almost weary under the deluge. After weeks of front-page publicity, the Government at Washington suddenly became interested in the plight of its ward, the defendant. Attorney General William DeWitt Mitchell ordered United States District Attorney Richard Harkness Templeton of Buffalo to assume Lila Jimerson's defense. Mr. Templeton reluctantly presented himself at the trial in the state court. The state prosecutor, Guy Moore, proud of his numerous first-degree convictions, fairly shouted when he beheld Templeton in the court room.

" I deeply resent," he bellowed, " this eleventh-hour and unwarranted interference by Washington bureaucracy! I object to Mr. Templeton's unfair interjection into this case. He has no right here! I request the court to ask him to get out."

Mr. Templeton replied by asking for an adjournment of the trial so he could prepare a defense, as he was comparatively new to the case. The judge, however, took this to be his cue to explode:

"The Attorney General of the United States," he shouted, between raps, " is not running this court. Motion denied."

With the sad result that Templeton from then on assumed a very minor part in the defense. In the first place, his presence was the result of the tepee-born, Kaw-blooded Vice President Charles Curtis asking the Indian Bureau to interest itself in the life-and-death struggle of one of its wards. When questioned by a reporter as to his interest in the case, the Vice President replied it was " only casual."

The New York newspapers discovered that artist Marchand had not accomplished an unusual feat in his seduction of an Indian woman. The Cattaraugus Reservation has become a rendezvous-ground for the bucks of Buffalo. Many prominent citizens of the city, so the papers reported, are known to be at large nursing " bad colds " as a result of their latest attempt to subdue the Indian.

5

I conclude this chapter with a simple statement by Dr. George A. Dorsey, author of *Why We Behave Like Human Beings*, which may be applied as a just indictment of the Indian Bureau for the present moral condition of its wards. " Caught young," he stated, " no other animal can be as effectively tamed, civilized, socialized, humanized, as the human."

The Indian Bureau has never educated the Indian into a civilized, socialized, or humanized Caucasian. Yet the Indian, as an untamed savage, never raped his daughters. The uncivilized never committed incest. The unsocialized satisfied his sexual appetites normally. For example, the Southwest tribes today are not as weak morally; their women's maternity is not as enfeebled as their northern sisters, because they live more closely to the old standards which prevailed before the white man's arrival.

The old frontier belief that the best Indian was a dead one has survived, at least in the minds of Washington officials: As soon as all the Indians have died off the better they will be, morally and physically. Hence, their logic concludes, why properly educate the living?

XX

THE SILENT TOMAHAWK

1

If the red slayer think he slays,
  Or if the slain think he is slain,
They know not well the subtle ways
  I keep, and pass, and turn again.

"Brahma" — Ralph Waldo Emerson

I FIRST conceived the silent tomahawk idea from a nineteen-year-old Indian dying of tuberculosis. He was in the last stages; his breath was double-quick and his heart fluttered in spasms like the throat of a canary. It seemed as though he would expire any moment, but his deep eyes burned on, fiercely like two nuggets of coal in a white plaster skull. His mind was nimble in his ramblings, as he lay on his cot, talking.

"White man pay some day," he gasped. "Soon every Indian be filled with germs — soon the white man comes crowding around him. Then Indian use tomahawk of revenge, tomahawk of disease. Then, some day, when white man's body all sick with syphilis, TB., trachoma — he might open his eye . . ."

As I walked out of his hovel I could see his eyes burning in his pallid face, and there came to me the vision of a new Indian warrior, with strange, new weapons. He bore no tomahawk, and carried no bullet pouch, but his aim was as straight as the arrows of his forefathers. And his harvest was richer, for his revenge was abundant. I could see him silently stalking through the files of white faces, uttering no war cry as he strode, and the scalping knife in his belt was bloodless. But everywhere white faces disappeared and the ranks became thin. Like the figure of death he stalked, and he smote down fellow creatures by the mere presence of his black, infectious body. . . .

2

The Indian death rate according to the United States Census, has increased 62 per cent from 1921 to 1925, the last year for which the Census Bureau computed mortality percentages. Although the Indians' death rate is three times as high as the Whites' no vital percentages have been issued since 1925. Since that year a comparative census has been verily stifled. Death, however, has never taken a holiday in the Indian country. Reservations are fast becoming cesspools of disease to infect neighboring communities and tourists. Indians are rapidly becoming germ-carriers, wandering freely about like flies. Soon they will menace the Caucasian who has been the cause of their afflictions.

Citizens from every state in the nation have gone into the West during the tourist season, and more will go with each coming summer. They visit Indian festivals and behold Indians dancing in native costume. In the great Southwest fiestas are held among the Pueblos; the Hopi and Navajo tribes annually hold their sacred dances. In the Northwest among the Chippewa and the Pottawatomi, it is the powwow. In the Dakotas it is the rodeo. In Montana, Washington, Oregon, and California it is the same. Even the Red Lilacs of the Senecas are providing the inquisitive of Buffalo with something far more spectacular than St. Vitus's Dance.

When Santa Fe revived her ancient September fiesta a few years ago she employed the services of many neighboring Indians. In 1930 Santa Fe staged an elaborate pageant, commemorating her 325th birthday. To quote an AP bulletin of September 1st: " Hundreds in gala costumes celebrated Santa Fe's 215th annual fiesta. . . . Indians of four tribes from the painted desert were in the *market place.*" Mingling. Although the Southwest Indian is not as disease-ridden as his northern brother he nevertheless, victimized by the present medical neglect, will soon be as menacing. Through this neglect not only are helpless Indians being dealt death-blows, but innocent Whites as well. If the Indians' Silent Tomahawk ever becomes noticeably effective nobody but the white man is to be blamed for spreading and then not controlling his communicable diseases.

Governor Franklin D. Roosevelt of New York State was conspicuously crowned chief of the Iroquois tribes near Saratoga, New York, before a tremendous crowd of interested spectators, elbowing their way beside silent-faced Indians.

Hotavilla, one of the many Arizona pueblos, is much frequented by interested Whites. The famous Snake Dance at Walpi is another mecca to which tourists flock from all parts of the world. In addition to the Snake Dance of the Hopis there are the festivals at Gallup, New Mexico, in which both Navajo and Pueblo Indians participate. Albuquerque is the leading commercial center between Denver and El Paso and many are the pale faces that congregate there. For the benefit of the traveling stranger in their midst the promoters stage a grand-stand Indian show, usually entitled " First American." Circle tours of the Indian country are nationally advertised from June to September, and hundreds upon hundreds of bus loads are daily exposed to contact with syphilis, tuberculosis, trachoma, and other infectious diseases.

Mingling. Conspicuously mingling with Indians who are tomahawking, unwittingly, unconsciously tomahawking.

At these dances, fiestas, pageants, powwows, festivals, and grand-stand shows the tourists stand side by side with Indian spectators and participators. At the 1930 seventeenth annual Menominee Indian Fair, held from September 9th to 12th, I saw an Indian boy with open lesions who was pointed out as having a plus four Wassermann, conversing with a family of sight-seers. At the Wabeno County Fair I saw an old tuberculous Pottawatomi depositing tubercle bacilli sputum recklessly on the ground, among the milling Whites. At the Pine Ridge Rodeo a middle-aged Sioux woman, half blind from trachoma, was selling hot dogs to the crowds and intermittently wiping her perspiring face with her hands.

The Winnebago Indians of Wisconsin roam like gypsies about the State, attending county fairs and the like, while their death rate from tuberculosis is fourteen times higher than the white folks to whom they sell their beads and buckskin. On the main highways running to Superior and Duluth the Chippewa hold weekly powwows to catch the wandering tourist. On the Apostle Islands, not far from Ashland, the Red Cliff band regularly stage a widely advertised pageant.

When Ex-President Calvin Coolidge went among the Black Hills, the Sioux bestowed its usual honor in the usual way. Several thousand American citizens witnessed their President become a Sioux chief. They gathered into a vast crowd of inquisitors, clicking cameras like machine guns not only at the President but at every Sioux who would pose. Promoters who stage coronations, rodeos, fiestas, and powwows are largely to blame for this systematic spreading of diseases among both Whites and Indians.

When Ex-President Calvin Coolidge went along the Brule River for his next summer's vacation, the Chippewa were likewise asked by newspapers to bestow a chieftainship on the President. There would be much publicity, they argued, many wealthy photographers, many tourists wanting beadwork. But Charles Armstrong, the uncrowned chief of the Bad River Chippewa, refused to allow the silent tomahawk to descend on hundreds of innocent whites.

"You expect us to tool ourselves in the ways of the white man," he told a Duluth newspaper, "but still you want us to put on feathers and paint for such things as this. It is an insult to Indians who have attempted to become civilized."

And thus many tourists were denied the pleasure of viewing the Brule Indians don their war paint, tighten their drums, and make the President of the United States a big chief, or a medicine-man, or something.

It is not enough that Indian communities are focal points for communicable diseases and thus endanger the health of neighboring towns and tourists, but in addition they have become exploited, advertised meccas that actually beckon vacationists to come, intermingle, and suffer the consequences.

Walter V. Woehlke, managing editor of the *Sunset Magazine* of California, has also observed the terrors of the silent tomahawk. " In twenty states west of the Mississippi," he wrote, " the Indian today is probably killing and incapacitating, merely by his presence and contact, more white people than his immediate ancestors did with arrow or bullet or tomahawk."

3

Hendrik Willem van Loon, the eminent historian, has drawn the opposite picture of what might have happened, if the Indian's civilization had progressed more rapidly than the Caucasian's:

" The American Indian never achieved the wheel. If he had (given the extraordinary mathematical possibilities of his savage brain), would not Europe to-day be a vast Indian colony, with a few reservations for slowly decaying groups of measle-ridden Germans and Frenchmen and Lithuanians? ”

And then would not those diseased Europeans employ the use of muffled rifles in a vain attempt to revenge themselves upon their Indian conquerors?

V
PROPERTY

XXI

THEY ROB US YET

1

IF you should by chance tour in the vast Southwest Indian country you undoubtedly would be routed over the direct tourist trunk line from Tucson to Phoenix, Arizona. About fifty miles out of Phoenix, after driving one monotonous mile after another, the last looking like the first — all bare desert, your eyes would suddenly be confronted with a magnificent stone and concrete bridge. Nearly a quarter of a mile of it would loom out of the empty air at you, as an unnatural, man-made spectacle, completely out of harmony with the loneliness of the landscape. You could not help but be impressed with its brilliance, its expensive up-to-date structure, massive and pretentious. A conspicuous brass tablet would catch your eye, and you would read the names of two Indian Commissioners, responsible for its construction. When you would leave the bridge your automobile would move over a modern gravel road, better than most state highways. But you would notice a few feet away the endless stretches of lifeless sand, which would seem to mock the gravel, because there are so many trillions upon trillions of grains. You might even glance at the river you just crossed, and notice its shallow depth, its dry beds over which water rarely flows, and never interferes with automobile fording more than two or three days a year.

Perhaps all this would arouse your curiosity and after going westward a few miles you would stop at the small Pima Indian Town, four miles up the dry river bed. There you would see Indians crossing the river, as their fathers have forded it for centuries. You might even ask one of them why he does not use the magnificent bridge, probably constructed for his benefit. He would answer you in good English, saying: " What for? Why should I travel eight miles out of my way just to cross the river on cement rather than dry sand? " Not satisfied you might ask him how many Indians would ever use the great bridge, and he would reply: " Not one in a thousand."

Other people besides you have become curious over the Pima bridge. The Honorable James A. Frear remarked in the House on January 4, 1927, as follows:

When we asked whence came the beautiful bridge with its ornamental lamp posts and heavy stone railings far out in the desert, we were told it was a bridge and roadway that would cost nearly a half million dollars, built across part of the Pima Reservation, and forming part of the direct tourist trunk line between the two cities named, and was built in connection with an irrigation dam at the same point. The extra cost for the bridge was estimated by reservation people at several hundred thou-

sand dollars. . . . I asked who paid for the bridge, and was told
that they had heard it was part of an irrigation dam project and
that the Indians were expected to foot the entire cost of bridge
and ditch that in all probability will reach nearly a million
dollars.[1]

When this bridge was built the Pimas for ten successive
years had planted crops only to see them wither and die on
the desert soil. When they have been able to get a little
water they have been good farmers, taking all prizes in
state and county fairs. But they have been starving because
the Whites have taken all their water on the upper reaches
of the Gila River. The Government built a storage dam
but failed to put any laterals down to the Indian land. The
Pimas have been so treated by Whites whose lives they have
saved, for it is the proud boast of those gentleman Indians
that they have never shed a drop of paleface blood. In the
early days they sheltered white settlers; and took them,
dying of thirst, into their homes and nursed them back to
health. Finally, after a weary, death-watch wait the Pimas
will see their lands watered from the Coolidge Dam. Those
lands will have a large value, but the allotted Pimas, dead,
and dying five times faster than the Whites, are compelled to
leave their land in the control of the Indian Bureau. They
have no choice, for that is the law; a son can not inherit his
father's land, if he is an Indian. Those lands are being
rapidly sold to white men, and the proceeds are being used
to pay for the magnificent bridge! The heirs are to get the
remnants, but there will be no surplus after a third of a

[1] Hearings Before a Subcommittee, etc. Pursuant to S. Res. 341. 1927.
P. 17.

million is paid for the bridge. The Pimas are again to live on hope — hope of getting money from the sale of their land. But as for the land itself, now well-watered and at last fertile, their land, their ancestral land, they can not inherit.

Such is the plight of the Pimas, who were dying at the rate of 59 per 1,000 per year from " slow starvation and heartbreak " when the tourist bridge, constructed solely to encourage tourist traffic, unused by the Pimas, and built at the cost of a third of a million, was charged against this impoverished tribe as a reimbursable debt.

Henry A. Johnson, an educated Pima, has sent the Senate subcommittee pictures of the bridge, which confirm the verbal descriptions as given in the House of Representatives and quoted above. Accompanying the pictures was a letter sent from the Gila River Indian Reservation, Sacaton, Arizona, dated February 8, 1927, and addressed to the Hon. James A. Frear, which reads as follows:

Dear Mr. Frear: . . . I am also enclosing herewith pictures of Sacaton diversion dam and bridge, which not one Pima Indian ever knew from the start of the bridge, and even now, as to why this was built without first consulting with the Pimas that the construction charges is to be reimbursed by the poor Pima Indians.

The Pima Indian Tribal Council held a meeting with the Santon district Indians on January 27, 1927, and we asked the United States inspector, Mr. H. H. Fiske, and our superintendent, A. B. Six, to be present at that meeting, and not one Pima's right hand shown up in favoring the bridge and its cost to be paid back by the Pima Tribe . . . This highway cuts the Pima allotments in two and without any compensation to the allottee nor ever was talked about the compensation for the allottees by the superin-

tendent in charge here or the State. Really all these are highway robbery, and I agreed with you that an investigation must
be made at once by the United States Congress.

Surely the Indian Bureau is a rotten, dirty — mistreating the
American Indians. . . .

Very truly yours,

Henry A. Johnson (Signed)

Santan District Councilman [2]

The meeting referred to by Mr. Johnson, in which not one
Pima favored the building of the bridge at Indian expense,
was held as a result of criticism; however, it took place
three years after construction had begun.

When Senator Lynn Frazier conducted his investigation,
following that of Congressman Frear, he discovered an
action which was a Bureau indictment of its own pretentiousness at the expense of the Pimas. When he saw the
bridge he walked over it, measured its dimensions, and
discovered that dozens of large-sized, decorative light bulbs
had been suddenly removed. This action had followed Congressman Frear's remarks in Congress with regard to the
Bureau's extravagance to the hardship of starving Indians.

Curious in connection with the Pima bridge has been
the attitude of the Indian Rights Association of Philadelphia, organized to do " non-partisan work for Indian civilization and citizenship." Mr. Matthew K. Sniffen, secretary
of the association, has unconditionally stated that: " The
Pimas understood the proposition and favored it." Further,
he cut down the cost of the bridge from $400,000 to $100,-
000, making an error of 300 per cent.

[2] Hearing Before a Subcommittee, etc. Pursuant to S. Res. 341. 1927.
Pp. 17–18.

Concerning Mr. Sniffen's curious attitude and his more curious statements, John Collier of the Defense Association has said:

Mr. Sniffen is not ignorant. He visited the Pima reservation only a year ago. He was a guest of the Rev. Dirk Lay, head of the Presbyterian Indian Mission on the Pima Reservation. Mr. Sniffen is a devout man; he preached in Dr. Lay's church to the Indians.

But Dr. Lay, for twenty years a resident missionary among the Pimas, a man of truth who discovered that in one township containing a third of the tribe one-fourth of the Indians have died in a four-and-a-half-year period, this honest Dr. Lay wrote on May 12, 1928:

The only expression that has ever come from the Pimas in this bridge matter was made before Inspector Fiske and Agent Six and it was a strong protest against the payment for this bridge.[3]

Former Commissioner Meritt, whom Mr. Sniffen so valiantly attempted to defend in his organization's white-washing campaign, out-rode his Sir Galahad. When Mr. Meritt was embarrassed with challenging questions regarding the Pima bridge, while appearing before the Oakland Forum of California in November, 1926, he declared that there was no Pima bridge, he denied it ever existed.

2

To cite only one of the several companion cases of such legalized robbery there is the Lee's Ferry Bridge, costing

[3] *American Indian Life*. Bulletin No. 12, June 1928. P. 14.

$200,000, one-half to be paid by Navajo money, without tribal consent.

Will Rogers, in one of his daily news quips, spoke out of turn and in so doing told the truth. From Laguna, New Mexico, under date of November 7, 1927, he wrote the following:

They struck oil on the Navajo reservation more than three years ago. I foolishly asked: "How often do they get their payments for their oil royalty?" Well, they haven't any yet. They took a million of it to build a bridge across the Little Colorado river so the tourists would not have to drive so far to see the Grand Canyon. The Navojos paid for the bridge and a Navajo has never crossed it yet. If the Indian's oil royalties hold out they will have enough to build the Boulder Dam for the whites. Poor Lo. I suppose I will be recalled for telling this, like McGruder and Summerall.

Yours,

WILL ROGERS.

The National Park Service and the Fred Harvey Transportation System have long desired a bridge across Lee's Ferry. The State of Arizona also wanted the north and south rims connected so that money-spending tourists could have freer access to the canyon. However, when ex-Senator Cameron of Arizona heard of the Indian Bureau's advice to Congress to build the bridge and make the Navajo tribes pay for it, he broke faith with and gained the silent approval of his party by declaring, before the assembled Senate, the project to be "highway robbery."

Theodore Roosevelt has dubbed that lonely land in northern Arizona "the God-forsakenest spot in the United States." That is Lee's Ferry, bound on the west for forty miles by a vacant, treeless desert, on the east by the Navajo reservation on which one can travel thirty-five waterless miles before seeing a sheep or a lonely hogan.

Congressman James A. Frear has described the location of the bridge in a diary entry of September 22, 1926:

> Only one settler was met, about halfway to the ferry. . . . During the last thirty-five miles of the drive to the ferry we did not meet a soul on the road or see a tree or a single water hole. It was deserted excepting for a few scattered cattle during the thirty-five miles. Not a half dozen settlers live within thirty-five miles of the ferry, we were told.
>
> We crossed at the ferry over the Colorado with Deputy Sheriff Moon running the rope ferry. He said the place was the last hole in creation; that he could handle all the traffic and averaged about two cars a day ($3 each) during September.
>
> We drove along the south side of the Colorado River for about fifty miles (on the Navajo Reservation), and it was as deserted for the entire distance as on the north side. . . .[4]

So gloomy and morbid is the vacant, void desert of only sand and sky but no landscape, and so obvious is the day-light "robbery" that the Indian Rights Association ventured to criticize the Indian Bureau. Mr. Matthew K. Sniffen visited the proposed site in the summer of 1926, and noted that "not an Indian lives within twenty-five miles of the site on the reservation side, and the nearest settlement across the river is about eighty miles distant." Further, he concluded, "it is a white man's proposition, and no stretch of imagination can justify using $100,000 from the Navajo funds for such a purpose."

[4] Hearings Before a Subcommittee, etc. Pursuant to S. Res. 341. 1927. P. 15.

Representative Frear, knowing the Indian Rights Association to be " very conservative, rarely questioning any action of the Indian Bureau," has declared that not only the Rights organization but all witnesses agree " that no Indians or Whites live or can live anywhere near this bridge."

Senator Bratton of New Mexico, thoroughly acquainted with the facts of the Lee's Ferry Bridge, has added his voice to those of the protesting few, by publicly denouncing the bridge as " unjust, inequitable, and iniquitous." On the Senate floor on February 17, 1927, he spoke into the *Congressional Record*, saying:

I am informed that the Indians are universally opposed to it; that they never consented to it, but that against their desire and over their protest it is proposed to take from them $100,000 and to establish a policy which may lead in the future to taking from the Indians sums vastly greater than the amount in this case.[5]

Ex-Senator Cameron of Arizona, besides stating that not ten Indians use the bridge, has asserted that " it has been proven that the Navajo Indian Tribe has never, does not now, and never will derive any benefit from the Lee's Ferry Bridge. . . . Why does the Bureau of Indian Affairs get behind a proposition to rob these poor Indians? Yet I call it highway robbery."

Needless to say the " robbery " was accomplished.

No Navajo was called to Washington to testify to his tribe's sentiment, before Congress, the Indian Bureau, or an investigating Senate committee. The fraud was perpetrated on the Indians without even their consultation.

[5] *Congressional Record*, Sixty-ninth Congress. P. 3840.

What of the financial status of the Navajos? Nearly $900,000, under the title of reimbursable charges, have been chalked against the tribe by Congress, on the sole recommendation of the Indian Bureau. About $450,000 of this mortgage are for white men's bridges, white men's highways, and white men's water systems. The status of the Navajo tribal fund, when the Lee's Ferry Bridge item was entered on the books with the others, was $116,000, against which $700,000 of reimbursable charges already stood.

While heaping these burdens unconstitutionally on the backs of complaining Indians, the Indian Bureau in accompanying breaths has declared the Navajos to be the most backward of any tribe in the country. Little wonder. Ex-Commissioner Sells, in a rare streak of confession, acknowledged several years ago the negligence of the Bureau. Testifying before the Snyder investigation of the New Mexico and Arizona Navajos, he stated:

The Indians of the Southwest, including the Navajos, the Napes, the Apaches, the Pimas, and the Papagoes, have all been considerably neglected. They have had very little help from the Government. . . . The Navajos have gone through all sorts of trouble.

The Navajos are bizarre as Old World gypsies, and yet as dignified as only the American Indian can be dignified. That ancestral dignity, however, is fast decaying beneath shoulders newly stooped with the unaccustomed diseases of oppression, robbery, and the loss of spirit: The white man's mark of an encroaching civilization. In addition to these disheartening diseases of the soul and the will, there are the white man's afflictions on the Indian's body: Starvation and the coughing of the tuberculous. On the quiet desert you can hear that coughing, echoing from the Navajo Mountains, the Rainbow Bridge, or the Monument Valley. On the Painted Desert you can hear that coughing, never blending with the awful beauty.

The Navajo's suffering dates back to the moment the white man began his relentless " subduing," in 1863–64 by United States troops under Kit Carson. To quote the words of President Grant's Indian Peace Commission: " In the transporting of the prisoners to Bosque Redondo such great hardships and terrible exposure were experienced that many died, and the few who were allowed to retain their flocks and herds lost most of them in crossing the snow-covered mountains." For four long years the white man's reign of terror descended upon the unsuspecting Indian with an unforgetable frightfulness that still burns as a dark story in the memories of a hundred tribes.

Today those nomadic shepherds, as picturesque as their ancient trades-kin of Galilee, are attempting to perpetuate their artistic and husbandic livelihoods in the face of tremendous changes in the economic life about them. About 2200 Hopis possess approximately 1,100,000 sheep and goats along with 50,000 cattle with the result that their reservation is pitifully overcrowded. The Board of Indian Commissioners in 1922, accepting the minimum standard for grazing acreage, declared that " a steer or horse must have forty acres at least and a sheep or a goat eight acres." Accepting this minimum standard the entire Navajo reservation, approximately half the size of France, should be devoted entirely to the grazing sheep and goats. This obviously has not been done; there has not been sufficient water. Only one's imagination can depict the result of such overcrowding.

One great Navajo voice is begging: " We need land. We need more range for our sheep. We need water holes; our lambs are dying every year. We also need a wide, intelligent market for our artistic productions. Our hand-woven blankets are bought by weight only. Let our money, held in trust at Washington and which we have never seen, be used for reservation improvements. Let it dig us wells, buy us sheep, and make our reservation better for Navajos, not for white tourists. We are poor; we need help, but now we must pay for the white man's bridge."

3

The Pima and Navajo bridges are not lone cases. Only two instances of the Indian Bureau's scandalous methods of robbing the Indians have been here disclosed, while it is Congressionally estimated that the charges against tribes for the erection of white men's bridges and approaches alone reach several million dollars. " Others have been referred to in speeches I have made," stated Representative Frear, " and in the case of the San Juan Bridge the facts are practically like those quoted in the cases above [Pima and Navajo]. I have been on the bridge [San Juan] and the Indians declare it is a white man's bridge built at Indian expense."

William Madison, " of superior intelligence," was born in a wigwam on the White Earth Reservation, and despite this handicap has managed to educate himself thoroughly. He wrote Congressman Frear that he had " in no way overstated conditions — rather have not given them strong enough." Mr. Madison went on to tell the Congressman of an additional case. He told of the Mescelero Apache Indians of New Mexico, who, being financially unable to send a representative to Washington, asked him to protest the building of an eighteen-mile highway through their reservation, and charging them $107,000 for the job. The Bureau added insult to injury by importing Mexicans to construct the road.

A decade ago the Indian Bureau acknowledged to the Indian Affairs Committee of the House that more than three million dollars of reimbursable charges had been improperly placed upon the Indians, without their consent and usually without their knowledge. The Indian Bureau simply obtained from the United States Treasury money for bridges, roads, and irrigation systems largely for the benefit of Whites and told the Treasury to charge it to the Indians. By 1919 the mortgages on the tribes had exceeded $23,000,000, of which $8,000,000 had already been collected. In Montana alone the reimbursable charges laid against the tribes for irrigation, of which two-thirds has been wasted, are approximately $15,000,000. In that state one tribe, the Flatheads, have been forced into a $7,000,-000 debt for irrigation, reservoirs, canals, laterals, and salaries. Only 33,000 acres have been cultivated, and mostly by Whites, thus making the cost of irrigation $152 an acre. The Indian Bureau guessed wrong as to the amount of water available for irrigation by 320 per cent. However, the Flatheads have been charged with their error to the tune of $5,000,000.

By 1928 the Indian Bureau had succeeded in charging $37,967,315.86 out of $41,291,000 appropriated as a reimbursable debt on the Indian tribes — a pitiful story which will be treated in the following chapter.

4

On May 23, 1930, immediately following the Senate Investigating Committee's hearing of the Phoenix flogging cases, an AP correspondent asked Commissioner Rhoads the latest developments concerning the " white elephant " bridges in the Southwest, charged to the Indians. I was standing beside the Commissioner and heard him reply, after a few nonchalant puffs on a cigarette: " Well, they haven't paid for them yet."

XXII

CHARGE IT TO THE INDIANS

1

ON January 21, 1930, the Senate Investigating Committee of the Committee on Indian Affairs summoned Commissioners Rhoads and Scattergood to disclose their administrative attitude with regard to the reimbursable charges illegally made against the Indians. Chairman Lynn Frazier called on the head of the Indian Bureau to open the investigation with his comments. The following two sentences consisted of his statement: " Mr. Chairman and gentlemen of the committee, I am coming here more to learn than to tell you how it should be done. I am altogether new to this, and I am very much bewildered by the complexity of the whole question of reimbursable debts."

The Senators impatiently twisted in their seats. They had come to get a positive opinion, upon which future policies might be directed. Senator W. B. Pine turned to the Commissioner and asked: " Have you someone in your organization that can advise the committee what your organization thinks ought to be done? " Mr. Rhoads replied that the question was " a very complicated matter that will have to be studied quietly and thoughtfully."

Again the disappointment of the Senators was noticeable. Senator Pine's colleague from Oklahoma, Elmer Thomas, attempted to relieve the Commissioner's embarrassment by asking him a helpful question: " Don't you think each particular case would have to rest on its own merits and be worked out as an individual proposition rather than to apply some general formula? "

The Commissioner of Indian Affairs answered: " I rather think so. I think there will probably be certain general underlying principles that will be guiding."

That was all. He took no more advantage of the loophole than of another one presented to him, this time by Senator Pine: " There is considerable confusion, isn't there, because of the fact that Congress has passed different laws and attempted to meet special conditions on different reservations? "

Mr. Rhoads' reply was still far from illuminating: " Yes, sir. There are general laws, and there are special laws, and they are sometimes conflicting."

" Nothing will come of nothing." So the good senior Senator from Oklahoma tried again, but this time more specifically:

Senator Pine: In Montana we found one reservation where the Government was attempting to collect construction charges against a piece of inherited land that had been

bought by a white man and deeded to him free of obligations. There seems to be considerable confusion because
the Government apparently has no well-defined policy.

The Chairman: We also found in Montana, on one or two
reservations where a good deal of money had been spent
for irrigating projects, especially on the reimbursable
plan in connection with Indian land, and after several
years they are now recommending abandonment of those
projects. It seems to me there should be no question in the
case of that kind as to the duty of Congress to take care of
the reimbursable charges of that nature, at least, against
Indian property.

Mr. Rhoads: It would seem so. Perhaps some of those
projects will have to be reorganized and some of them will
have to take up the loss.

The Chairman: The Fort Peck Reservation, especially,
as I recall, had come to the conclusion that it wasn't practical and that it shouldn't have been started in the first
place, but several million dollars were spent there — I
have forgotten the exact amount — before the Government
engineers came to that conclusion.[1]

The Senators were not willing to waste a morning; they
were conducting an investigation and supplying the facts
at the same time, because nobody else would. To continue
viewing their specific charges, we read:

The Chairman: In this report that I have before me there
is a statement in regard to irrigation on the Blackfoot Reservation. Here the statement is made that the problem
presents a hopeless situation. [Over $688,500 have been
wasted.] And the same statement is made in regard to the

[1] Hearings Before a Subcommittee, etc. Part 6. Jan. 21, 1930. P. 2198.

project on the Fort Peck Reservation. It is designated as a hopeless failure. It would seem to me that in cases of that kind there is nothing else for the Government to do, for Congress to do, than to cancel any reimbursable debt of that kind, at least, that has been charged up to the Indians. Then, in the list that we have, there are roads, bridges, and items of that kind from which apparently little value is coming to the Indians. Most of this has been for the benefit of tourists in continuing through roads that happened to run across an Indian reservation, or bridges on Indian reservations on these roads. What is your opinion, Mr. Commissioner, in regard to reimbursable features of that kind, whether for roads or bridges?

Mr. Rhoads: Well, in general, I should think it ought to be based on whether it is for the benefit of the Indians, or for the benefit of the general public. I would be persuaded to charge up to the Indians all these roads and bridges that run across their reservations.

The Chairman: Well, it seems to me that it has to be a strong stretch of the imagination to consider that a bridge costing several hundred thousand dollars was for the welfare of the Indians.[2]

Mr. John Collier, in the course of his testimony to the Committee, disclosed to the Senators that Congress in 1914 " very casually " legislated that the past gratuities, some of which dated as far back as 1867, should be immediately turned into reimbursable charges. " It is a question of constitutionality," Mr. Collier pointed out, " and of

[2] Hearings Before a Subcommittee, etc. Part 6. Jan. 21, 1930. P. 2199.

justice, a matter, first of all, for Congress to decide whether or not it was equitable and fair to pass retrospective legislation that wouldn't have been constitutional if it had been applied to white people and had turned all these gratuities into liens."

Senator Burton K. Wheeler of Montana burst into indignation upon learning of this historical phase of the problem. " It seems to me," he declared, " that it ought to be perfectly clear to anybody that where the Congress of the United States — where the Government issued to them a trust patent, that that should be given free and clear of any incumbrance; at least, there was a moral duty on the part of the United States to keep that promise."

The executive-secretary continued describing the situation: " that actually, day by day, allotted Indians have died and the allotment has been put up for sale, and the lien is paid from the sale price. The tabulation submitted by the Bureau shows that over $1,000,000 has already thus been taken from the Indians, and it is going to roll up faster and faster, and it amounts to a collection of substantially all the value of the land in many cases."

Senator Wheeler asked Collier a question, which he admitted should rather be asked of Commissioner Rhoads, but desiring direct and instantaneous information he asked the secretary of the American Indian Defense Association. The Senator asked whether reimbursable appropriations were still being asked of Congress by the Indian Bureau, and whether they were being made a lien on Indian property. " They are," he replied, " and indeed, they must, under the general policy."

" Why must they? " Senator Wheeler insisted.

" Tradition," was the answer. " The attitude of the House Appropriations Committee, and tradition."

" I am going to serve notice on them now," asserted the Senator, " that I am certainly going to fight any reimbursable funds going through the Senate where they are made a lien on Indian lands. Whether it is based on tradition or on anything else, it isn't based on justice, and I am not going to stand for it, if I can help it."

In attempting to place the responsibility for the numerous past misadventures in irrigation projects, bridges, and highways, Senator Wheeler was of the opinion that the evil lies as much with Congress as with the Indian Bureau or the Reclamation Service.

" There is a great deal of the evil chargeable against the service," Mr. Collier concluded, " that has gone on for a very long term of years — spending, spending, and spending on projects known to be failures, spending extravagantly on projects doomed to be abandoned at an early date, making, for example, a heavy capital investment when the capital is going to be wholly wiped out by a reservoir. [Over 50 per cent of the $272,000 expended from the San Carlos tribal fund for irrigation has been spent on erecting structures, pumping stations, and the like within the Coolidge Dam Reservoir site.]

" The evil is chargeable, of course, to the appropriation committees, who authorized these items, as well as to the [Indian] department, and I merely want to make that statement as a saving clause. In my own observation, and I have been on most of the reclamation projects, the most distressing element is the allotment law and the reimbursable system. But the Indian Bureau, either through engineering blunders or economic miscalculations, is somewhat to blame." [3]

2

Let us look at cases wherein the Government charged the land with irrigation items, after issuing trust patents to the Indians which provided that at the end of the trust period the land could be conveyed to the allottee " free from all charge and incumbrance if said Indian does not die before the expiration of said trust period." Those charges, it must be remembered, were originally gratuitous and were made reimbursable only by a retroactive law.

Nearly a million dollars was spent needlessly on the Fort Peck irrigation system. Thirteen years before the Government's own expert engineers advocated complete abandonment of the project the Indian Bureau was told by the Fort Peck Indians to cease operations until the already constructive units proved valid. What of those Indians who were robbed of a million dollars, taken from their pockets without their consent?

William Madison, secretary-treasurer of the Society of American Indians, visited the Fort Peck Reservation during the time when the project was going forward over the objections of the Indians. What he observed can only be described as disgraceful to the Indian Bureau.

[3] Hearings Before a Subcommittee, etc. Part 6. Jan. 21, 1930. Pp. 2712–7.

The first Indian family he visited was " Runs Through " and his wife " Night Hawk Runs Through." He found this old couple living in a tent which was the sole habitation they had:

I found this old man and his wife busy drying horse meat which they were preparing for food and the only food they had. They informed me that they had secured it from the dump grounds of the town of Wolf Point. . . .

The tent occupied by Runs Through and his wife was about six or seven feet square and slanted all the way from the ridge pole to the ground. There were two bed comforts, on the ground, a box with a couple of tin plates and tin cups and a bread sack. The horse meat that they were drying was hung upon poles, and this was the whole of their estate.

Mr. Madison next visited Two Woman Armstrong living in an old, dilapidated log shack:

This old log shack, which is her home, has a dirt roof and a dirt floor. She said that she had no articles of furniture, and no food on the premises and that when she asked the sub-agent at Wolf Point for help and food, he did nothing for her and advised her that she could drown out gophers for meat to eat. That he was particular in advising how she should do it.[4]

Mr. Madison told how this old, indigent woman owned 2,190 acres from which she has never received a cent of income. Those acres have been completely under the supervision of the Indian Department, and she did not know whether they were being used, leased, or grazed upon. She had heard rumors of cattle grazing upon her lands, but repeated calls upon the agent in charge brought her neither satisfaction nor money.

[4] Hearings Before a Subcommittee, etc. S. Res. 341. 1927. Pp. 73–74.

DIRT FLOOR, DIRT ROOF, NO WINDOWS

AN INTERIOR, ABOVE THE AVERAGE

William Madison has told of numerous instances among the Fort Peck Indians wherein injustices of old standing have not been rectified while new ones occur every week. Medicine Cloud is now penniless because the Great Northern Railway emptied a roundhouse sewer on his property, thus killing his herd of 132 cattle. There are dozens of similar cases. Heartbreaking cases of Indians paying $3.25 a bushel for seed from the Fort Peck Agency office while the same seed was only $1.25 per bushel on the open market. Untold graft in the leasing of 80,000 acres of tribal and individual lands to Frye & Company, a private cattle concern, without the Indians' consent. Indians complained to Madison of the cattle company stealing Indian cattle and branding them. Of the lease — the Indians get less than fifteen cents per acre per annum for the grazing of cattle on their lands. Yearly, this amounts to $96 for one section of land. The Fort Peck Agency expects its Indians, whom they are supposed to supervise by a benevolent guardian, to live on such a meager pittance. The result has been inevitable: horse meat and gopher meat, tents and dirt cabins.

In the meanwhile the Indian Bureau spent a million dollars of the tribal fund, in its past and present shrinking status, for an irrigation project condemned to uselessness sixteen years ago.

3

The Fort Peck Reservation is in Montana. So is the
Crow, where nearly $2,000,000 has been spent on an irri-
gation project, necessitating three-quarters of a million
as a maintenance and operation cost. What benefit was this
extravagant expenditure to the Crows? As a result, in 1926,
they irrigated only 535 acres. The Fort Belknap reservation is also in Montana. Its reimbursable irrigation fiasco
has cost through the year 1927 nearly $600,000, spent for
the purpose of irrigating 17,000 acres, of which the Indians, however, cultivate merely 1,805. Both these projects
have been previously reported by Federal irrigation ad-
visers as " hopeless," containing " many useless and unnecessary structures." Commissioner Rhoads has acknowledged that the experts' recommendations for abandonment
have not been followed by his department. This acknowledgment was made after Senator Wheeler had informed
the Commissioner and the Committee at the January 21,
1930, meeting that " I don't know of any Indian reservation in Montana where the irrigation system has been of
any benefit to the Indians. I think the only thing done was
to benefit the white settler out there, but it hasn't been of
any benefit to the Indians, and it has amounted to confiscation of their lands in many cases."

Fairly recently Rhoads handed me a memorandum for
the press, dated May 15, 1930. Among the paragraphs of
impressive figures I read this sentence: " Appropriations
for Indian irrigation are increased by $545,000, to be
spent largely in Montana and Washington."

XXIII

THE PUEBLOS HOLD THE BAG

1

THE Rio Grande is a playboy Nile. It is an erratic river, as the dwellers on its unreliable banks will tell you. The citizens of Albuquerque, New Mexico, for instance, will inform you how the city, located in the river bed, has had several serious floods. They will tell you that they live in constant fear of the whole city being destroyed by floods. Or, you can listen to the glib officials of the Santa Fe Railroad. They will inform you that their roadbed, which runs parallel to the Rio Grande for about 150 miles, is in constant danger of being flooded and their tracks seriously affected. You can also talk with the residents of other towns along the river, Algodones, Bernalillo, Los Lunas, Socorro, Domingo, or Belen, and you will hear a singular plea: We need flood control works on the Rio Grande.

You will undoubtedly agree, as I have, that necessary

flood control works should be constructed. And they are being constructed, but who pays the bill? The Santa Fe Railroad? The citizens of the river towns?

Let us look briefly at the history of the Rio Grande Pueblo Conservancy Bill, a measure drafted by the political interests of the urban centers along the river. In 1926 a bill was introduced at Washington for the necessary flood control works, which contained a provision that nothing should be done unless the Indians consented. This was intended to be a well-seasoned bait with which the confidence and financial support of the Indians was to be obtained. The bill failed; the Indians had rejected the proposal. They had been farming for centuries through an adequate irrigation system of their own invention. They did not need flood control works and saw no reason why they should be involved in another white man's project for the benefit of white men. The Pueblos were no fools, but the conservancy district proved craftier. Those white politicians realized that they could not pass their desired legislation unless they obtained the endorsement of the Pueblos involved. So Senate Bill 700 was drafted and offered to the Indians for their approval. It provided that the Pueblos' existing irrigated acres, totaling 8,346, would remain free from debt incurred in the erecting of the flood control works. It also provided " that in determining the share of the cost of the works to be apportioned to the Indian lands there shall be taken into consideration only the Indian acreage benefited which shall be definitely determined by said Secretary and such acreage shall include only lands feasibly susceptible of economic irrigation and cultivation, and materially benefited by this work, and in no event shall the average per acre cost for the area of Indian lands benefited exceed $67.50."

The Indians agreed to Senate Bill 700. They saw that legislation was inevitable; they had seen for centuries how the white man ruthlessly got that which he wanted. They also knew that such legislation could not help but affect Indian lands, so they renewed their expressions of faith in the American Indian Defense Association and thus prepared to guard their rights during the course of the legislation for the bill.

Judge R. H. Hanna and Mr. Fred E. Wilson, magnanimous attorneys for the Pueblos, wired John Collier on January 20, 1928: " Indians opposed any reimbursable debt but feel if such debt unavoidable the safeguards contained in bill are absolutely necessary."

The first action on the bill was taken by the Senate Committee on Indian Affairs, which reported unanimously in favor of its passage as approved by the Council of All New Mexico Pueblos. The Senate likewise unanimously approved. Next, the bill went to the House, where Louis Cramton succeeded in jockeying through a motion absolutely violating the promises that were made to the Indians in order to get their endorsement. Thus the protective features, insisted upon by the Indians, were struck out without an explanation.

The Cramton amendment exempted the original 8,346 acres from reimbursable charges, but it placed, however, on the additional 15,000 acres a charge of $109.50 per acre, a higher charge than that which was made against the acres of whites. Whereas the second provision of the bill read that " in no event shall the average per acre cost for the area of Indian lands benefited exceed $67.50." No betrayal, no fraud, could be more obvious.

2

The Indian Bureau, as a guardian of its Pueblo wards, agreed to the cost per acre of $67.50, when it knew the same work could be done for $35 or $40.[1] Further, while still the Pueblo's guardian, it countenanced without even a questioning expression the latest figure of $109.50.

Chairman Frazier of the Committee questioned any cost in the first place by quoting Dr. W. J. Spillman of the Agricultural Department as saying that " the Indians were out in the Rio Grande valley before the white man ever came there and have every moral right to it. The white man came along and took the water away from them and now they go to work to develop the water which the Indians originally had and charge them for the water rights and are making them pay more than they possibly can, which is absolutely wrong."

Dr. Spillman also stated:

I think that if the original principles involved in the bill are not adhered to, it ought not to be passed. Unless the original principles can be adhered to, I would oppose this bill as a vicious piece of legislation. It would mean that the Indians could not possibly pay for it. Anyone with experience in irrigation matters knows that the white man would not pay for it. If they want to

[1] Hearings Before a Subcommittee, etc. Part 2. Feb. 17, 1928. Pp. 63–5.

put the Indians in a position to redeem themselves and make them civilized, they can never do it in this way, as it is entirely unjust to the Indians.[2]

Senator Frazier received telegrams from the Fortnightly Club of Baltimore along with scores of that city's women. Judge Hanna and the Executive Committee of the New Mexico Association on Indian Affairs also wired objections to the Cramton amendment. But the simplest and most realistic plea came from Sotero Oritz, President of the Council of All New Mexico Pueblos:

My dear Senator: We Pueblos will be ruined if debt of one and one-half millions placed on our lands be collected from proceeds of land, which means crops, as quickly as Indian Bureau decides to collect it. We kindly ask your honor that conservancy bill be recalled and considered. This is desire all Pueblos, which is truth.[3]

3

On March 1, 1928, the Senate voted on Bill 700. A bare handful of courageous Senators vainly attempted to influence an assembly that had been thoroughly canvassed by lobbyists. Senator Robert La Follette of Wisconsin addressed the poker faces: " Much work has been done on both sides of this Chamber to line up Senators for the bill," he asserted. " That has been accomplished by *ex parte* statements. Perhaps the votes have been gathered in to ' put across ' this injustice to the 3,500 Pueblo Indians — peaceful, civilized Indians — who over the years of written history have never waged warfare against the United

[2] *Ibid.* P. 60.   [3] *Ibid.* P. 59.

States. They are a simple, agricultural folk. Under the laws of New Mexico they are disfranchised. They can make no protest at the ballot box for what may be done here in their name.

"Mr. President, if this can be done, if such an injustice may be perpetrated in the name of the Indians, then this Chamber has about-faced, and we must prepare to wage continued battles against the encroachment of the white interests upon the interests of the Indians, as was the case when my illustrious father came to this Chamber in 1906. Single-handed and alone he fought time after time against legislation which contained contemplated injustices against the Indians. . . .

"Mr. President, we are now told that the votes have been gathered in to perpetrate and consummate this injustice. If that be true, and if the roll call shall demonstrate that fact, then in a few years we shall be called upon to pass remedial legislation to undo this injustice which is contemplated with regard to these Indians." [4]

Citizens who take their voting privileges for granted will perhaps be jarred by the statement of the dynamic Senator from Wisconsin to the effect that the Indians of New Mexico do not vote, according to the constitution of that state, although they were awarded United States citizenship in 1924. Senator Cutting of New Mexico arose to defend the integrity of his state: "The Pueblo Indians of New Mexico have the same rights which they had under the Mexican Government," he stated, "namely, that they

[4] *Congressional Record.* Seventieth Congress, First Session. February 29 and March 1, 1928.

may vote if they pay taxes." The Pueblos can still recall the tyranny of the Mexicans. Under a newer flag they live on reservations, made non-taxable by the Government, and so they do not vote.

In the preliminary hearing held before his Committee Senator Frazier counted a one-vote majority for the bill as amended by Cramton. He spoke lengthily on the Senate floor before that body cast its well-oiled vote, in a futile attempt to rectify the ill judgment of his Committee. " It seems to be the attitude of some people," he declared, " that the Indians do not amount to much; that they have no rights to be considered. They have been crowded back out of the way to make way for civilization, and some people in the past and some people still seem to feel that the Indians should be further crowded out of the way to give the best of their lands to the white people, who might culti- vate them and make better use of them, in a way, than the Indians are making."

In addition, those acres burdened with a $109.50 per acre debt will be ultimately confiscated, according to Sena- tor Frazier. " There is something in our Constitution," the Senator continued, " which says that property may not be taken away from our citizens without due process of law, but the Indians apparently are not considered in that con- nection . . . the Indians obviously are not considered as coming under the Constitution of the United States. It would seem so at least, not only in this case," he concluded, " but in hundreds of other cases in the treatment of In- dians in this great Nation of ours." [5]

[5] *Ibid.* March 1, 1928.

Despite all this testimony and evidence, despite Senator La Follette's warning them that even the 15,000 acres " will ultimately pass from Indian ownership " because of the $109.50 debt an acre, despite his telling them that " there is no justification for the claim that $67.50 per acre of benefits is to flow to these 8,346 acres of land. Despite his warning them that " It is the urban communities of New Mexico which are interested " and not the Indians. And despite his final reminder that the bill as amended " is a breach of faith with the six Pueblo Tribes involved." Despite all these facts the Seventieth Senate in its First Session on March 1, 1928, passed the bill as amended by Cramton.

4

In the meanwhile, Louis Marshall, " a Prince in the House of Israel," an exceedingly magnanimous gentleman ever interested in the plight of minorities, became aroused over the betrayal of the defenseless Pueblos. He appeared upon the field of battle when the guardian of the Indians, the Indian Bureau, was forcing a crisis upon six tribes by demanding they pay $600,000 or more for flood control works needed by the Santa Fe Railroad, the City of Albuquerque, and other towns on the Rio Grande, but of no advantage to the Pueblos.

" It will become my duty," stated Mr. Marshall, in a letter to the Commissioner of Indian Affairs, dated May 18, 1929, " to see that this matter shall not be railroaded through even if it becomes necessary to seek the protection that the Indians are entitled to from your Department, through action of the courts and arousing the conscience of the American people."

Mr. Marshall first became interested in the Pueblo case through his friend, Mr. Robert B. Ely, secretary of the Economics Club of New York. Mr. Fred M. Stein, of New York City, also interested Mr. Marshall, who soon discovered that the contract, approved by Congress, between the Interior Department and the Middle Rio Grande Conservancy District, placed a debt of $150 an acre on about 11,000 Indian farmland acres. He also discovered that an additional lien was being placed on 15,000 benefited acres. In all, this amounted to $600,000 in excess of the legitimate sum, which " will be used to reduce the assessment against the City property of Albuquerque, against Albuquerque as a municipality and against the railways."

The result of executing the contract, Mr. Marshall observed, will be to dispossess 3,500 Indians of one-half of their arable land. In all cases their acreage debt will be greater than that placed on white acreage. On two-thirds of their land it will be double. On forty per cent it will be treble the white acreage debt. For centuries the Pueblos have been self-supporting, but never profit-securing farmers. According to the tabulation of the Institute for Government Research, which in turn was based on Indian Bureau records, their income per capita per annum is $31.00. From this fact alone one can see the Pueblos are penniless, and being without funds they can not pay the huge debts placed upon their lands. The result is inevitable: Six tribes will be landless within a century.

In order to perceive the proper perspective with regard to this robbery one intimate observer has written that it " far surpassed the Lee Ferry and Pima Bridge raids in the total of money to be extorted from the Indians. And the money is to be collected from the Indians beginning immediately, which is not the case with these earlier examples."

As fraught with injustices as the Conservancy Act contained, when signed by the President of the United States on March 15, 1928, those injustices have been inconsequential to the new ones fostered into the bill by the Interior Department, through the prompting of the Indian Bureau.

The new scheme is fraught with menace to the Indians, by taking nearly half of their arable land and renting it to whites and applying all the rental fees on the Indian debt. The result of this action will be to alienate the land for two or more centuries from the Indians, who have tilled its soil before Lief Ericson ever sighted the North Atlantic. Through this action of the Pueblo's guardians they are denied every protection insured to white farmers and property-owners by the Conservancy Act.

5

When Louis Marshall appeared before the Senate Investigating Committee on January 8, 1929, he did so merely through his " interest in the downtrodden "; he thus presented himself as the gratuitous attorney of six Pueblo tribes. He explained his presence to the Senators by simply saying, " Briefly, it seemed to me that the Indians were not properly protected and safeguarded."

Senator Wheeler asked the eminent lawyer: " In other words, you think this legislation was far more beneficial to the Santa Fe Railroad and to the towns than to the Indians? "

Their conversation has been recorded as follows:

Mr. Marshall. Infinitely. The Indians were a very small fraction, so far as interest is concerned, compared with the vast interests — not with the agricultural communities even, but of the general community living in that district. The white farmers, together with the Indians, of course, were interested in the irrigation for agricultural purposes, but the great benefits were urban as distinguished from agricultural.

Senator Wheeler. And, of course, you understand that those are the people whom we legislate for down there?

Mr. Marshall. It sometimes happens that the people in the cities are more active and have more influence — vulgarly called pull — than have the people who live far away from the busy marts of life.[6]

Among the many illuminating facts which Mr. Marshall disclosed to the Senators was the assertion that the Indians lost most of their acreage, which they held since the recording of history, " through the negligence of the Indian Bureau, as I understand it, as shown by legislation."

For many months one of the country's greatest lawyers protested the contract, a logical, legalized protestation

[6] Hearings Before a Subcommittee, etc. 1929. Part 3. P. 1124.

which in turn was denied and overlooked by the petty minds in the Indian Bureau.

Referring to that final stage of the fight, Mr. Marshall said the following: " During that period of denial this contract was signed in a great hurry, after certain facts became known."

This Conservancy contract was signed on December 17, 1928, a few days before Mr. Marshall was to make his plea; this was done under the pressure of the Indian Bureau and the Conservancy District. Besides the obscure language of the contract, it charged the Indians approximately twice as much for each acre benefited as the amount to be paid by Whites. That is, $71.72 have been demanded of the Indians for each improved acre to the white man's $36.75 for the same acre benefited.

Louis Marshall did not consider his tasks defeated by this victory of the Indian Bureau, Congressmen, Senators, and District politicians over the Indians. He had not forgotten his pledge to the Pueblos. He still saw an oppressed minority. He saw their ancient culture, condemned to die, yet struggling on in face of death warrants. He saw their sacred religion, centuries old, outlawed to die, yet strong in death. He saw the Juggernauting machinery of a mighty Government thundering down upon those defenseless farmers and grinding out of their bodies and soil hard earned money meant for bread.

If the camels would not tread through the eye of a needle, he would alter the species of camels. The much heralded " reform administration " was partly achieved through Louis Marshall's efforts.

With increased vigor he attacked the contract which made the Indians pay three-quarters of a million dollars for flood control works solely benefiting white farmers and white urban centers in New Mexico. During the year previous to his death he poured the energy and concentration of weeks into the case. His briefs and testimony have been described by John Collier as having " the quality of a trumpet challenge to the imagination and the conscience."

When Louis Marshall sailed for Europe in the summer of 1929, justice had not yet been dealt to the Pueblos. A square deal was awaiting the resumption of his energies upon his return from Europe. But when Louis Marshall returned to New York, he was in a black box, and the Pueblos' hopes had died with him.

Months later Secretary of the Interior Wilbur made a decision which has since lessened the Pueblos' hardships. Intimate students of this case, however, have informed me that there is no telling when Wilbur's decision will be reversed, as neither law nor ballot box protects the Pueblos. Nevertheless, a temporary victory has been secured. After a two-year fight the tide has been momentarily stemmed. The Pueblos have moved from the loss of land to the gain of land, loss of water to the gain of water, loss of autonomy to the gain of autonomy, from a threatened disintegration to a higher integration. Their one hundred per cent victory has proven that success is possible by fighting; after a two-year siege a buttress has fallen, with the aid of their own competent lawyers, not selected by the Indian Bureau. Numerous forts await assailers recruited from the ranks of both Congress and the citizenry.

6

As a crafty chicken-hawk waits until the guardian farmer strolls off the chicken-yard before he swoops upon his prey, so waited the enemies of the Pueblos. The Indians' champion had not been dead three months before a new menace, in the shape of the Simms Pueblo bill, arose against them. It threatened the very life-core of each Pueblo; it would govern them through rules and regulations made by the Secretary of the Interior. By destroying the Pueblos' ancient constitutional system it would strike a death-blow to the tribes. This was planned by hoping to set up an Indian bureau-appointed governor as supreme within each tribal group, regardless of merit or custom, and by setting up above this governor a magistrate also chosen by the Commissioner of Indian Affairs. This measure was proposed by the New Mexico Association on Indian Affairs and by the Indian Welfare Committee of the General Federation of Women's Clubs. It is obvious that those organizations were merely mouth-pieces for the politicians of New Mexico, whose memories still contained the stubborn battles waged by the Pueblos during the Middle Rio Grande Conservancy District fracas. It has been also disclosed, however, that this death-blow bill was drawn up by the Indian Bureau's own employees in New Mexico, namely, H. J. Hagerman and Walter Cochrane, hired as protectors and guardians of the Pueblos. Judas, thou art not dead.

On June 18, 1930, the All-Pueblo Council met and

unanimously voiced a stern condemnation of the Simms bill. This protest was sent to Washington, but no intervention has yet occurred.

7

Now the long-suffering but battling Pueblos have been struck another blow, the latest of a long series aimed to reduce this last stronghold of the cultured Indian. The sequence of events is revealing of how the " accursed system " does its work.

These tribes are wards of the Indian Bureau. With the knowledge and acquiescence of the official guardian, thousands of white squatters crowded on to the Pueblo farm lands, so that in 1919 the *bulk* of Pueblo land was held by Whites, while a number of Pueblo tribes had been reduced to the starvation level. Indian ownership was undiminished and intact but Whites occupied the land.

In 1919 it happened that the office of Indian Bureau Attorney for the Pueblos was filled for about one year by an eminent jurist, Richard H. Hanna, who had been previously Chief Justice of the State Supreme Court for seven years. Hanna saw his duty and performed it. He filed suits in ejectment against the squatters. His test case was tried in 1921 in the Federal District Court of New Mexico but the Court mysteriously withheld its decision.

The mystery was solved in 1922, when Judge Colin R. Neblett wrote a letter to the Sandia Pueblo, stating that he had withheld decision because the United States, as plaintiff in behalf of the Indians, had requested him to withhold it. Technically the Court's action was a proper one. The

Attorney General who made the request was Harry Daugherty. The Secretary of the Interior who arranged for Daugherty to make the request was Albert ,B. Fall.

Fall and Daugherty made no secret of their purpose. New legislation was being prepared, which would defeat the Indian case. Fall wanted the Court's decision, necessarily a decision in favor of the Indians, held up until the new legislation was enacted by Congress. That new legislation was the infamous Bursum Bill of 1921–22. The Senate passed this Bursum Bill on misinformation and later recalled it on motion of Senator Borah. Then in 1924 a compromise bill was passed, providing that Whites claiming Indian lands could stay there and become entitled to a quit-claim deed against the Indians if they had been in open, notorious, adverse possession for 35 years prior to the date when the Act of June 7, 1924, became law. Also, they were required to show that they had paid taxes continuously, as proof of good faith and as notice to the world that they had been claiming against the Indians.

The Act of June 7, 1924, required that the Department of Justice, in all cases where the White settler could not qualify under the Act, should bring suits in behalf of the Indians. The Pueblo Lands Board was created as a judicial and fact-finding agency, and this Board construed the Act as requiring that the payment of taxes by the settlers must have been made contemporaneously and must have been completed before notice was served on them by the Act of June 7, 1924. The Department of Justice joined in thus construing the Act, and the Indians were content. They would lose much land, but they would gain back some land besides being compensated by the Government for part of the land which they would lose.

The Indians could have rejected the Act of Congress and brought independent suit, outside the retroactive measure of the Act of June 7, 1924, and under this independent suit all of the lands would have been recovered to the tribes. They chose, however, to proceed under the Act of 1924, and have adhered to this choice through the long ensuing struggles.

When the Department of Justice went into the trial Court with its suits in behalf of the Indians, the trial Court reversed the construction of law which the Lands Board and Government adopted, and held that settlers who had failed to qualify for ownership before the date of the Act of June 7, 1924, could retroactively qualify after that date, and even could retrospectively qualify after the Pueblo Lands Board had completed its findings and had filed its report calling for their ejectment. The Circuit Court of Appeals, in an opinion of somewhat indefinite character, sustained the trial Court. These actions by the lower court had been anticipated by the Indians and their friends. The hope of the Indians lay in the Supreme Court.

And at this point, on July 10, 1929, the Department of Justice returned to the policy of betrayal of the Indian wards which had been attempted by Fall and Daugherty in 1922. The Department of Justice waited until the period for appealing the Taos land case to the Supreme Court had almost expired and then notified its agents in the field that no appeal should be taken; the hostile action of the lower courts should stand and should be riveted on Taos Pueblo and on all the Pueblos.

Thereupon the Taos Indians hurriedly pressed an independent suit, now on its way to the Supreme Court, designed to secure a final construction of the law from the Supreme Court. The Supreme Court will not be able to dispose of the case before its Autumn term of 1931.

The Department of Justice now is bringing to trial, in rapid succession, all the remaining Pueblo cases. The trial Court is knocking out the Indian claims through applying its disputed construction of the law. The Department of Justice is refusing to protect any of the results even to the extent of lodging a formal appeal and holding matters in *statu quo* pending the action of the Supreme Court. All the cases are passing to final judgment, and are being foreclosed irretrievably against the Indian wards.

The Indians have a last line of defence. They can bring their own suits in ejectment, going outside the Pueblo Lands Act and asserting that no claim to any of their lands has become vested in any white person through time, tax payment, or any other cause. The Pueblo Lands Act expressly reserves to them the right to bring such independent suit, and their unextinguished and primary rights are unaffected by the Act of 1924.

But the cost of such procedure will run into tens of thousands of dollars. The Pueblo tribes, though self-supporting, are possessed of no money at all. Hence, it is probable that the action of Attorney-General Mitchell will be successful and that the attempted betrayal of these tribes, begun in 1921 and 1922 by Fall and Daugherty, will be completed in 1930–31, by President Hoover's Attorney General.

8

All over America today there are greedy, covetous hands reaching out into every Indian reservation, to clutch at Indian property, to steal timber, oil, water-power, grazing lands, irrigation systems, cattle ranges, and what not. But has the Indian Bureau raised a fatherly hand of protection? What have they done, for instance, to protect and help the Pueblos?

The twenty Pueblo groups in New Mexico, living in twenty-five towns along the Rio Grande and over the Arizona desert, do not need the Indian Bureau. They do not need the Department's routines, its archaic officials, its ignorance and jealous interests. Those have been a dead weight about their necks long enough — a veritable handcuff. Instead, they need the Department of Agriculture. They need state agricultural colleges, state schools, and not the distant Indian boarding institutions. They need farm loan boards. At Taos, one Pueblo, the Indians borrow their seed in April and repay in October at an interest of one hundred per cent. At other Pueblos they surrender half their corn as payment for getting it ground. Give them fair play.

But the Indian Bureau will never relent its hold upon the Pueblos. Since that is inevitable the Bureau at least should cease its devastating policies: It should no longer diminish Indian land holdings; it should cease attacking and attempting to destroy the culture and spiritual life of the Pueblos; it should no longer hinder those qualities which develop citizenship and manhood, namely, the privilege of making one's own decisions and casting one's own policies; it should cease executing through an elaborate, extravagant personnel a uniform policy regardless of the vast divergencies among the tribes; above all, it should end its monopoly of control.

XXIV

CHEATING INDIANS AND THE PUBLIC

1

ONE of the most scandalous actions that has occurred in this century with regard to the affairs of the Indian has been the embittered struggle over the Flathead power-sites. Perhaps this case will appear infinitely more scandalous to the American public when it learns that its national welfare has suffered twice as much as the Indians'. The Flatheads of Montana were cheated out of one-half of their prospective income. The result of the battle has been a bare fifty per cent victory for the earliest settlers, while the public and its regulation of utilities have been dealt a hundred per cent defeat.

To the case. Although a strict censorship prevailed until the cheating was consummated and the license issued, I have had access to a sworn record of over 3,000 pages, the hearings before the Federal Power Commission, which have only recently been printed as Part Ten of the Senate Investigating Committee's record.

It is more than curious to reflect that the public eye was considerably focused on the Muscle Shoals project for several years, and the public welfare therein involved was safeguarded and benefited by that publicity. Whereas, in western Montana there lies a huge reservoir, far more natural than the Muscle Shoals site, which tumbles an energy of 210,000 horse-power down a deep gorge in the Flathead River. The ultimate potential power of the Flathead gorge is well over half a million, which places the project in the Niagara-Boulder Dam class. The Muscle Shoals furnishes less than 200,000 of prime water power; the Government power at the Shoals could be sold for $20 per horse-power-year, which the newspapers boisterously proclaimed to be an exceptionally low rate, paying Government interest-rates but yielding no profit. The obscure Flathead energy, hidden in the quiet of western Montana, could be sold at $15 per horse-power-year, pay interest on private rates, meet the earnings on its investment, and yield $240,000 a year of rental to the Indians, who own the sites. When fully developed the yearly rental to the Indians could be over $315,000. If accomplished under public development a sales price of $13 per horse-power-year could cover the rental, all capital costs, and amortization.

In addition, the acres surrounding this stupendous power-site are rich in ores that can be manufactured into zinc, copper, and chemicals with the aid of cheap electricity. Further, the soil is of such a character that it can be readily made into fertilizers, also with the aid of cheap

electricity. Consummating these possibilities is a hungry
market at its back door, stretching from the Pacific Coast
into Ohio, where farms are demanding additional fertilizers year after year.

In summary, the Flathead sites provide the cheapest
imminent development of power in the whole United States.
Next to the oil fields of the Osages, the timber stands of
the Klamaths and Menominees, they remain the most valuable resource the white man has left to the Indian. To that
same white man they could lower his power rates throughout the entire Northwest and make his State of Montana an
exceptionally industrial state, provided the sites are intelligently developed. To the Indian, it could furnish him
not merely a permanent income, but steady employment
near home.

Truly, this presents an impressive picture, which is of
incalculable importance to the Nation. Why then a censorship?

To explain that phase of the case let me introduce the
characters in this silent drama, and let us watch them perform. On one side of the stage is a private concern, the
Electric Bond and Share Company, coupled with Governmental organizations, the Indian Bureau, the Interior Department, and the Federal Power Commission. On the
opposite quarter stand the Indians, organized into the
Flathead tribe, and the American Indian Defense Association.

To the drama. In 1859 the United States Government,
through a treaty, confirmed the Flatheads' ownership of
the power sites. This was further confirmed in the course

of subsequent Congressional acts, ordering the withdrawal of the site area from allotment and reserving it solely for the Indians. In addition, the tribe was guaranteed all rentals if the sites were rented under the Federal Power Act.

But an uninformed Congress in 1926 ignored the tribal ownership while legislating a Cramton-devised appropriation bill. Immediately following this trickery a hurried contract was signed on February 17, 1927, between the Indian Bureau and the Montana Power Company. This contract provided for a rental fee of $1 per horse-power-year, to be split between the Government and the Whites living in the Flathead Irrigation District, whose legal or moral claim on rentals from the sites is absolute zero. The Indians came in for only a minor part in the split. This secret contract was unearthed through the vigilance of Senator Borah, and through his and other Senators' criticisms was nullified in March, 1928, by an act of Congress.

Concerning this contract the Montana Power Company has testified under oath, and the Secretary of the Federal Power Commission in writing, that those parties did not initiate this agreement to cheat the Indians. It has since been proven that the attempted despoliation originated with the Indian Bureau, the supposed guardians of the Flatheads. Of the Indian Bureau's officials who originated the robbery, John Collier in 1930 has said: " Those immediately responsible for this action are still employed in the Bureau."

2

What of this Montana Power Company? Can it be absolved of all sin in connection with the 1927 contract?

Let us glance at the power-monopoly existing in the State of Montana. Linked with the Montana Power Company is an interlocked chemical-fertilizer-metallurgical monopoly. The Montana Power Company and the Anaconda Copper Company are both headed by John D. Ryan. The American Power and Light Company in turn owns the power-monopoly, which, in turn, is but one of four tremendous holding companies which constitute the gigantic organization known as the Electric Bond and Share Company. This monstrous company earned a gross income in 1930 of $53,263,165, out of which $41,095,006 was a net income. In the Company's report to its stockholders published on September 27, 1930, which I have before me as I write, the total assets at June 30, 1930 were $989,241,-203.37 — a gain of $45,694,891.33 in one year. According to the statement of the board of directors on page five of the report, the four large holding companies owned by the Electric Bond and Share Company are: American Power and Light Company, American Gas and Electric Company, Electric Power and Light Corporation, and the National Power and Light Company. To read from the report: " The subsidiaries of these four holding companies supply electric power and light and other utility services in thirty-one states of the United States." What a monopoly! Incalculable.

But to return to the Montana Power Company, the immediate bad actor in this melodrama. That company takes each year an excess profit of 4.7 per cent on its assets, that is, profit above the legally permitted earnings. This has been accomplished by the Montana Power Company slashing its earnings through the giving of reduced rates to its affiliated Anaconda Copper Company. In other words, taking money from one pocket and depositing it in another, but keeping the valuable pants on all the time.

Montana consumers, it has been stated, have thus been " squeezed " out of $2,100,000 above the legal return. Almost the majority of the Montana Power Company's sales have been to the Anaconda Copper Company, which only pays 3.82 mills per k.w.h. while other industrial customers pay from 10 to 20 mills per k.w.h. Thus the Anaconda Company is able to eliminate competition and yet exact a high monopoly rate from domestic as well as industrial consumers.

This, then, is the impregnable, iron-clad power-trust — a veritable wolf in sheep's skin — into whose clutches wandered the unsuspecting Flathead lamb, led by a rope in the hands of the Indian Bureau, the supposed shepherd of the flock. In 1927 it looked like a successful slaughter until Senator Borah smelt blood.

3

Shortly after the Senate's hard-won victory of March, 1928, the Flathead tribe, fearful of the further designs of the power-monopoly, solicited Mr. Walter H. Wheeler, an independent engineer from Minneapolis, to make a bid on the sites. He proposed an initial development of 214,000 horse-power, and guaranteed a sales price of $15 per horse-power-year at wholesale to all consumers at long-term contracts. Those customers would have been industrial, chemical, metallurgical, and fertilizer companies. Mr. Wheeler offered the Indians a yearly rental of $240,-000, which was a gain of more than 280 per cent, while the public gain was more than 100 per cent. Wheeler's $15 per horse-power-year rate was more than 100 per cent below the industrial rates of the Montana Power Company, and yet remained a liberal return on his investment.

When Wheeler submitted his bid the Flatheads became elated and signed a contract with him for the development of *all* the power-sites. For once, in the history of the State of Montana, the power monopoly was threatened.

The Montana Power Company, driven by Wheeler's unprecedented competition, asked for a license for only *one* of the five sites, but which, incidentally, is a key site, controlling the remaining four. It refused to develop more than 68,000 horse-power, and offered the Indians only $68,000 a year rental. This stinted bid was rendered through the Rocky Mountain Power Company, a dummy corporation owned by the Montana Power Company, and which is under guarantee to sell solely to John D. Ryan at any price he sets.

Fearful that this meager bid would not pass on its own merits the Montana Power Company resorted to post Civil War tactics in a Herculean effort to drown out Wheeler. It launched itself on a lavish spending orgy. According to authorities they " paid out thousands of dollars to parsons, rabbis, and priests, to Deaconesses' homes and Y. M. C. A.'s, to commercial clubs and wool-growers' associations, and to individual Indians, Indian ' fixers,' Indian picnics, and Indian powwows. Fake petitions were circulated by the company and its paid agents, including bought Indians. These petitions called for the instant, unconditional grant of the power-sites to the Company."

When the meaningless petitions were sent to Washington they were promptly verified by the Flatheads' superintendent, Charles E. Coe, prominent Indian Agent. In addition, the petitions were placed in the Congressional Record to disgrace that truth-loving document by none other than Congressman Louis C. Cramton of Michigan, who always has managed to appear upon the scene, like Mephistopheles, at the most congruous moments for rendering evil.

When the Rocky Mountain Power Company filed its pre-license costs with the Federal Power Commission, supposedly based on necessary investments to be charged against the power consumers, it listed the hundred odd items of bribe-money.

At this point in the drama I must introduce the two " reform officials," Commissioners Rhoads and Scattergood. Along with these two came a new Federal Power Commission with a new secretary. " With their coming, the betrayal of the Indians and public was speeded up," drily remarked one observer of the melodrama.

Not satisfied with the effect of the fake petitions the Montana Power Company increased its activities on the Flathead Reservation, but the Indians refused to be demoralized. One of the activities of Superintendent Coe, the local guardian, was to organize a fake " Flathead Indian Association " and head it with paid chiefs of the Montana Power Company. Conscientious Indians protested to Commissioners Rhoads and Scattergood, but to no avail; they instead assumed complete responsibility for Superintendent Coe and his shady enterprises. In addition, they refused to allow the Flatheads to reimburse A. A. Grorud, their humanitarian attorney, who had been working since 1927 without fees or expenses. By this refusal the Commissioners adhered to the disreputable policy of the " resigned " Burke, who likewise refused the Flatheads an expenditure of their own money for their own cause. In addition to supporting Coe's canned association, Rhoads and Scattergood announced that the official Tribal Council of the Flatheads, which had vigorously opposed the power-monopoly, was by them no longer considered official. By this biased action the Commissioners hastened the destruction of the Flatheads' collective tribal life, a life that blossomed in Montana long before English Pilgrims thought of going a-Mayflowering.

4

Wheeler, on the basis of this honest bid, asked for a permit which would enable him to sign contracts for his market. No one disputed the overwhelming advantages of his proposal. He was only met by the following argument: " You can not sell the power; you can not attract the industrial market." To which the Indians and Wheeler answered:

" Grant the preliminary permit, on the strength of which customers can be signed up and finances demonstrated. In three years, or less if the term of the permit be abbreviated, proof or disproof will have been furnished."

But no permit was granted. Instead, Wheeler was notified in October, 1929, to appear before Bonner, the Secretary to the Federal Power Commission, but not before the Commission if he desired to show why the power-monopoly should not be granted a license on its 68,000 horse-power project. Through Senatorial protests the hearing was transferred from the Secretary to the Commission. Wheeler, at a cost exceeding $10,000, built up a smashing *prima facie* case. This was delivered under oath. (See 2,000 pages of sworn hearings of the Federal Power Commission, November and December, 1929). But still no permit was granted.

At this hearing Assistant Commissioner Scattergood did an unprecedented thing for an Indian Bureau official. Under his brilliant cross-examination the gigantic excess profits of the power-monopoly were exposed and established in the record. The Montana Power Company admitted that it expected, if it obtained the license, a revenue of a net twenty per cent from the number one site of the Flathead group, which would amount to more than $900,-000 a year. The right of the Flatheads to share in these excess profits was also established.

But at this point in the drama the screws were applied, and Mr. Scattergood, blushing from the embarrassment of his unfashionable procedure, made a hasty exit and from then on remained hidden somewhere backstage. To reëstablish himself in the good graces of his political superiors

Scattergood later prepared a memorandum, proposing the dummy scheme by which the public and Indians were cheated. In departing, he, as a conscientious guardian of the Indians, urged applicant Wheeler to withdraw from the competition![1] A curious procedure after he had brilliantly disclosed the power-monopoly gains. He further proposed that Wheeler make some sort of proposition with the power-monopoly so that he might become aligned with them as an engineer or stockholder. This conversation between Scattergood and Wheeler has been confirmed by the Assistant Commissioner of Indian Affairs before the Senate Investigating Committee.[2]

Instead of presenting himself before dolers of justice, engineer Wheeler found himself confronting powerful political forces. Just how deeply sank the roots of that political weed can be estimated from the following correspondence between John Collier and the Honorable Ray Lyman Wilbur.

On April 22, 1930, the Executive Secretary of the American Indian Defense Association wrote the Secretary of the Interior: " In our conversation of some days ago, dealing with the Flathead power site matter, you made one remark which has puzzled me and I have since consulted the record. The remark was to the effect that the large use of power by the Anaconda Copper Company had the effect of giving all other industrial users in Montana a very low rate which otherwise would be impossible." Mr. Collier went on to explain carefully that the Anaconda Copper

---

[1] Hearings Before a Subcommittee, etc. Part 10. 1930. Pp. 3414–5.
[2] *Ibid.* Pp. 3433–4.

Company pays on an average of 3.82 mills for its power bought from the Montana Power Company, whereas the average sales price for the power of the Montana Company is 7.336 mills. " It follows," wrote he, " that the consumers other than the Anaconda Copper Company and the Milwaukee Railway are paying in excess of ten mills as a minimum." The authentic source for his facts was the recorded hearings of the Federal Power Commission, pages 1405–11 inclusive.

Ray Lyman Wilbur signed a letter of April 23, 1930, to Mr. Collier, which read: " You evidently misunderstood my remark, which is the subject of your letter of April 22. I referred to domestic users, not industrial users."

Whereupon the Executive Secretary of the American Indian Defense Association again patiently delved into the sworn record for his irrefutable facts. His next letter to the Secretary was dated April 26, 1930. It read: " But from the facts developed at the Power Commission hearings and from the published rates of the Montana Power Company, it would seem that the domestic users suffer even worse than the competing industrial users as a result of the discriminating rates enjoyed by the Anaconda Copper Company. . . . The power house rate of the Montana Power Company to the Anaconda Copper Company is $17.50 per h.p. year. The rate to other industries for 24-hour power is $36.25 per h.p. years."

It is 1931 and Wilbur has not yet replied to the last quoted letter, nor can he make a reply.

5

Throughout the spring of 1930 the actors in the Flathead drama moved rapidly and sensationally. The engineers of the Federal Power Commission drafted a proposal, which drew the most impossible conclusions from data wholly fictitious. It completely favored the Montana Power Company's claim to the total discredit of the Indians' rights. This scheme only considered a low rental up to 68,000 horse-power, the sworn maximum of the Montana Power Company, and upon reaching that figure the rental magically leaped $6.53 skyward. The Commission's engineers explained this as " an energy-charge." When John Collier exposed this scheme it was hurriedly withdrawn, and the officials involved attempted neither a defense nor an argument.

Proposals at that time began to appear like rabbits. The next scheme was Secretary Wilbur's and was actually delivered to the Montana Power Company by his hands. This latest offer ignored applicant Wheeler entirely and proposed to the Indians a minimum rental of $104,400. Again to John Collier befell the task of analyzing this proposal and finally attacking it, which was done successfully through the People's Lobby, the National Popular Government League, and Senator Lynn B. Frazier. The Interior Department announced that the Montana Power Company had " rejected " the Department's latest proposal, in which the Indians' rental was to be derived from the profits of the dummy Rocky Mountain Power Company. The curious fact must be remembered that the Government no longer considered it had any control over the excess profits of the dummy. They have been held to be beyond even governmental acknowledgment of their existence. To put the fact plainly, the interests of the Indians have been tranferred from the Indian Bureau and the Interior Department into the spacious yet ever-hungry lap of the power-monopoly.

The result of the Hydra-headed proposals with their Herculean slayings was to produce finally the desired psychological effect. The Interior Department and the Montana Power Company succeeded in reducing the patience of the Federal Power Commission. Finally, on May 23, 1930, the Montana Power Company accepted a license on its own terms, namely, the paying of a maximum of $175,-000 a year to the Indians, and an average of $140,000 across the next twenty years.

By this singular action the Federal Power Commission and the Interior Department, prompted by the Indian Bureau, have destroyed the accumulative public rights, which have been previously guaranteed by the Federal Water Power Act. Those officials have chosen to surrender to the Montana Power Company's scheme of a dummy licensee. Regulation has been nullified. The license was actually issued to the dummy, who, in turn, has been required to sell monopolistically to its owner, the Montana Power Company. This right has been vested for the next fifty years. Governmental or private competition has been permanently outlawed. Not even Congress can alter or recapture the public authority that has been signed away. Only the courts can now rectify this wrong. The Indians, who have witnessed this confiscation of their rentals to the estimated amount of at least $5,000,000, can only appeal to the justice that dons a black robe. It would be useless to seek any further protection from their betrayer, the Indian Bureau.

There is a greater injury to the Indians than the dissipation of their rental values of $100,000 a year and upward. The Montana Power Company has announced it will develop no industries at or near the Flathead Reservation; instead it has planned to transmit its power 140 miles to Anaconda. The Flathead Indians are in desperate need of employment. Their farm life has been stifled under a tremendous reclamation failure, which has placed on their backs a debt of many millions. The Indian Bureau, not satisfied with this lien, has already started to accumulate one still greater. The revenue from their power-site rental will go toward paying for this failure and toward the construction of another. In the meanwhile, the Indians, paper-rich, are compelled to leave their reservation and seek employment elsewhere.

Engineer Wheeler would have undertaken the development of diversified industries near the power-site, where the Indians live. Secretary Wilbur and Commissioner Rhoads have been preaching eloquently for the need of jobs for the Indians near their homes, and yet by their action, not their empty words, they have destroyed the one possibility for industrializing and Americanizing the Flatheads.

XXV

MEN OF BENEFICENT SEED

1

IT was long after sundown when I reached the northern boundary of the Menominee Indian Reservation. The car sped over a well-graveled road, which pierced a dense, virgin forest; my headlights illuminated the immense bellies of fat, old trees as the car swung around the curves. It was refreshing to see trunks and foliage, after driving all day through a denuded land which only sprouted dead stumps, the ghosts of primeval giants.

As I traveled over the reservation road, once an old military wagon trail, I began to notice conspicuous signs placed along the way. A row of virgin pines were left standing in the highway, and their trunks were labeled "Five Pines." A lone tree was dubbed "The Sentinel Pine." Creeks and waterfalls were christened with euphonious titles, such as: Burnt Shanty Rips, Shot Gun Eddy, Dells of the Wolf, Smoky Falls, White Rapids, Big Eddy

Falls, and Wayka Ribs. A boulder on the side of the road bore the poetic name, " Spirit Rock." Frame houses were likewise advertised by posters telling the motorist their histories, what famous traders were purported to have slept there, and what Indian families were then living within.

After the traveler has been subjected to this propaganda for twenty-nine miles he reaches the town of Shawano, where he is presented with a pamphlet published and distributed by the Shawano Chamber of Commerce. He learns that the Menominee Indian Reservation is known as " Wisconsin's Playground." He reads of a veritable pantheocracy on earth: " Many streams are stocked with brook and rainbow trout which not only furnish them [the Indians] a means of livelihood, but a playground where they could roam at will and enjoy the green forests, pure air, and sparkling spring water which nature so abundantly endowed this territory."

By this time the traveler has become so intoxicated with the beauties of the reservation that he joins thousands of fellow inebriates, who weekly descend upon the Indians. I have been told that on certain holidays their number swells well over 5,000. All of them travel over the reservation roads and are subjected to the advertising placards, and so believe the Indians to be well, contented, and prosperous.

But as I sped over that rejuvenated military road I was not thinking of the mythical, mighty Menominee fisherman, robust and healthy. I knew their high rate of venereal diseases and tuberculosis. It was a wholly different phase of the problem with which I was concerned when I stopped before the superintendent's cottage in Keshena, where the Government agency for the Menominee is located.

Superintendent W. R. Beyer is of a caliber well above the average Indian agent; he is well-educated, intelligent. Being primarily interested in the educational and field phases of the Menominees' lives he has come to know them intimately and thoroughly. He visits each family in its home at least once a year.

" Their intelligence? " he repeated my question. " As a whole the intelligence of these Indians is high. There are only thirty pagan families out of 1600 on the reservation. The Menominees are way above the average Indian's intelligence."

The next day, in Superintendent Beyer's office, I substantiated his evaluation by examining industrial reports of individual Indians as well as surveys regarding their general tendencies. In all, they disclosed a different, more industrious, far more serious Indian than what is pictured by the Chamber of Commerce and the roadside propaganda. I found, according to the statistics, that although lumbering is their most important means of revenue, not more than slightly above fifty per cent of the timber employees are Menominees. Of the laborers employed the year around only 43 per cent are Indians. The industrious Menominee then has turned his energies to farming in such proficient numbers that in 1930 there was a twenty per cent increase in the acreage cultivated. I learned that they are splendid gardeners, with about 175 families supporting their own tables, and about fifty families doing commercial gardening, and over two dozen selling milk and cheese from their own herds. No Indian family on the reservation lives in a tent; the majority of the houses are of the latest frame construction.

I discovered that out of 1,928 Menominees, men, women, and children, 850 are self-supporting as a result of their own industry and thrift, fifty more partially support themselves, and another fifty are indigent. More than half of the tribe read and write English, while almost all can speak the white man's language.

Only one Menominee Indian in 1930 was arrested for theft.

The Indians' homes, barns, and corrals are evaluated at $150,000, their livestock and poultry at $50,000, their horses at $26,250, and cows at $21,000.

I picked cases at random while skipping through the Industrial Status Report. Paul Vigne, in addition to cultivating 54 acres, owns six horses, two ponies, nine cows, ten heifers, fifty chickens, sixteen pigs, one Ford truck, and one Buick car. " Paul," wrote Superintendent Beyer, " has a large family and they are all good workers. This family is self-supporting through their own efforts."

I spent my first evening on the reservation in attending the evening session of the seventeenth annual Menominee Indian Fair, organized, sponsored, and operated solely by Indians. " The Menominee Indians cordially invite the public to their fair," the premium booklet read. " Those who come to see us will find collected some of the best things produced on the Menominee farms and in the homes located thereon . . . exhibits of livestock, grains, fruits, vegetables, cooking, sewing, fancy work, and splendid Indian babies."

I spent several days at the Menominee Indian Fair, and observed concessions and food shops efficiently managed by Indians. All the exhibits were Indian. The entire fair management was Indian. I watched the young women stroll about the fair grounds looking more like beautiful Spaniards in the latest American dress than Indians. The mothers disclosed their innate taste for good colors in the clothing of their children and themselves; even the young men dressed neatly.

There is no one more immaculate than an Indian, when the Indian chooses to be immaculate. In addition, I did not notice or hear of a single case of drunkenness.

What, then, is the Menominees' problem? Although they are industrially and financially better situated than most tribes they are not politically content. What is the cause of their trouble?

2

Seated in a comfortable armchair overlooking the dashing Keshena Falls, is Chief Oshkosh, honorary chief of the tribe. He is old and failing fast, but he looks at the swirling water and his talk is clear.

" We Menominees," he says in a dignified, educated voice, " have always been acknowledged as an independent nation even as early as 1732 when we were recognized by the French and British. While other tribes were being segregated and confined to limited territories, where eighty per cent of them lost their homes through the forced allotment of their lands, we remained here. We saw the New York Indians being pushed into our territory; and we saw our neighbors, the Winnebagoes and Pottawatomies, in turn being pushed into Kansas and Nebraska. But we did not wish to be moved westward to make room for the Whites and eastern Indians. Uncle Sam went to the other tribes, and said, ' I'm a big man, you're a little man, and I'll be your protector. You stay in that pen. You need no money. I'll feed you and watch you.' And in that manner killed the initiative of those tribes. I say Uncle Sam has made a rich man's son out of the Indian. ' White man do it all,' he says, and quits work because his ambition is smothered.

" Who is to blame for the Indian being lazy? He was not a lazy man before the white man came; moreover, in the old days he knew he would starve if he got lazy and quit the chase.

" No, the Indian should be allowed to solve his own political problem. Dump an Indian and a white man into a stream and the Indian will get to shore just as fast as the White."

Chief Oshkosh looks at me with his pale, fading face. " As long as the Indian Bureau at Washington," he says, " continues to protect the Indian they hurt him. We have been told that we can not have a voice in our affairs; but we are going to organize the tribe into a united membership, like a corporation, so that we can help control our destiny. For the Government has made a failure of our affairs; millions of dollars' worth of our property has been destroyed.

" We can not possibly handle our affairs worse than the Government. We Indians are one of the few self-supporting tribes in America; we have never asked the Government for a cent. Instead, we have paved the state roads here, and built schools for our children, and now run a lumber mill, costing us $35,000 a month to operate.

" But it has been the Buffalo Bill-Cody-Custer type of literature which has discolored the public's mind, and has given them all their ideas about Indians. I want to interest the public in the wrongs the Indian Bureau officials are continually doing. Washington runs our mill and cuts valuable timber, but no money is made. The reason? Washington holds the reins; Hammer, the superintendent of the mill, had to be taught the business by us Indians.

" The solution? If the Menominees be incorporated, as we desire, then the Indians will have a voice in the spending of their own money. In addition, our reservation won't be broken up into allotments, and consequently be lost through grafters and Indian Bureau officials."

Chief Oshkosh is failing. You can see it in his face as he sits in his armchair, peacefully staring at the tumbling falls. His mind flees into mystical lyricism as I take my leave.

" The trail is straight, well-broken," he whispers. " I can hear the drum a long ways off. I will go West to the setting of the sun. . . ."

3

What of the Menominees' grievances? What of their attempts to incorporate? Younger men, more active than Chief Oshkosh, have taken upon themselves the burdens of the tribe. Through their tribal council they have for many years protested the Indian Bureau's mismanagement of their affairs. The Menominees' dissatisfaction has arisen from the fact that they pay the salaries of incompetent white men, while the efficient among their number are not given employment; in many cases they have been black-listed. Vastly more fundamental than these complaints has been the Menominees' charge that their lumber industry has been so badly mismanaged that millions of dollars have been lost to the tribe. In fact, they have demanded an audit of the mill books, but the Indians have been refused an accounting of their own money. For sixteen years there has been an illegal cutting of the Menominees' forests and for twenty years the books have not been regularly audited. " We charge," the tribal council has stated, " that fearing our claim that profit and loss statements of a padded show-ing of profits for 1927 and 1928 will be substantiated, the Bureau officials now prefer to admit that they received less for their lumber than it cost them to produce it during those years."

The Menominees protested to Edward E. Browne of Waupaca, Congressman from the Eleventh District, who went to Commissioner Rhoads. The Commissioner's answer was as follows:

During the past two years several investigations have been made by representatives of this bureau and the Interior Department. While there have been some differences of opinion among these investigators as to the advisibility of certain plans of the management, all the reports indicated that the affairs of the Menominee Indians were being conducted honestly and in general efficiently. Assistant Commissioner Scattergood made a special investigation at the reservation in July last as a result of which he was convinced there was nothing essentially wrong with the administration of affairs at Menominee.

What of this investigation by Scattergood? Six days after he had taken office in Madison, Wisconsin, Secretary Wilbur dispatched him on his first official assignment as a " reform " appointee. Wilbur had just received the report of an impartial, scientific investigation, headed by the best cadastral engineer in America, Ernest P. Rands, in which the Menominees' charges of mismanagement were substantiated. So Scattergood proceeded to the reservation. He spent one and a half days consulting solely with the officials of the Indian Forestry Department and the Indian Bureau, who were accused of mismanagement. Satisfied with their side of the case he returned to Washington without having consulted with the Indians who made the charges. He arrived in the Union Station with a whitewash brush in either hand. The Rands report died. Friends of the Indians have termed it a " grandiloquent gesture." Scattergood's report was given preference " for the morale of the service." Commissioner Rhoads, in his above reply to Congressman Browne, repeated the battle-cry of the Old Guard: " We must stick together." He likewise completely negated the Rands report, and forgot the unaudited books and the unanswered charges.

Blocked by their own guardian, frustrated by officials whom they pay to safeguard their interests, the Menominees have come to regard the incorporation of the tribe as their only means of salvation. They desire to be free of the Indian Bureau's shackles, so that they might independently sue the Bureau for the millions lost in mismanagement. In October, 1929, the tribal council voted to incorporate.

The idea was not originated by them. In 1927 the Institute for Government Research suggested the incorporation plan for Indian tribes, because it would enable them to manage their own affairs efficiently, and because, in the case of the Menominees, the allotment of their land would be an unfair distribution of their natural resources. Yet with millions to their credit on the Indian Bureau's books, some needy families have been compelled to take boxes of clothing from the Camp Fire Girls of Oshkosh.

By incorporation the Menominees know they can demand an audit of the mill books, not by the Indian Bureau's own officials as has been the practice, but by disinterested Certified Public Accountants. They also know that they can demand a stop to the injustices heaped upon the Indians living in the South Branch District, who are compelled to pile pulp wood four feet six inches high, making every eighth cord an extra one for all those delivered at a station seven miles distant.

In order to incorporate the Menominees must secure from Congress an enabling act, allowing them to hire lawyers to draw up the corporation papers. Although the Menominees were awarded United States citizenship in 1924 they are still wards of the Indian Bureau, and as such are not permitted to hire lawyers. The gist and humor of the case is that the Menominees must get approval from their guardian to hire lawyers to protect them from that guardian.

4

An agent of the Menominees lives in a large white house, overlooking a small mill town, of which he is in complete charge. The Menominees consider him a more formidable enemy than the Chippewas were to their grandfathers. This agent hires and fires Indian employees. He operates the mill and maintains his own system of bookkeeping. It is rumored that when the Menominees become incorporated and have a voice in the administration of their affairs he will have to leave.

On the noon of September 10, 1930, I rapped at the front door of the large white house. A sweet-faced woman in a plain house dress answered my knock; her eyes bore a sad expression. After leading me into her living room she went to the head of a flight of stairs, and called to someone that " a gentleman is here to see you." The unseen recipient of her information did not know who was calling on him, whether it was Commissioner Rhoads, his almighty boss, or an Indian, a common day laborer about the mill. He only knew his caller to be " a gentleman." After a few minutes of silence the woman again went and inquired of her lord whether he could descend.

" No," growled a rough voice, " can't you see I'm busy? "

She approached me with a half-smile on her face. " He'll be down shortly," she said, and disappeared.

After a fifteen minute wait Mr. Hammer came down the stairs. His face was stern, hard, aggressive; his nose long and thin; his eyes cold, angry; his voice belligerent, pugnacious.

We left the house for his office. On the porch he abruptly accosted a small boy at play with a fierce " What are you doing? " The child, apparently his son, was ordered into the house. We proceeded.

At his office I was informed that the Menominees were paid an annuity of $200 each in 1928, one of $100 in 1929, and they were not to expect a dollar in 1930. The future looked as barren as 1930.

" The peculiar thing about these Indians," said the robotical Hammer, " is that a man earning $6.50 in the woods would prefer to earn $3.25, one-half as much, provided he could work at home with his family.

" But the younger fellows are of a keener type," he concluded, " they are coming along better."

Upon inquiring into the gross cost per year for the operation of the mill I was informed that the figure was $583,000. Chief Oshkosh, who worked for many years in the Forestry Service of the Indian department, previously informed me that the Indians believed they were paying only $420,000 a year for the operation of the mill.

5

I returned to the fair grounds in Keshena where Congressman Browne was addressing the assembled tribe. A slight, quiet-faced man was talking earnestly from a platform.

" The Menominees voluntarily raised over a company of troops in 1861, another in 1898, and in 1918 more Menominees volunteered for service than from any corresponding population. If you people are intelligent enough to fight for the United States, voluntarily, when you were not her citizens, then you surely should be given the power to govern yourselves.

" There has been so much long-distance bureaucracy and red tape that there is no doubt but that the progress of the Menominees has been impeded. You must go to Washington to get permission to have a delegation to secure attorneys. You must go to Washington to get permission to send your young to college and that permission is difficult to obtain."

At the conclusion of the Congressman's address I sought out Ralph Fredenberg, the tribe's leader in the fight for incorporation, and undoubtedly the best educated Menominee. I found him to be better dressed than the average white man and his talk far more coherent and picturesque.

" Water finds its own level," he said, after we had seated ourselves on the running board of a car, away from the fair crowds. " But the Indians haven't been allowed to seek their own level. Everything that is done on the reservations has been thought out by some white man in distant Washington. Laws made for Indians of the Southwest are not always applicable to the Indians of the Northwest. In Haskell there are 86 different tribes represented, each with a distinct language; yet all are governed under the same regulations and laws. In the administration of the states such a rigid policy is not carried out; Maine does not legislate for Texas. Therein lies the weakness of the present system of handling the Indian.

" You heard Congressman Browne just say that each Menominee is worth at least $10,000. I'll add that there is $2,400,000 to our credit in the Washington treasury. But all that does not mean a thing, for there is still poverty here. I can show it to you.

" The feasibility of incorporation? I tell you there are Menominees who can fill all the responsible positions on this reservation. Yes, there are enough well educated, intelligent Indians to safeguard our own interests."

Upon leaving the reservation I stopped at the St. Joseph Mission and interviewed the gentle-souled Father Englehart, who has learned the face of every Menominee during the past quarter of a century.

" The children are as bright as white children," he confirmed. " These are capable, intelligent Indians, who know what they are doing. Many have gone to college and should be given an opportunity to work for their people here on the reservation. The case of Miss Alice Oshkosh, a refined lady, is but one instance of where employment has been again and again refused.

" Yes, of all the Indians I know, the Oneidas, Chippewas, Munsees, and Stockbridges, these Menominees are the most intelligent."

I explained to Father Englehart the corporation idea of three commissioners, one a judge of a United States district court, another appointed by the Indians, and a third by the Indian Bureau, who would supervise over a board of directors, composed of Menominees. The Indians would hold stock in this corporation.

" Yes," said the veteran Franciscan, " I believe that corporation idea would work."

But the fate of the Menominees does not lie with intelligent white men, familiar with the problem. It lies with distant Congress, and Congress has already denied the Menominees their freedom.

The real cause of the Menominees' failure, as pointed out in the July, 1930, issue of the *American Indian Life*, " was a devious opposition and obstructionism within the Indian Bureau, led by Assistant Commissioner Scattergood." But Representative Cramton was the individual responsible for preventing the Menominees' enabling act from reaching a House vote. What was the extent of his argument? He voiced it on the floor of the House:

" I am opposed to incorporation and these new fangled ideas."

XXVI

THE KLAMATH DISGRACE

1

A STOCKY Senator, square-faced and rugged, stood
upon the floor of the Chamber, and in no uncertain
terms announced to his colleagues that the manner in which the Klamath Indians have been governed is a
national disgrace.

That fearless speaker was Senator Lynn J. Frazier, Chairman of the Senate Investigating Committee. His speech has
been recorded in the Congressional Record of February 25,
1930.

" Mr. President," he said, " I am frank to say that, in
my opinion, after investigating and after visiting that
reservation . . . the way the Klamath Indians have been
handled is nothing short of a disgrace — a disgrace to the
local agency officials out there; a disgrace to the Indian
Bureau; a disgrace to the Department of the Interior; a

disgrace to Congress, and to the United States Government itself."

On the morning before his address Senator Frazier received a letter from Edward B. Ashurst, a prominent attorney at Klamath Falls, which borders the reservation. The letter set forth the present situation accurately and fully.

" The Indians at this time," wrote the lawyer, " are making a courageous effort against great odds to regain control of their tribal grazing lands in order that they may be self-sustaining.

" In this fight they are opposed by power livestock interests of southern Oregon, who have at their command great financial resources, and with these resources these livestock men have secured the support and backing of local newspapers, banks, and civic organizations."

The Klamath Reservation is located in an excessive elevation, so that timber and grazing are the only Indian resources; agriculture is impossible amid the perpetual frosts and cold spells. The Indians' grazing land has been leased to cattle and sheep concerns against their protests, and, as Senator Frazier pointed out, to their complete detriment. " The cattle have been stolen in some instances and the superintendent has failed to get any action in favor of the Indians," Frazier told the Senate, " and so they have practically been put out of business."

Inspector Trowbridge of the Indian Department investigated the Klamaths in 1928, and reported that the cattle and sheep leases should be abandoned, so that the Indians themselves might be allowed to graze their herds on the grass when it returned to normal. Almost needless to say, Inspector Trowbridge's recommendation was not seriously considered by the Indian Bureau.

Lawyer Ashurst supplied a reason for the departmental favoring of white interests in preference to its wards. " The superintendent of this reservation," he wrote, " has a very difficult position to occupy and fill. If he takes a stand in behalf of the Indians, in opposition to the livestock interests, to the timber interests, or the power interests, he, through political influence, is soon removed. . . .

" I feel that the department can not serve the interests of both the outside wealthy stockmen and the Indians. If they take a stand in behalf of the wealthy, influential stockmen and against the Indians, in view of what is taking place here, I am certain that things will come to light which will be a discredit to them."

The battle the Klamaths have been waging has been extremely unfair; the odds have been and still are too great against them. Their worst enemies have been the white men in charge of them, and the white parasites who live off their timber and land. As Mr. Ashurst expressed it: " The local newspapers are carrying on a strenuous and unfair fight against them; men of wealth and local influence are being induced to take a stand in behalf of powerful and wealthy outside stock interests and against the Indians."

2

What of the more specific rôles the Government has assumed in this drama of disgrace?

At a recent hearing held before the Senate Investigating Committee, Chairman Frazier asked Mr. Kinney of the Indian Bureau what punishment was meted out to the men who had been discovered taking money from the timber interests while employed at the Klamath agency. (Mr. Kinney had previously testified that Bureau officials had been caught pocketing bribes from timber concerns, which were purchasing Klamath timber). Mr. Kinney replied to the Senator's question by stating that the men were compelled to return the money to the companies. That was their only punishment. Senator Frazier has observed that the sops to Cerberus " are still on the pay roll on the Klamath Reservation."

More disgraceful than this action has been the not unprecedented procedure of the Klamath agency officials in arranging and accomplishing a stuffed Indian vote made with regard to their tribal problems. On Saturday, February 15, 1930, Mr. T. W. Wheat, clerk in charge of the Klamath Reservation, called the Indians together at Williamson River for a meeting, at which they were given instructions that the voting would be solely confined to the proposed forestry bill. At the conclusion of the voting on the said bill the majority of the Klamaths left the hall. Of the shady balloting that then took place the Indians' executive council wrote the following to Senator Frazier: " But Mr. Wheat, by a preconceived plan, arranged that a few Indians whom he had favored remained at the meeting house after the others had gone. After many Indians had gone, Mr. Wheat, and those working under his direction, caused a vote to be taken for the recall of our delegates and the leasing of our grazing lands. The vote . . . does not represent the wishes or the sentiments of our people. . . . We strongly protest against the unfair and fraudulent means which have been resorted to in securing this vote for the leasing of our lands and the recall of our delegates."

Attorney Ashurst has confirmed the Indians' account of this meeting in his letter: "I have, since the meeting, been well informed as to the trickery resorted to in securing this vote and feel it is my duty to advise you of the circumstances under which this vote was taken. . . .

"The fight that Mr. Crawford and the other delegates are making for the Indian stockmen of the reservation is meeting with the approval of 90 per cent of the Indians, but they are fighting against a combination which is hard to combat.

"Your committee [Frazier's] should take steps to see that the Department of Justice makes some investigation into this situation. And if this was done, they would find that considerable sums of money are and have been paid to a few of these councilmen for their vote against their people, and these councilmen are, while serving as councilmen, officials both of the Government and of the tribe, and these men who have bribed these Indians to sell out their people could and should be prosecuted for the bribing of Government officials."

Trowbridge, an honest inspector in the Service, reported in 1928 and again in 1929 regarding the above conditions, and added additional charges of gross mismanagement of funds and property. Unlike most Bureau inspectors he made constructive recommendations for obliterating the wrongs, but quite like the Indian Bureau no corrective action has been launched.

Finally, on February 7, 1930, the Senate Investigating Committee made a preliminary report (No. 158) in which they recommended to the Indian Bureau that the superintendent and the chief clerk " should at least be removed from that reservation." In 1928 the Committee discovered that each Klamath, man, woman, and child, was contributing $213 out of the tribal fund for agency salaries and expenses — a tax rate even intolerable to white communities. The Committee strongly objected to " an extravagant and extra-ordinarily inefficient administration by the superintendent, and second, to the efforts of the superintendent and certain of his subordinates to block the expression of the tribal will, to interfere with elections, and with the conduct of the tribal council and to discredit the Indians." The Committee declared of the superintendent, Arnold, and his finance clerk, Wheat, that " their retention in the Indian service in any capacity appears to the Subcommittee as a highly doubtful procedure, but their continuance at Klamath Reservation appears to the Subcommittee indefensible."

Commissioner Rhoads took no action on this report.

When recently discussing the Indian situation with Senator W. B. Pine in his office in Washington, he mentioned the Klamath case. " Our committee," he told me, " has strongly demanded Superintendent Arnold's resignation of Commissioner Rhoads. His reply was that he was 'going to make an investigation.' Why, his own files are full of investigations, by his own inspectors, by the Indians themselves, and by our committee.

"Those Klamaths are equal to the intelligence of white people who have been living in that territory for many years. One of their number is the district judge at Klamath Falls. They also have their own business committee. Yet their Bureau physician, Doctor Rogers, is racially prejudiced against Indians, although his salary is paid with their money. At our meeting on the reservation I observed that he ignored the Indians and refused to converse with them. They have demanded his discharge for he is their employee, but the Government has failed to fire him. In addition, he has refused to call on sick patients and has allowed them to die. A case of that sort was brought to the attention of Superintendent Arnold, and then to Commissioner Rhoads. Our committee likewise demanded his discharge, but Rhoads still keeps Arnold and Rogers out there."

3

The story of the Klamaths' loss of their timber through a " legal robbery " is too long to enumerate here. With their own cattle starving because the sheep of white men have eaten their grass clean to the fences, the Klamaths have watched the last tribal timber stand also dissipate into the hands of Whites. When they wired the Indian Commissioner protesting against their timber being sold at about $3 per thousand when the market price was $8, the following reply was received: " You people have no voice in your timber. I will sell the timber to whom I please at any price."

In 1918, following a five year period, the Klamaths lost 450,920,000 feet of timber, through a beetle pest and the wholesale negligence of the forestry service of the Indian Bureau.

The Indian Bureau today is continuing its capital disregard for the protection of Indian property. Indian timber, worth $130,000,000, is safeguarded from forest fires by a 1931 House appropriation of $50,000, or 1/2600th of the value of the timber.

Not as a panacea for all their ills, but as a positive means of constructive relief, the Klamaths are today looking toward the incorporation of the tribe with an undying hope. Senator McNary has introduced Senate Bill 4165, which the Indians pray will be voted on in the next session of Congress. The Menominees plan to mould their incorporation along the lines of the Klamaths, who have been the pioneers in this attempt to cast off the bonds of the Bureau. As Nelson A. Mason, clerk of Committee on Indian Affairs, wrote me, other tribes are beginning to view incorporation as their possible salvation. " This Committee," writes Mason, " has proposed a bill for the incorporation of this particular tribe [Klamath], however, it being understood that practically all Indian tribes of the United States are interested in such legislation."

Incorporation, above all other solutions, helps decentralize the Indian Bureau's tenacious hold on the Indian.

Senator Frazier, in his address in the Chamber, summarized the plight of the Klamaths, whose grazing lands have been leased from under them to white men, whose timber has been sold to lumber interests, whose money has been spent building roads for the sole benefit of those lumber interests and for a worthless irrigation project, costing up to date over $200,000 with additional expenditures every year. In concluding, the Senator from North Dakota stated: "Mr. President, so long as the Indian Bureau, the Department of the Interior, and the Congress of the United States sit back and allow conditions of the kind I have described to continue it seems to me impossible ever to better the condition of those Indians."

As the stocky, square-faced, rugged fighter of the Indians' cause wearily sat down, Senator Burton K. Wheeler of Montana obtained the floor. " I desire to ask the Senator," he said, " if the conditions on the Klamath Reservation are very different from the conditions that he found on practically all the other reservations."

" Oh, no, Mr. President," replied Senator Frazier, instantly arising to his feet. " Much the same situation exists, on a great many other reservations."

VI
CLAIMS

XXVII

YOU REMEMBER US NOT

1

CHARLIE CAMERON shuffles up a dusty road on the Bad River Reservation. Old Charlie Cameron, eighty-year-old Chippewa, with the purest Indian blood of any. Three-quarters Chippewa. Damn good nowadays.

Charlie Cameron, you have always wanted. Eighty years of gnawing want, weighted with a dull hope. The hope of a treaty, a broken treaty. Treaty of 1855.

First they told you: " Go, Chippewa, pick eighty acres. Washington will make them your allotment."

Five years later they told you: " Move on, Chippewa, this is not your allotment. You have not been living on your eighty acres. Plenty white men here to buy your eighty acres. Move on, Chippewa."

Move on. Move on. Ever moving Indians. First the Pigfoot Settlement, then Pickford, near Sault Sainte Marie.

Move on to the Shawville Mission, then to Bay Mill. No allotment, no home. Move on, Chippewa.

Charlie Cameron, the Indian boys and girls at the Bay Mill school were Indian boys and girls. They loved the running air of fields and woods. When the school bell rang for recess they rushed the door like buffalo calves stampeding. Your daughter, Emily, Charlie, sat in the back row; sat, and was caught on the outgoing flood on the first day recess. The shouting colts hurled her on the cement doorstep and broke the knee-cap.

Move on, Chippewa, move. Come into Wisconsin with the brother Chippewas. But moving is hard when daughter Emily lives in a wheel chair . . .

Charlie Cameron, you shuffle in the dust as if you lived your life walking. Charlie, with your bent back, leather face, and white shreds of hair above your lips; Charlie, sit here in the shade with me, as you did last year when I came. Tell me of the men your mother, Ke-Way-Ah-Bun-O-Quay, Returning East Woman, used to talk about.

" Long tam 'go Chip'wa live by Big Falls at end o' great string o' laks. Town now call Buffalo. When Georg Wash'-ton fight Rev'lutionarie War three Chip'wa be his scout. Zhin-Gaw-Bay-A-Sin, dat means Much Rock, was wan scout."

" Charlie, was he your great-great-grandfather? "

" Zhin-Gaw-Bay-A-Sin had daughter who had daughter who was Ke-Way-Ah-Bun-O-Quay, Returning East Woman."

He shuffles off to beg food for supper. Charlie Cameron, descendant of a Chippewa scout for George Washington, wanting and starving. Eighty years. Now alone in a shack at the end of the town, weeding other Indians' gardens for a meal and coffee.

Charlie Cameron, George Washington said he would not have won his Revolutionary War if it were not for your great-great-grandfather and his brothers.

Charlie Cameron, son of the American Revolution, Washington owes you eighty acres. America owes its existence to your ancestors, but it owes you several hundred dollars in Chippewa treaty money. Treaty of 1855.

2

There are a thousand Charlie Camerons. The United States Court of Claims is beseeched with their pleas. Senator Frazier has stated that there are hundreds of tribal, not individual, claims, begging for acknowledgment. Before the assembled Senate he stated the following:

In the past, treaties have been made with the Indians by the United States Government. . . . In every session of the Congress since I have been here the Indians and their representatives have come before the Indian Affairs Committee and asked for the privilege of going into the Court of Claims to establish claims against the United States Government for violation of treaties, and many of those requests have been granted; and there are many cases now pending in the Court of Claims of the United States to test out the violation of those treaties.[1]

Senator Frazier continued by stating the time when he

[1] *Congressional Record.* March 1, 1928.

investigated the affairs of the Minnesota Chippewa Indians, whose treaties had been violated by an act of Congress, which had been sponsored by the Minnesota representatives. The gauntlet of procedure, through which a tribe must run in order to present their claims, has been fully described by the following case of Senator Frazier:

The result of the investigation was that the committee recommended the passage of a measure to give the Chippewa Indians of Minnesota the right to go before the Court of Claims and establish their claims there against the Government of the United States. The bill was passed in the Senate. It went over to the House and was referred to the Committee on Indian Affairs over there. That committee changed the measure considerably, and it came back here amended so that the attorneys for the Chippewa Indians claimed that it would be useless. It was referred back to the Committee on Indian Affairs here, and we put up a fight, and the bill was put back in its original form, and finally passed; and the Chippewa Indians, through their attorneys, have cases filed in the Court of Claims to establish their rights.[2]

Senator Frazier concluded this case by asserting that he *" might go on almost indefinitely and cite cases where the Indians have been defrauded."* In this discussion of Indian claims we will not go on indefinitely, which I confirm is almost possible.[3]

[2] *Congressional Record.* March 1, 1928.
[3] For further information see the five-page petition submitted to the Senate Investigating Committee, beginning with the allegation "That the Chippewa Indians of Minnesota have and claim various grievances against the United States growing out of the act of Congress of January 14, 1889," et cetera. Hearings. Part 5. 1929. P. 2031.

3

Scattered throughout the Upper Peninsula of Michigan are groups of Chippewas, who once lived in a picturesque Indian village on the banks of the St. Mary's rapids. Today they are living in the direst poverty, in the worst destitution possible. No Government field nurse or doctor circulates among them, and as a consequence of this neglect they are rapidly being decimated.

Old, indigent Indians have told me, spaciously moving their arms around the horizon, that not long ago thousands of their fellows were living healthily. Today one sees only the remnants.

In 1820 Governor Cass of Michigan acknowledged the Chippewas' right to the land on which their village was camped, by granting them a perpetual right to its 36½ acres. Those days, I have been told by aged Indians, were a paradise. There was plenty of whitefish in the St. Mary's River; the Indians removed tons every day by merely dipping their nets in the rapids. At two and three cents a pound some made as high as $75 a day, or between three and four thousand dollars a season, which supported them throughout the winter.

But such happiness was doomed, as almost every Indian happiness has been doomed. On July 31, 1855, the United States Government accomplished a treaty with the Sault Indians, which permitted Washington to negotiate with the Indians for the sale of their lands. The cause of this sudden interest on the part of the Government was founded three years previously, in 1852, when a state lock was constructed for conveying boats between lakes Huron and Superior. This lock was built on Indian land without their consent. The Government, in 1855, through some strange fit of conscience, began negotiations with the Indians for their land.

The Chippewas, however, were reluctant to relinquish their perpetual right. The Government officials, on the other hand, were not to be stumped by a tribe of Indians, who merely loved the land they lived on with an undying love, hard for the bureaucrats to comprehend. Locks had to be built for the trade, and the nature-devotion of an obstinate tribe was not to hinder construction. So the Government officers packed a few of the chiefs into a boat and sailed for Detroit. I have been told by old Chippewas that those kidnapped chiefs were given a "hot time." Made drunk with liquor and women, six of them signed away the rights of the twelve chiefs who consummated the 1820 treaty. This Detroit affair, for a time, was kept secret; the Government was fully aware that the true representatives of the tribe had not been consulted.

What of the compensation of the August 2, 1855, or Detroit treaty? One of the signing chiefs was given an island for his personal use. All six were given lumps of money. But what compensation was doled out to the tribe itself? Each Indian was given $19.01. Upon being informed that they had sold their perpetual right and the $19.01 was their share, the Indians were dumbfounded. Many refused to abandon their village, saying that they had signed no treaty. The Bureau officers threatened them with soldiers; the Indians were told their village would be burned and bullets would kill their women and children, if they did not move. The Chippewas had no choice. The "White Father" was strong with his thousands of muskets. Silently they removed the buckskin from the tepee poles, folded it into bundles, and shuffled quietly away.

But leaders of the tribe went down fighting; they would not be silently beaten into submission. Letters were written to the Indian Bureau, protesting the ridiculous sum of $19.01 for the valuable site. George W. Manypenny, then Commissioner of Indian Affairs, wrote the Chippewas on October 14, 1856: "I have awarded all that I believe it to be worth."

Today more tonnage passes through the locks at Sault Saint Marie than through the Panama Canal. The Treasury of the United States receives its major waterway revenue from the Soo locks. In addition, it is estimated that the Government receives $75,000 a year from power plants for the use of the Indians' water — Indians, who were only given $19.01 a head for the most valuable 36½ acres west of Niagara Falls and east of the Black Hills.

New leaders of the scattered Michigan Chippewas are today writing the Indian Bureau, but with no more success than their predecessors. The wrong has not been rectified. In the meanwhile " Crookneck " Brown lives in a crumbling shack by the city dumping grounds of Sault Saint Marie, his wife sick, his family hungry and poorly clothed. There are hundreds of " Crookneck " Browns.

4

Antoine Francis, you are a good Indian. You have seen and talked to fine white people. You want to paint your house, improve your house. Good thing, Antoine Francis, but watch Maggie Sharlow, Maggie of the Lost Tribe.

David Blackbird, your grandfather, bought the land your house is on. Bought it from John Frenchman, the great log runner. Played with logs like toothpicks. John Frenchman had a son John Frenchman; white folks called it junior.

Then came Maggie Sharlow, running all summer like a heated bitch with first young Diver then Livingston.

John Frenchman Senior, John Frenchman Junior, living two arrow shots away, is sick and dying in the fall. Maggie, Maggie, big in the belly, why do you walk those arrow shots? Why do you keep the Frenchman house throughout the fall? Four weeks go like the autumn leaves, and Senior Frenchman is dead and buried. Four weeks follow like the fleeing geese, and Junior Frenchman, ailing, lies beside his father. Dead in November. Dead at the close of fall.

Antoine Francis, spring is here. Up and stirring. Buds are out in May. Maggie's belly's thin and shaggy. Buds are out in May. Buds have fathers, many fathers. John Frenchman's child, she is screaming. Do you hear that, good Antoine Francis? A black sheep's in the Indian fold.

" Certainly, Maggie's baby is the heir to the Frenchman's estate," so say the Government officers. Antoine Francis owns a home on the Frenchman estate. Antoine Francis, give your home to Maggie.

But you have spent $1300 on improvements, and the price old David Blackbird paid to Senior Frenchman, Antoine. The Government owes you $1300. Walk into the office of Farmer Dohn; he has your money in a slip of paper, waiting for your signature.

Antoine Francis, do you not know the ways of white men? White men called the Indian Bureau employees. White men's ways run deep. The check is turned over, face downwards. Dohn offers you a pen. Write your name on the back, Antoine.

Antoine Francis, you are an Indian, a damn good Indian. You have endorsed your check for $1300; but do you not see Dohn put it back into the safe, turn the combination, and stand smiling at you: "I'll keep it here. That will be all now, Antoine. Thank you."

Yes, he should thank you. Pierce the safe door with your hard, steel glasses. Glasses called the Indian eye. See your check, drawn on your savings, the savings of a lifetime. What are the numbers that you read there? Yes, two — seven — eight — zero. Yes, two thousand, seven hundred, and eighty dollars. $2780! Antoine Francis, why do you crumble like a corn stalk in the snow? . . . Why are you cold like ice in the noonday heat? . . .

5

The above tale is all fact. Anyone can read it in either the law records at Madison, Wisconsin, under the title: 60F in Equity, April 16, 1928, case of Maggie Sharlow and Ke-de-Kwe-Simon versus Veronica Raiche and Joseph

Raiche; or, you can read the confession of the Indian Bureau employees in the expurgated portion of the Senate Investigating Hearings, Part Five, held at Lac du Flambeau, Wisconsin, on July 10, 1929.

There are countless other claims of individual Indians against the Government through the corruption and graft of Indian Bureau officers — too numerous to even enumerate.

Of the dozens of tribal claims perhaps the most sensational is the one most recently disclosed by the Senate Investigating Committee. Philadelphia, Mississippi, is the center of a number of Choctaw communities, and in that locality the investigating Senators have discovered " actual peonage."

The Treaty of Dancing Rabbit Creek of 1830 established the rights of the Choctaws; they were granted 140,000 acres of land. By various devices about 70,000 acres of their inheritance have been acquired by Whites. The Indian Bureau has been issuing patent-in-fees to the Choctaws, but the deeds to lands aggregating 25,000 acres have never been delivered to the Indians. The Whites, consequently, have been living on Indian land, the titles to which have never yet been divested from the Indians. The Government has made itself a party in this defrauding of the Choctaws; the Bureau has not ejected " squatters," nor has it prohibited Whites from securing title by " adverse possession," which is in this case contrary to the law.

" As a result," said Senator Lynn Frazier, in the December 2, 1930, issue of *Labor: A National Weekly Newspaper,* " many are now living as ' share croppers ' on land rightfully their own. They are kept constantly in debt and not allowed to leave one landlord for another until these debts are satisfied. The system of peonage is so well established that we found evidence that a standard price had been set for the transfer of an Indian family from planter to planter. One old Indian had worked 20 years for the same planter and was still in debt, although he was unable to account for the manner in which these obligations have been incurred."

The "standard price" for a transferal is $600, which "buys him over for the next year." Those Mississippi Choctaws have been and still are living in slavery, comparable only to pre-Civil War days in the South. They are dealt with as horses or cattle — more like the auction-block slave of New Orleans — than as humans. They are given a bare living for their work, but can not share in the profits of their own land and their own labor. They are good farmers, the white landlords will tell you; they raise much cotton, like their darker brothers-in-the-spirit. They can not, or dare not, quit their labors; they are held until their indefinite indebtedness is paid. Since the landlord does all the bookkeeping, the Indian never gets any money and consequently can never pay his debts. Not at any time, however, are they legally in debt. This imprisonment for civil debt is contrary to the Constitution.

Dr. R. J. Enochs, superintendent and physician at Philadelphia, Mississippi, wrote his superiors at Washington with regard to this unlawful peonage. He was told that the matter was "none of his business." At the December, 1930, hearings of this case the entire Washington office was present, but no official knew anything about the situation.

The Yakima Indians in the State of Washington have a claim against the Federal Government for the manner in which Superintendent Evan W. Estep has conducted his corrupt leasing-ring with neighboring whites, all of which has been exposed in Part One of the Hearings.

The Sisseton Sioux on the Sisseton Indian Reservation in Northeastern South Dakota have a singular claim against their superintendent, Willihan, who likewise conducted an alleged leasing-ring with confidential whites.

The Yankton Sioux, in the southeastern part of the same state, have made like complaints against the manner in which Chief Clerk Dixon leases Indian lands. Arthur Stone has told me that his wife's heirship land has been leased to whites over his head, making it difficult for him to farm with his acreage divided.

There are thousands of Arthur Stones on dozens of reservations; there are, moreover, scores of tribal claims; but there is only one Indian Bureau, with apparently only one policy.

What is that policy? In the exceptional exertions of George T. Stormont, Court of Claims counselor from the Department of Justice, we see that policy clearly reflected. Although Stormont has spent a lifetime in the Department he has dismissed only six cases in 12 years. Functioning at a one-claim-in-two-year rate it will take 172 years for Stormont and his successors to dismiss the 86 cases now listed. During the fiscal year of 1930 eight claims were filed against the Federal Government from tribes located in California, Oregon, Washington, Nebraska, Oklahoma, and Montana; it will take 16 years alone to dismiss these cases. If one may assume that no more claims will be listed after 1937, and those filed till then will be done so at the rate of only eight a year, the last Indian claim will be dismissed in the year 2210 A.D. At the present speed of decimation there probably will be no Indians alive when that final decision is surreptitiously handed down.

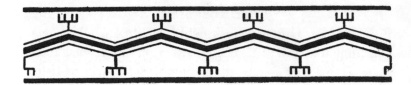

XXVIII
STILL FORGOTTEN

1

I HAD traveled almost half a mile beyond Mole Lake before I realized that I had overdriven the camping ground of the Lost Tribe, so unassuming were the desolate shacks of those forgotten Indians. As I swung my car around and retraced the road I thought of how my oversight was so similar to that of the Indian Bureau. During the past three-quarters of a century the bureaucrats have paid little attention to that forbidding cluster of huts.

I found the members of the lost band more intelligent than I anticipated. Their history sounded coherent, their arguments logical, and their plea restrained and unemotional.

"The Government in 1860 originally surveyed a reservation for us," Willard Ackley told me, "which was to be twelve miles square, comprising more than four townships. That is a fact, because Roe Vaughn, who lives not far away, helped survey the land."

"We were a large band then," spoke up his old father, Dewit Ackley, "and numbered about 2,000." His eyes wandered from our group. "Now," he said, "there are only about 150 of us left."

Through a wholesale medical and industrial neglect on the part of the Indian Bureau the Lost Tribe has decimated more than 13 times over.

The Indians sent a petition to Senator Frazier, stating their case, its history, and their hope for some favorable action. In July, 1921, and again in December, 1928, they had made previous complaints; the May 21, 1929, petition to the Senate Investigating Committee was their third, and most recent.

"While we are members of the same tribe," they wrote, "and descendants of the tribe that made treaty with the Government in 1854, we have at no time been justly compensated as have the members of the other bands. The enrollment of this band, which was made officially by the Government on August 2, 1920, has meant nothing to us so far. At least this band has benefited in no way by such enrollment. Further, that none of the good promises made by the Government inspectors and representatives have been carried out." [1]

Interested in their history, I asked the members of the band, who had assembled during my conversation with the Ackleys, of any additional Federal recognition.

[1] Hearings Before a Subcommittee, etc. Part Five. July, 1929. P. 1983.

" Two of our old chiefs, Ma-ge-zee and Kay-she-wa-be-sah-she, were given medals by the Government," they answered. I recalled the Indian Bureau's custom of giving old chiefs large silver medals as a sign of recognition and friendship. In many cases the Bureau considered its obligation fulfilled upon the presentation of those ornaments.

" But after our chiefs died there was nobody to fight our case," they continued. " We were recognized and then forgotten."

Inspectors from the Bureau, however, have called on those Indians from time to time; they have repeatedly assured them of a reservation, but nothing has materialized.

Inspector Wooster of Washington, the Indian Bureau's latest delegate to the Lost Tribe, has told me that in his opinion the band has no claim; he recommended that only 13 out of the entire tribe of reservationless Chippewas should be recognized. This reversal of the previous inspectors' decisions has had the effect of a dash of cold water on the partly frozen Indians. They have lived on hope for almost seventy years, only to find that today, in this " reform administration," the white man's words are more dirtied than ever with lies. Since 1860 the fathers of the Lost Tribe have retold their sons the promises made to Chief Ne-geek, the sage Moses of the band; but the fathers in 1930 have sat before their attentive sons, and no word has passed.

How does the Lost Tribe manage to exist today? I visited them in the fall of 1930, after Wooster had made his report. Hopelessness had mingled with desolation. A month before the medical examiners in the Crandon-Wabena clinic told me that they had never seen such specimens of neglect. They said that dirt was caked on their bodies, and vermin of all sorts were in their skin and hair.

I found most of them living in tents. Some lived in old bark shacks, totally inadequate to keep out the cold in winter. The men were constantly seeking employment. The indefinite state of their livelihood has had a bad influence on them, morally and physically.

Once the tribe owned large, virgin forests, but a lumbering concern from Escanaba, Michigan, and another from Shawano, Wisconsin, descended upon them and swept their forests as clean as a sand beach. "We would have had a fine reservation, like the Menominees, if the Government fulfilled its promise," Willard Ackley said to me, and his face animated as he spoke of the Menominee Reservation.

Aside from their government troubles the Lost Tribe has had to deal with a more formidable exploiter in the personage of a certain man whose particular racket has consisted of extracting exhorbitant fees for letters written to Washington. The band, as poor as it is, has already paid him the equivalent of $125 in labor, rice, and cash. "He wants $300 now before he sends any more letters," one member informed me.

Pat Monroy, an Indian of Mole Lake, Wisconsin, has written an unexploiting letter, intermingled with sympathy and humor, with regard to his neighbors, the Lost Tribe. He wrote the following to the Lac du Flambeau agent, supposedly in charge of the band:

" And nothing don't seem to do them any good, and of course there's no one looking after them. And I am a thinking that they will be killing each other.

" I really don't know just how we can stop them. The men are fighting their wives and I don't think that's right.

" I would like to know what can be done in order to settle them down. If you can help out any way about giving them a law. . . ."

2

Of all the groups of Indians, who today hold pieces of paper, " dirtied with a lie," the case of California's first settlers is one of the most hopeless and pitiful.

When the United States annexed the State of California there were between 100,000 and 150,000 Indians residing in the fair land of advertising agencies. Upon the discovery of gold, the white man, ever the Indians' Machiavelli, swooped upon the first natives. The Whites wanted the land; so in 1850 and 1851 the commissioners appointed by President Fillmore negotiated 18 treaties with 119 different tribes of California Indians. The treaties called for the surrender of land covering the greater portion of the state, for which the Indians were to receive reservations totaling 7,500,000 acres. The 119 tribes, trusting the envoy of the President of the United States, signed the treaties and relinquished their lands. However, the Senate, influenced by California's gold seekers and pioneers, refused to ratify the treaties. The 7,500,000 acres rapidly disappeared into white hands, but no compensation of any sort was paid the Indians. Today, those negotiations are still known as the *Eighteen Lost Treaties* — a black page in a dark book of treaty-making.

Driven from their cultivable lands by endless waves of emigrants, the Indians were pushed back, back into arid wastes, back into rock-infested mountains. Eph Cummins of Calaveras County has enacted a typical scene of what befell the California Indians. Cummins nine times cleared and cultivated a small portion of earth, and eight times he was driven off his land by white settlers, who assumed control of his acreage. Each time he cultivated a new plot it was on land more remote and less desirable than the preceding selection. His ninth choice was on land so arid that no white man wanted it, and at last Cummins was hounded no more and he lived in peace, won at the expense of poverty.

Conscience-stricken, the Government has from time to time set aside small tracts, known as Executive Order Reservations. What has been the nature of those lands? They have been the least desirable of the public lands — those portions which the white settlers have refused to buy or homestead. Investigations have coincided in the belief "that a very small portion of the land that has been set aside for Indian use, in the form of reservations or of allotments to individual Indians, can be cultivated and even that which is arable is almost without water."

"Some of the allotments," wrote the 1920 Board of Indian Commissioners, "are so thickly covered with bowlders that it is possible to walk over acres without setting foot on soil."

The *American Indian Life's* fourth bulletin has summarized the status of California's hopeless Indians as follows:

" Landless, or with worthless land, and for the most part homeless, the California Indian has been reduced to a deplorable economic level. Naturally this process of dispossession, with its solemn promises made and broken, has left a deep psychological mark on the race — a mark that must be taken into account in all efforts to understand and to help the Indian of today."

Americans of circus-tastes, who have gone by the thousands every year to view the medicine shows of Hollywood, see the pretentious, conspicuous movie palace of Jackson Barnett, an illiterate, wealthy, and robbed Indian of Oklahoma, and believe California's 18,000 Indian survivals fare as well.

The solution? Progressive legislators of California have seen the hopelessness of Federal administration. The Swing-Johnson Bill would provide for state education, health, and relief. But the California Indians, being Federal wards, must first be released by an act of Congress, through the recommendation of the Indian Bureau. This approval and enactment have not yet been secured. The Pharaoh has not been willing to let God's children go free. . . .

3

In another case, where the Indian Bureau has doled out a reservation to postmortuary Indians, the land so granted has turned out to be highly unsatisfactory. For over a century the Seminole Indians of Florida have been homeless.

While in an unusual conscientious quandary the Indian Bureau recently granted the remnants of the tribe a reservation, which, however, is today being questioned as to its utility. Lawrence E. Lindley, associate secretary of the Indian Rights Association, wrote me the following under date of September 16, 1930:

> I am under the impression that very few if any of the Seminoles are now occupying this land set apart for them and I believe the question has been raised as to whether the reservation is very valuable to them under the present conditions.

No wonder; it was staked out in swamp lands and everglades.

Paramount among the instances where the Indians were granted a reservation, only to have it taken away without compensation, is the pending case of the seven Sioux tribes, who have not yet been paid for the Black Hills — a case discussed in the first portion of this book. However, in passing, the opinion of Congressman Cramton with regard to this claim might be repeated. He has stated that " if the Indians get a judgment the money should be used for maintaining schools and agency buildings." The Sioux, on the contrary, have a grievance against the agency offices now maintained on the Yankton Reservation, which they claim to be already overloaded with superfluous employees and equipment. Over ninety per cent of those Indians have been turned loose, but the personnel has not been reduced accordingly. " In fact," Ben Vandal said to me, " I was in the service twenty-five years ago and they had as many employees then as now."

The Sioux living in North and South Dakota have additional claims with regard to 40,000 head of their cattle, which were shipped out of the country by Government officials with neither the consent of nor any compensation to the Indians. Mrs. Gertrude Bonnin, President of the National Council of American Indians, has been working on this case for some time. Her additional claims are as follows:

On the Omaha and Winnebago Reservations in Nebraska the non-taxable Indian lands, held in trust by the Government, are nevertheless taxed with the inevitable result that they are rapidly being sold for non-payment of taxes. The Indians are helpless, for their land is leased through the Government office for less than the taxes.

On the Uintah and Ouray Reservations in Utah the Indians once owned a beautiful valley, in which five streams had their headwaters. In 1902 the Government allotted some of the land to the tribes, and opened the balance to settlement by Whites at $1.25 an acre, whereupon the State of Utah assumed control of the water in the five streams. In 1906 Congress passed an act which provided for the construction of an elaborate irrigation system, costing well over a million dollars. When this was completed the old Indian canal systems, which had adequately met the Indians' needs for years, were destroyed. The entire irrigation system was placed upon the backs of the Indians as a reimbursable debt, and later it became a lien against their individual allotments. Yet the Indians, whenever they desire their own water from the ditches which are charged to them, must first secure permission from the Whites. The maintenance charges, nevertheless, are also yearly listed on the red side of the Indians' ledger; those charges are constantly accumulating against the tribes' land. At present the Indians' acres are being consumed by Whites. In time, they will be homeless.

Another case, another claim, another long wait.

XXIX

SCRAPS OF PAPER

1

THE dome of law looms loudly over the Venice of the West. More loudly than its twin dome of learning. On one warm, quiet morning, July 8 of the year 1929, legislative hullabaloo gave way to the hearing of a restrained, dignified plea from a broken people.

Senators Frazier, Wheeler, and La Follette, of the Senate Investigating Committee, sat in the State Capital Building at Madison, Wisconsin, and listened to William Skenandore, an Oneida Indian and chairman of his tribe's council.

"We are not going to ask you," he stated to the Committee, "to appropriate a penny to feed our mouths or to clothe our backs, although we are in destitution and receive an annuity of 56 cents a year to provide for our clothing, domestic animals, farming implements, household utensils, and to pay the instructors. . . .

"All we are going to ask you is to see that our cases are

carefully examined, and should you find that wrongs have been perpetrated . . . make such suggestions and recommendations as would be conducive to the protection of these Indians. . . .

" We are making the same plea to you at our time of distress as was made to the Oneidas by Maj.-Gen. Philip Schuyler at the time of the distress of the American people to free themselves from the tyranny of taxation without representation."

What is the case of the Oneidas? Their tribal council has succeeded in recording over a dozen closely printed pages of testimony in the Committee's hearings, all of which is too lengthy and detailed to warrant repetition here. (Those interested see U. S. Senate Hearings, Part Five. Pp. 1918–1930.) However, two paragraphs of the Oneida's plea are worth quoting whole, as they serve as an appetizer to the entire document:

We are not only going to show how the fee simple patents to the Oneidas have been issued to them, regardless of their competency as interpreted to the Oneidas here by a Senator in 1909, which is one of the causes of the present pathetic conditions of the Oneidas, but we are also going to show that our constitutional treaty and lawful rights have been disregarded, violated, ignored, and trampled upon, caused, as you will see, by a desperate, despotic, oppressive, and adroit bureau, which has reduced the Oneidas from a powerful, loyal, self-supporting, progressive, and merciful people, to insignificance, as to-day they are helpless, ignored, their man power sapped and looked upon by the bureau with contempt, contrary to the strong friendship created in the early struggles together for freedom, and guaranteed to be perpetual.

We are also going to show instances that the bureau has practiced deception and corruption, and has not only deceived the
Indian, but has also deceived Congress as to our status, which
was responsible to have Congress enact laws in conformity to the
recommendations of the bureau, which has been the cause of untold suffering, losses, and embarrassment on the part of the Oneidas, which you are going to hear and see directly from them.[1]

The Oneidas' original rights in New York State had been
so trespassed by 1821 and 1822 that they, together with
the St. Regis, Stockbridges, Munsee, and Brothertown Indians, migrated to Wisconsin to live on 1,300,000 acres
which they bought from the Menominees and Winnebagoes
with their own money.

The Oneidas' troubles began in August, 1887, when
they finally succumbed to the unctuous inducements and
bribes of the Indian Bureau, who offered the Indians a
twenty-five-thousand-dollar cash consideration if they
would accept allotment. The tribe accepted allotment, however, " only to define the limits of the property of the individual so that no one else could trespass upon it." The
Indian Bureau, on the other hand, did not value the Indians'
opinion, for they compelled 2,700 of them to take allotments with the sad and inevitable result that all but 21
were put on the tax roll. Of the 2,700 who were unwilling,
in fact, unknowingly, taxed — " most of the Indians have
lost their land."

The case of Henry Doxtater is but one of several thousand: He and his family were ejected by the sheriff from
their home, because they could not pay the taxes imposed

[1] Hearings Before a Subcommittee, etc. Part Five. July 8, 1929. P. 1926.

unconstitutionally upon their dwelling. They were forcibly removed " with fire, gas, and ax, contrary to the protection guaranteed in the Constitution, in Article VI, section 1, that 'all debts contracted and engagements entered into, before the adoption of this Constitution, shall be as valid against the United States under this Constitution as under the Confederation.' "

Of the claims, enumerated verbally before the Committee, there was one with regard to the treaty of 1794, under which " we were to get annuities, and it was reported on January 12, 1927, that there was 500 names that were not paid out."

Statler King, also of Oneida, Wisconsin, addressed the investigating Senators, saying: " We feel that we have some claims against the Government under our treaty rights, but it seems we can not do anything. . . . The Government have not kept their treaties with the Indians, and we are losing our lands and being taxed and are having a hard time getting along — many of the Indians have no homes and are in destitute circumstances." [2]

The Chairman of the Oneida Tribal Council, by specifically setting forth what action was necessary and what his people desired, has summarized the case of the Oneidas:

" What we want is a jurisdictional act to be passed by Congress permitting us to go into the Court of Claims so that claims based on the various treaties I have mentioned may be determined. We have been trying to do that but when the Indian Bureau found it out they served notice on us."

[2] Hearings Before a Subcommittee, etc. Part Five. July 8, 1929. P. 1930.

2

What of the New York Indians, descendants of the mighty and cultured Six Nations, who were not carted westward by the Government?

Recent hearings by the Senate Investigating Committee have exposed many exceptional conditions existent among the Indians of the Nation's wealthiest state.

For example, it was discovered that on the Salamanca Reservation, which contains a city of 10,000 population including large railway yards, factories, hotels, and business districts, the land within the city limits has been granted on a 99-year lease by an 1892 act of Congress. The enactment, as usual, did not guarantee protection to the Indians in making the lease. The urban Whites, with the aid of whisky and bribery, succeeded in doping the Indians, in true melodramatic style, to the point where they signed for a total rental of $8,000 a year. A prosperous city of 10,000 pays eighty cents per head for the use of its land for twelve months. Unfortunately, the lease has 61 years yet to run.

This Salamanca leasing scandal shows the need for a veto power over such property transactions and corporate affairs, invested possibly in a joint commission of Indian, Federal, and State authorities.

The Senate Investigating Committee discovered that the city of Syracuse was preparing to secure the Onondaga Reservation by force so that it might build a flood protection dam. The citizens of Syracuse believed it infinitely cheaper to take unprotected Indian land than to deal in the open market with intelligent Whites.

The Senate hearings also disclosed Indian land as involved with white manufacturing industries, power-sites, and flood control districts, of which many titles are clouded by the Indians' primal ownership.

The *Courier-Express* of Buffalo recently ran a series of articles dealing with the conditions among New York's Indians. They exposed the neglect of the health work, the inadequate education, and the meager roads provided for the Indians' transportation. Arthur C. Parker, an Indian and curator of the Rochester Municipal Museum, in his final article declared the New York reservations to be the " white man's shame."

The articles were not wholly destructive; they pointed out the positive need for a plan to aid Indian farmers, financially and educationally; they also disclosed the general need for vocational training.

There are about 5,000 Indians in New York, many of whom claim they are not subject to either State or Federal supervision. They are anxious to establish their status. The Snell Bill (H. R. 9720) would do that precisely, by transferring to the State of New York Federal jurisdiction over the Indians. The United States has obviously been vested with the authority to supervise New York's Indians, but such supervision has never been fully achieved. As it is today they live " under a twilight jurisdiction." Both the Federal and State governments claim all and nothing in the same breath.

New York Indians have been in the position of an unwashed orphan, uncared for by either its step-father or step-mother, and apparently unwanted by both.

3

You will find the Wisconsin Winnebagoes camped along the state highways, living in bands like gypsies. They sell wild berries and baskets. They travel during the summer from one berry patch to another, picking strawberries, blueberries, June berries, cranberries, raspberries, and any sort of berry they can find. You will see them following the county fairs about the state, selling their wares and dancing at powwows. With the first cold draught of winter they disappear. Nobody knows how they live through the severe Wisconsin winters. This much, however, is known: Every spring fewer and fewer of their number reappear upon the waysides of highways and at the powwow grounds of fairs. Soon, like the nomads that they are, they will fold their tents for the last time and stoically steal away, never to return in this unhappy hunting ground.

Such was not always the status of the Winnebagoes. Once they were the mightiest tribe in the Middle West, owning the land between Lake Michigan and the Mississippi, comprising the states of Wisconsin, Minnesota, and Iowa. It was a magnificent stretch of territory, rich in resources of timber, lead, zinc, and copper, not to mention the thousands of tillable acres — an empire within itself. Those lands of Canaan were relinquished to the United States Government in a series of treaties, beginning in 1818. Thousands upon thousands of acres of hardwood and white pine forests, along with the water power rights on the Wisconsin, Fox, and Black rivers, and countless acres of farm lands were all signed away.

What was the Indians' compensation? For the birthright to their lands they received far less than the proverbial mess of pottage. First, about 300 of the vast tribe were given a reservation in the Turkey River country, which was soon taken from them when the value of the land became apparent. Finally in 1863, when the Federal government felt the Winnebagoes had become a general nuisance, a report was circulated among the Indians, saying that they were to receive a reservation in Minnesota and South Dakota, on the richest soil those states afforded. After the Winnebagoes had assembled, awaiting their migration, the Federal authorities held them in security for a year, and finally, with the aid of soldiers, forcibly removed them by water to the mountainous portions of desolate Nebraska, on land the Omaha Indians no longer desired.

I have talked to old Indians, who as children were members of that terrible death march, one of the blackest scenes in the history of Indian affairs. They have told me of their journey into the wilderness, of their hardships as pitiful as those endured by another band of God's children, when they wandered toward a promised land.

" The soldiers scared us with their guns and fierce looks," I have been told. " We children and the old folks trembled all the way. Over half died on the journey and many died out there. We had never been away from home before."

Many fell by the way, never again to stand beside their

brothers. With the passing of each week the lines grew visibly thin, until a mere skeleton of the tribe was finally deposited on the dreary soil of Nebraska.

The moment the soldiers took themselves back to civilization, the Winnebagoes began to return quietly to the land of their birth. Some stayed behind, but many retraced those terrible steps. Like Sitting Bull, who said that he would rather have his freedom with the game scarce than life on a reservation with rations, the Winnebagoes sought to keep burning within themselves their spiritual love for the earth the Great Spirit gave them.

The Winnebagoes have valid claims against the Government of the United States, which have not been settled. Congressman Merlin Hull of Wisconsin, in addressing the Senate Investigating Committee at Madison, has stated: " Some of my best friends are Winnebagoes and they have been trying for 25 years to get their treaty rights. . . . The treaty rights of the Winnebagoes have been violated in many instances and no adequate recompense, if any, has been made."

In an interview with Superintendent Dickens, after observing some of the Winnebagoes' deplorable tepees, he told me that he considered them the " worst beggars of all the northern tribes." " They were farming and getting along well," he said, " until the Government got out from under. Since then there has been no supervision or education. They have drifted about the state rather hopelessly; I am continually approached by additional Winnebagoes seeking aid. This winter will be a tough one, and many will suffer."

Of the Winnebagoes who remained in Nebraska their condition has been likewise described as "intolerable" by reports of Indian friends, including the forty-seventh annual report of the Indian Rights Association, published in 1930.

4

Mike White Eagle, hereditary leader of the Wisconsin Winnebagoes, is a chief without a tribe. He is a pathetic figure, more pathetic than the Man without a Country, for the sorrows of a thousand of his brothers lie heavy on his over-burdened heart. Chief Mike White Eagle, the wisest, most respected among an ill-reputed tribe, lives in squalid quarters. I have seen the table he eats off and the bed he sleeps on, and I know. Yet his home is a Spanish villa compared to the tepees of his brothers.

I go to him in his shack in Oshkosh, Wisconsin, where he works as a painter.

"My people," says Chief Mike White Eagle, "are scattered to the four winds. Once, before the white man came, we were wealthy, but now we are the poorest of all Indian tribes. We have no reservation; the old people have no way to earn a living. In the winter we all starve, even though the Government gives $3 a month for food.

"The agent bought land for a few, but it was Mississippi river bottom land and was always overflooded. One fellow had to tie a cable from his cabin to a tree, to keep his house from floating away. You can't farm under water. Even the Whites can't make a living there. A few got some other land, in Jackson County, but that was all sand and good for nothing."

" Could your people farm if good land is provided? " I ask.

" Yes," he answers, " we can if we receive intelligent instruction. Indians and white people are alike. They are the same people, only their skins are different.

" By our treaty rights the Government should give us a good home. When I write to the Indian office I get no answer. Mrs. Ben Hooper, a humanitarian clubwoman in town, went to Washington but it did no good. It is all red tape. We get no answer. We get no chance to live."

What a calm yet bottomless depth to that pitiful plea.

The chief tells me of law firms in Washington who have told him that they would take his people's claims against the Government for a twenty-odd per cent fee. " I never expect anything from those fellows," the Chief says.

" But present conditions are not right," he continues. " We should be given a reservation on the land where we were in the first place. The Government ought to send inspectors among us to see how we are living and trying to earn money. Last winter was a tough winter. This winter will be worse. Many will freeze. Many will starve."

As I take my leave he stands in the doorway of his shack, looking at me. " We want somebody," he says, earnestly, " to show the Government and the people how bad our condition really is. We want somebody to help us that way, so we might get a home, good farm land — a chance to live."

I look at him silently, nod, and go away.

XXX

ROBBING THE ROBBED

1

OLD TOM KESHICK, son of Big Chief Kee-zhic, sits all day on a fallen log. Sits and feels the mission of his blood. Big Chief Kee-zhic led his people, soothed and comforted his people. From the prairies he led them, like the white chief Moses, dying and wanting, to the woods, to the uncut woods of another land. A King's land. Canada.

Old Tom Keshick sits all day on a fallen log. Sits until he calls his daughters: "We go riding to our brothers." For many years the daughters take him riding over northern Michigan, all Wisconsin, calling on Chippewa, Ottawa, Pottawatomi. Year by year old Tom Keshick's paper swells, swells with the names of Chippewa, Ottawa, Pottawatomi. "Soon I go on Washin'ton."

Old Tom Keshick, it will do you no good to go to Washington. Others have gone to Washington. Chief Naw-

Nee-Nuck-Stuck and Shinwah, Pottawatomi great-grand-fathers, waited all morning, all afternoon, all morning, all afternoon for days, but never saw the Great White Father's son, his Secretary of the Interior. A thirty-five-million-dollar claim on Chicago's lake front land can wait in the vestibule. . . .

2

The Pottawatomi's story is a long story. Shortened, it says:

Under the treaty of 1833 the Pottawatomi were to cede to the United States all their land along the western shore of Lake Michigan, estimated at five million acres. In part payment of this cession the Government agreed to grant the Pottawatomi, Chippewa, and Ottawa living along the west shore, land west of the Mississippi, to be assigned by the President of the United States, and to be not less than five million acres. The Indians were to stay in their country three years before moving west. They were to have $170,000 for school purposes and blacksmith shops. About 50 delegates of the tribes journeyed to survey the Kansas land, to see if their people would be satisfied. Only about half of the delegates returned. Those that survived declared the land was not a fit country for Indians; it was flat prairie, while the Pottawatomi, Chippewa, and Ottawa were forest tribes and had lived in the woods for centuries.

However, at the conclusion of the three years of grace the Indian Bureau declared that a payment was to be made at a specific spot on a river bank. They told the Indians to bring their families. When the tribes arrived at the appointed place they were confronted with hundreds of soldiers, who crowded them into a massive steamboat. There was no payment. The soldiers threw the children onto the decks as though they were gunny sacks. The Indians were totally unprepared to take a long journey; they brought no store of food or water with them; in fact, they little suspected they were being " taken for a ride." The Pottawatomi died like poisoned rats. Most of them never walked off the boat. Of those that finally reached Kansas none were allowed to settle, for the land, as poor as it was, proved too valuable for Indians. They were chased about like stray dogs. Some became tired and moved into Canada.

Since 1833 the Government has failed to father the Pottawatomi, except for what supervision has been feebly attempted in the past twenty-odd years. All the while they were being herded about the country no schools were built for them, as was promised. It is no wonder that they today are one of the most backward of the tribes.

A Lutheran minister, E. O. Mostard, discovered that the Government owed the Pottawatomi $447,000, but the Indian Bureau did not acknowledge that fact for twenty years. When they finally did, the Indians' money was spent like running water. They bought forty acres of land for each Indian, and built him a home. Whites have thought this action of the Bureau to be fatherly and magnanimous. The Government, however, was spending the Indians' own money. Let us see how it was spent.

In the company of Dr. C. A. Harper, Wisconsin State Health Officer, I set out one afternoon in the late summer of 1930 to inspect the land bought and the homes erected

by the Indian Bureau for the Pottawatomi. Our guide
was the Rev. L. A. Dokken of Soperton, Wisconsin, a missionary of many years' experience, and was instructed by
us to select only typical cases. But this warning was unnecessary, for there was little variance between the homes.
We surveyed Indian land, bought by the Government, on
which it was possible for us to walk from one end to the
other and not once touch soil. We saw land through which
it is impossible to run a plow, so thick were the boulders.
We looked at one room shacks, housing two or three men
and women besides several children. At one mud-clinked
log cabin I noticed a shirt stuffed into a crack to keep out
the cold. The bedding on the beds looked foul, as did the
filth strewn about the floor of the shacks.

Reverend Dokken, after showing us a reservation of
hillsides, boulders, and brush, guided us to the home of
John Shawano, who was appointed chief of the band by
the Indian Bureau in 1914, to replace Dan Keshick.

On Shawano's farm, which we were informed is the best
of those purchased by the Government, the chief has been
able to cultivate only five out of his forty acres. His home,
also considered above the average, is feebly constructed,
almost to the danger point. The timber supports are placed
exceedingly far apart, the walls are too thin, and there are
large cracks in the ceilings. A narrow chimney provides a
potent fire source to ignite the enfeebled structure.

That has been the extent of the Indian Bureau's civilizing the Pottawatomi. They, naturally, have not become ac-
climated in the past twenty years. Now the Government in-
forms the Indians that they have no more annuities, that

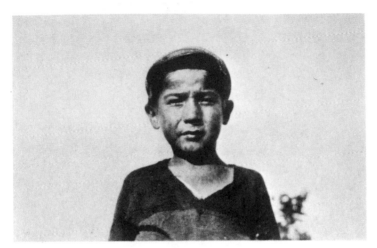

A TRACHOMA AFFLICTED SCHOOL BOY

FARM LAND BOUGHT BY A BENEVOLENT GUARDIAN

all their money has been expended on buying land and homes. But now that some of the Pottawatomi are still alive, what are they going to do?

Many are living on the hopes of realizing their claims against the Government, which would allow them to start life afresh. Many are dying with those hopes upon their mumbling lips. Old Joe Hale, an ancient Pottawatomi from Kansas, recently journeyed through several states in an effort to reach Daniel Shipherd of Carter, Wisconsin. Together they were to draw up the tribe's claims, based on their joint knowledge. But Old Joe Hale never saw Daniel Shipherd; 20 miles from his destination he halted, lowered his enfeebled body upon the roadside, and expired. The hopes of the Kansas Pottawatomi died with him.

But old Tom Keshick kept quietly circulating among his brothers until finally his petition was completed. One day Tom left his home, which the Government bought for him in a desolate quarter behind a swamp, and mailed a fat letter to Congressman George J. Schneider of Appleton. Six months later, on November 9, 1929, the Congressman wrote the following to Commissioner Charles J. Rhoads:

I am enclosing a letter dated May 9, 1929, addressed to me by Mr. Thomas Keshick of Laona, Wisconsin, with which he forwarded to me a petition signed by members of the Pottawatomie, Chippewa, and Ottawa tribe of Indians, requesting that compensation be awarded them in lieu of provisions made in various treaties with them . . .

Commissioner Rhoads answered on May 14, 1929:

The total amount due the 2,007 Wisconsin Pottawatomi was found to be $1,964,565.87 — $447,339 for those residing in the

United States and $1,517,226.87 for those living in Canada. The amount due those in the United States has been appropriated from time to time by Congress, but final action has not been taken with respect to the remainder of the claim. . . .

3

Old time powwow tonight. Every night. Soldiers' Field. Bright arc lights. Take a Michigan Avenue bus. See real Indians, imported from the north woods. Doing native dances. Seventy-five cents admission.

Next morning, three Indians sitting on camp stools. Sitting on Soldiers' Field outside army pup tents, stoically smoking. Tom Keshick. Chief Naw-Nee-Nuck-Stuck. Shinwah. They rise as one. "We go hunt Indian land."

Up the hot macadam road they tramp, jumping before the wheels of trucks and buses. Dodging traffic in their beaded buckskin leggings, left on from the night before. People stop and stare and wonder.

On a Michigan Avenue corner they halt, bewildered, holding their peace pipes in their hands. Up the deep canyons of brick and stone they look. Look at the tower of Wrigley, at the tower of the Tribune, rising like Keé-tchie Má-ni-dó, never-ending. Gas from rushing autos rises about them. Fills their nostrils. Fills their heads. The rushing autos make them dizzy, more dizzy than a week of dancing.

Slowly, they turn and retrace their steps.

XXXI

PASSING THE BUCK

1

THE Bad River in northern Wisconsin once held, in 1889, twenty-five million feet, jammed like tooth-picks. All moved in a roar. Moved and roared down the river, down, down to the quiet water in the bay.

It was Indian timber, every inch of the twenty-five million feet. Indians owned it, cut it, ran it, towed it along the lake to Ashland, Wisconsin, for cutting.

Then old Justus Stearns, in 1893, secured the exclusive right to operate lumber on the river, agreeing "to employ Indian labor in preference to other labor on equal terms."

Old man Stearns, why do you bring in carloads of Austrians, Poles, Finns, Swedes? Why does the population of Odanah leap from eleven to twenty-five hundred? Why are more white men living on the Indian reservation than Indians and their squaws? Why are white men working in the woods, and Indians sitting with their squaws?

Prices change from 1893 to 1903. But Stearns' prices do not change. Sixty-five cents per thousand for shingle timber. A dollar per thousand for green hemlock.

Charles Armstrong is a born headman. Charles Armstrong goes to Washington, showing prices from eight to sixteen dollars per thousand in the open market.

Charles Armstrong is an Indian. Indians love to roam the woods alone, looking for Keé-tchie Má-ni-dó, looking for some beauty. Wandering he spies a white man setting fire to green timber. He gives chase but loses sight of the fleeing figure in the green timber. Goes back, puts out the fire, and muses. Indians tell how Stearns' men take no care when they burn the rubbish in the woods.

I see 12,000 acres burning. Burning like matches in a safety box. Branches intertwining. Leaves touching. Burning like matches in a safety box. Two hundred million feet fallen and burnt. Burnt and rotting. Two hundred million feet.

Stearns buys burnt timber from sixty-five cents to two dollars a thousand. The Stearns Company has a large·payroll. It keeps Indians and calls them " chiefs." There are Moses White, Doolittle, Moccasin John, Silverman, John Shebaosh, or One-Arm-John. They go down the Bad River to condemn the burnt timber. Do you not know, Moses White, that the burnt acres are not on the Bad River? Do you not know, Moccasin John, that the burnt acres are on the White River? Do you not know, Shebaosh, One-Arm-John? Yes, they know. They all know how large is the Stearns' payroll. There are white tongues in red mouths.

I see the " chiefs " going down the river, condemning green for black, green for black. . . .

Charles Armstrong, do you remember that night we figured out that Washington bought the forests of northern Wisconsin and Minnesota for seven cents an acre through the treaty of 1837? Timber treaty. No, I have not forgotten.

I have not forgotten that the copper and iron lands were bought for seven and a half cents a share by the treaty of 1842. Mineral treaty.

Charles Armstrong, after we calculated that the great forests above Duluth were bought for eight cents an acre, you commented: " Liberal Washington. A one cent gain in 17 years."

Charles Armstrong, our old figures are like the Government's scraps of paper. Let me hear your story of today. Not the timber steals of last century. Tell me the story of today.

2

Charles Armstrong sitting in the office of the judiciary committee at Washington. Sitting alone in the outer office. Breathing after his fight with the claim agent.

Here I am . . . a humble being . . . representative of an ignorant race . . . trying to fight the brains of Wisconsin, the brains of Washington . . . legal brains, trained by years and money . . . mine is trained by the human heart of my people, by some God's sense of justice . . .

Worn. Tired. Weary. Charles Armstrong. The words of Senator Hoar, good words from Massachusetts, come like a cool wind at the close of battle, a wind that soothes: " If all the Indians in the United States had a representative like you, we would have less trouble. Instead we have white men, hired by the Government."

There are some kind white men. But few ever talk to Indians. It is to the misfortune of both.

Wisconsin claims the section sixteens in the reservation as State property for school purposes. Stearns Lumber Company backs the claim, for they have already removed the timber. But the sixteens are on the reservation, and Indians have their allotments on the sixteens. The Stearns Company has a large payroll, and its kept chiefs persuade Indians to move from their allotments. Others move in their places. Payroll chiefs . . . others . . . The Government Farmer accepts their filings. Accepts the filings of a Winnebago on Chippewa land, but rejects the Chippewas. Indian employees are not employed to watch the interests of the Indians when a lumber company's payroll is large. The judge decides against the claims. But the fight goes on. On and on. Charles Armstrong, like a dead leaf, haunts the United States Department of Justice. The Supreme Court decides. Decides for the Indian claims. Mary Zero, Winnebago, gets $23,000.

That is all. Nothing further. No timber scaled, no justice to the tribe. Two million dollars not repaid.

" Reverend Wheeler, good missionary, I can not get a lawyer in Wisconsin, Michigan, or Minnesota to right our claims. I can not get counsel in this pine range or in Washington. They are all tied up with lumber companies. Send us a lawyer from Illinois, where you live."

Comes a Swede. Short, fat, blondish. Never wears a collar. Yellow hair sticking from his chest, sticking over the dirty edges of his shirt. Lazy blond. Baby blue eyed Swede. Sits all day playing two-handed-rummy with an Indian woman. Teaches her how to play with the dirty thumbed cards. Teaches her how to play rummy in the day time. Teaches her how to love for him at night. Comes this man. Disbarred from Illinois courts, for actions "unprofessional, dishonorable, and criminal."[1] Comes to help the Indian. A fine lawyer with a fine record. Comes and sits.

First, he finds $9,000 on deposit since 1896 in the Wisconsin treasury to the credit of the Chippewas. Tries to have an act passed, giving Indians that money. Picking off the little things. Letting the big one go. Two million dollars. Letting it go.

Attorney-at-law Daniel Grady, Regent of the University of Wisconsin, is appointed by the State to present the Indians' and State's claims against the Government. Grady details him to make an estimate of the timber removed from the sixteens.

This short, fat, blondish man, wearing no collar, pushes himself over stump dotted wastes, scaling the ghosts of giant trunks, scaling stump heads. Government Scaler

---

[1] See Northeastern Law Reporter. Vol. 153. P. 348. — took the lifetime savings of a 52-year-old washerwoman, Miss Emma McWhoster, amounting to $1,025 — "money which he collected as her attorney and has failed to pay to her on her demand." He also took $110 from Mrs. Morrison, another client. The court charged him with "neglect, a failure to attend to the business which he had undertaken, and a disregard of his duty to his client." He was held guilty of professional misconduct warranting disbarment.

Burns follows the blond and his scaler. On a forty acre tract the Indian office had given credit of three hundred thousand feet removed. They find better than eleven million feet removed. Indian office reports one hundred thousand dollars due Indians. Grady puts the debt at two million.

Mr. L. K. Baker, President of the Stearns Lumber Company, becomes interested and visits Odanah. Grady gets a letter: " I think we are getting too much information for his comfort just now."

The tops of the trees are brightening. Soon the edge of the sun will be seen. A day is dawning.

Suddenly attorney-at-law Grady orders a halt. The Swede tramps out of the woods, Burns following. In the middle of the scaling they scale no more. The ways of some white men are strange.

Mr. Grady is a highly respected gentleman. The fact that the State of Wisconsin appointed him to protect its interests in the Bad River timber case substantiates the opinion held by that State's citizens. Politically he has been aligned with such Progressives as Senator Robert La Follette, Jr., and Congressman James Frear, who have fought the Indian's battle in both Houses. Representative Frear, incidently, was the first Congressman to take up his cudgels in behalf of the Indian. Mr. Grady's action regarding the scaling has been a puzzling point to friends of the Indian.

Over two billion feet have been cut from 115,000 acres of Indian land. The Government — some government — State or Federal — owes empty-bellied Indians two million dollars. Both are responsible. The Federal for not being a capable, careful guardian. By the negligence of its protection it is guilty. The State by the removal of the timber. Allowing Stearns and other companies to cut two billion feet of Indian timber. Two million dollars owed to the Indians by someone . . . owed . . . by someone . . .

From what is scaled comes the story. Let it speak alone. Let it argue for justice to all stumps. The nameless stumps not scaled. In one section the stumps say nearly 2,500,000 feet were cut. The books show 185,000 feet were paid for. Another section of stumps cry: A million feet cut. The books whisper: sixty thousand paid for. On the sections surveyed the stumps shout that 3,763,290 feet have never been legally purchased.

This is a sample. A very tasty sample. For a dollar an acre every reservation can be scaled. Finish scaling the sixteens. Scale every acre. For we have a sample. A very tasty sample.

3

Why was the order made to cease scaling? Why have not the remaining four sections been scaled?

Before the Senate Investigating Committee Daniel Grady expressed himself, twice verbally and twice in writing, to that effect " that large quantities of timber have been removed from the reservation, for which no compensation has been made to the Indians."

Very well on the obvious point that the Indian has been wronged. But on the question of responsibility for the robbery Mr. Grady is not so energetic a crusader. " I went as far in my investigation as my authority directed me to ascertain to what extent the State of Wisconsin was liable, but in obtaining this data I had to depend more or less on the figures obtained by Mr. Oliver M. Olson," he says in the record. Mr. Grady is positive that " somebody got the timber and did not pay for it." He believes that the Federal Government should stand for the loss, and thus let the State of Wisconsin go scot-free. In fact, he recommends " that the State of Wisconsin ought, through its legislature, request immediate and appropriate action on the part of the Government."

While Mr. Grady has been clamoring for Governmental action, certain facts have been known, which disclose the financial sufferings of the Indians. First, everyone knew that approximately seventy-five million feet were " lost to the Indians because burnt timber was not taken care of at the time it was burnt and killed, but it was left on the ground and worms got into it and it was never cut." Secondly, that the trespass on six section sixteens and swamp lands have been estimated at twenty million feet. Thirdly, that the Stearns Lumber Company, in all its transactions, " had the coöperation of the Indian agent and the Indian farmer, both of whom were silent partners of L. K. Baker in the lumber business." Fourthly, that Superintendent Everest was handed a check from the Stearns Lumber Company " for the sum of $23,885.77, and referred to by him as a ' Christmas present entirely unexpected.' " And fifthly, that the Bad River Indians are destitute and " are going to be poorer and harder up as time goes on." [2]

[2] See Senate Investigating Committee's Hearings, Part Five. 1929. Pp. 1891–1911.

In other words, everyone knew how the diseased, poverty-stricken Indian was robbed, who robbed him, and how much was stolen. With a heart overflowing with compassion for the suffering of fellow creatures, Grady wrote former Commissioner Charles H. Burke, charging two million dollars to the Indian Bureau. Mr. Burke retaliated by stating that the State of Wisconsin was more implicated and responsible than the Federal Government. The two million dollar charge was boomeranged into Mr. Grady's solar plexus.

I have read their correspondence in the files of the Indian Office at Washington. Burke on March 31, 1928, wrote:

You are aware that by the decision of the United States Supreme Court in the case of United States v. J. S. Stearns Lumber Company (245 U. S., 436), the title to Sections 16 was confirmed to the Indians and if the state still holds funds derived from the sale of land or timber within Sections 16 it would appear that such amount should be paid to the Indians . . . The Office would greatly appreciate a statement from you as to what the records of the state of Wisconsin show with respect to funds derived from Sections 16 and timber thereon and from so-called swamp lands or timber sold therefrom.

Daniel Grady, under date of April 2, 1928, replied in this fashion:

I have your letter of March 31 in reference to the claim of the Indians of the Bad River Reservation against the State of Wisconsin. I have heard of this claim being asserted, but have never been able to ascertain the facts in connection with it. However, I shall endeavor immediately to ascertain just what the record shows and shall be pleased to advise you as promptly as possible.

Nevertheless, Grady's sense of immediacy and promptness has not allowed him to advise the Indian Office on a matter with which he had been intimately familiar for over three years, ever since his appointment on February 9, 1925. Another three years have now passed and he has not yet replied to the Bureau's retaliatory charge, nor will he apparently make a reply.

Nothing has been done since. By his silence Mr. Grady has saved the State of Wisconsin two million dollars. By his sudden and complete refusal to further fight the Indian's case, he has proven a valuable citizen to his state. But how about the Indian?

4

The last time I sat with Charles Armstrong there was a silence hanging over us. There was nothing to speak of. Hope died still-born soon after its conception.

Charles Armstrong has seen false dawns. His heart renewed its beat when Reverend Wheeler sent a lawyer from Illinois. When Wisconsin appointed Daniel Grady its joint counselor with the Indians. When Grady announced the debt at two millions. And when Grady charged Burke.

But now Charles Armstrong's heart is feebly murmuring. It is eating itself out at the thought that, if his people had not been molested, they could have methodically continued cutting their timber themselves, taking 256 years and three months to make one complete circle. With pine growing 41 inches in diameter in 42 years, their logging would go on indefinitely. Dreams, idle dreams.

We sat in silence. Finally he spoke, and his speech was slow.

"I have seen lawyers come and go," he said. "I have seen scalers come and go; Congressmen, members of women's clubs and welfare groups — all have come and gone."

He ceased talking. The uncrowned chief of the dwindled band looked directly at me and said simply: "You are our last hope. I think you will not fail us."

VII
CONCLUSION

XXXII

WHAT IS THE SOLUTION?

THE Indian problem is the white man. " It has been to the everlasting disgrace of the Indian," Will Rogers has said, " that he allowed the Mayflower to land."

When sympathetic, intelligent administrators are placed in charge of the Government's wards, three-quarters of the perplexities and so-called problems will automatically disappear. Graft and corruption will exaporate only when honest men are employed. Of the present Indian Bureau personnel I believe that fifty per cent should be dismissed outright, twenty-five per cent placed on probation, and the remaining quarter kissed on both cheeks and gently led into a spacious pasture where they might spend the rest of their days free from nightmares.

" If it isn't the overhead it's the underhand expense," one Yankton Indian told me, which summarizes the need for a complete overhauling of the Bureau.

After the elementary correction of the personnel there remains the question of the Bureau's policy and attitude. " When will we learn," said Matthew Arnold, in an address advocating Irish home rule, " that what attaches people to us is the spirit we are of, and not the machinery we employ? " We have made the Indian an alien in his own land. I have had the only one hundred per cent Americans in the United States tell me that their spirits are so thoroughly subjugated that they are actually afraid to call their bodies their own. Did Goethe have Indians in mind when he exclaimed: " Here and nowhere is thine America! "

How, then, can we reincarnate the Indian's dead soul? John Collier's " way out for Indians " is as follows:

Abolish the guardianship of the United States over the Indian person. It is a survival from times when the Indians were enemies or prisoners confined under martial law on reservations serving as prison compounds.

Preserve the Federal guardianship over Indian property individual and tribal. Regulate that guardianship by statute; make it accountable to the courts; provide for its termination, whether for tribes or individuals, in the discretion of the federal court or through action by Congress after recommendation by the court. So amend the allotment law and other laws, as to permit joint or corporate landholdings and industrial enterprise by partnerships or tribes. Modern credit facilities to be extended to Indians; property and earning capacity, on initiative of the Indian borrowers, and after approval by the property guardian subject to court review, to be hypothecable against the loans. The spurious reimbursable indebtedness to be remitted through act of Congress.

Comprehensive Federal court jurisdiction to be established over civil and criminal matters on reservations; the court to be empowered in its discretion to recognize tribal custom and authority in matters internal to the tribes.

Transfer, with minor exceptions, all responsibility for Indian health work, education, social service, agricultural guidance and welfare to the states; the federal appropriations of tax-raised funds and Indian trust funds for these uses to be transferred to the states under contracts and to be supplemented through state appropriations.[1]

Collier's " way out," with a few exceptions, is comprehensive. I add that the pretentious, inhumane boarding schools should be dissolved into small reservation day schools. Such a dissolution would enable the children to live at home with their parents and experience a wholesome, normal childhood. This reëstablishment of family life, this preservation of the home, would greatly lessen the present unwarranted immorality. Today, however, the boarding schools are more over-crowded, more numerous, and more destructive than ever; they are forcibly taking children younger than before and in so doing are over-riding state statutes and the Constitution.

A final necessary reform is the question of Indian law. Mr. A. A. Grorud, investigator for the Senate Subcommittee on Indian Affairs, has handed me the following statement:

[1] *The Survey Graphic*, January 1, 1927. P. 455.

The Indian Bureau's weapon for chastising the Indians is that peculiar body of statutes called Indian law.

Indian law places the Indian wholly at the mercy of the Indian Bureau on the theory that the Bureau is a virtuous and industrious guardian. American politics make the Indian Bureau not a guardian but an exploiter and betrayer.

When the Indian tries to go into court against his guardian, the Indian Bureau, Indian law fixes it that the culprit and defendant, namely, the Indian Bureau, shall appoint the Indian's lawyer and control his actions. This complete supervision of all litigations must be restricted.

When the Indian is thrown into jail by an Indian Bureau employee, his appeal lies to the Secretary of the Interior, which is another name for the Indian Bureau.

Shall an Indian son or daughter be permitted to inherit the parents' money or land? The Indian Bureau decides, and if the son or daughter appeals, the appeal is conducted to the Indian Bureau. If the decision is erroneous there is no appeal or redress. On the other hand, if a previous decision is not to the liking of the Secretary of the Interior, he, according to a December 11, 1930, statement of O. H. Graves, Assistant to the Solicitor, " notwithstanding the decisions of former Secretaries, may reopen, revise, redecide, and entirely control its final disposition." In other words an Indian never knows when his estate is settled.

Shall an Indian child be torn away from parents and home and locked up for ten years in a boarding school under conditions of endemic disease and child labor, while his religion and language are effaced? The Indian Bureau decides and if the child or parent wants to appeal, he can appeal to the Secretary of the Interior, namely, the Indian Bureau.

Shall Indians be permitted to form themselves into organizations, whether for mutual aid or political action or for religious communion? The Indian Bureau decides and if its decision is not obeyed, the Bureau tramples the organization out of life. The Indian Bureau actually maintains regulations which define Indian religions as Indian offenses punishable by fine and imprisonment.

The Indian Bureau banks the Indian's money. It holds the check book. It pays out what it wants to pay out and can demand that the money be spent exactly as wanted by the Indian Superintendent. It may account for the money or not as it chooses and in numerous cases it does not choose.

And meanwhile, the Indian Bureau, through manipulating patronage and funds, exerts a dominant power with Congress, and steadily multiplies the statutes which decade by decade rivet the chains more completely on the Indians' limbs.

The Supreme Court has countenanced the atrocity as a whole by ruling that Indian matters are subject to the political branch of the Government and are not reviewable by the courts on the substantial issues. The Indians are the only people in the United States who for practical purposes are denied access to the courts and the protection of the Constitution.

And today, as before, the Indian Bureau and Interior Department are standing like rock against all efforts to bring Indian law into line with American traditions, constitutional conceptions or ideas of democracy, individual responsibility and cultural freedom.

Senator Elmer Thomas of Oklahoma issued me a statement which discloses the relationship of Congress to the Indian Bureau in this matter of reforming Indian law:

Under the present administrative set-up, the Indian Bureau is presumed to advise Congress as to the legislation necessary to enable the Federal Government to discharge properly its responsibility as the guardian of some three hundred odd thousand of our Indian citizens.

Yet, after one hundred and fifty years of Federal supervision, we find many of our Indians of today are not developed to that point where they can successfully compete with the white population in the struggle for a livelihood and existence. (This legislative-appropriative control keeps pork-seeking Congressmen favorable to the Bureau.)

The reason for this status of the Indian lies in the deplorable fact that Commissioner Rhoads' legislative achievement is actually below that of Burke's. Two hundred good appointments will not compensate for Rhoads' lack of a constructive legislative policy; by both his inactivity and warped activity he has succeeded in blocking and wet-blanketing his own suggested reforms. In December, 1929, he wrote four letters to Congress, outlining a new, revolutionized body of laws which would free the Indian while yet preserving Federal responsibility for Indian welfare. Those letters were nationally broadcasted —

they were a grandiloquent gesture. Rhoads contradicted his own legislative remedies in a letter of May 5, 1930, which has been placed in the Congressional Record. " I do not know of any law or regulation," he wrote, " which restricts the civil rights of Indians to a greater extent than in the case of anybody else for the common good."

Rhoads and Wilbur have received " an accursed system " from their predecessors; they, too, are passing it on to their successors, unregenerated, unaltered.

Former Governor Alfred E. Smith published his pledges to the Indians when he was running for the Presidency in 1928. Aside from any irrelevant political implications which those pledges might have borne, they are nevertheless worthy of enumeration here as a summary of the necessities which must be accomplished:

The Indians shall have an accounting for all their moneys.

Their moneys shall be used according to their wishes and not otherwise.

The control of the Indian Bureau over Indian funds and Indian life shall be curbed.

The Indians shall be given schools at their homes.

The Indians shall be given ALL THE CONSTITU-TIONAL RIGHTS. This means:

No more putting Indians in jail by the superintendent.

No more interference with Indian religious observances.

A day in court for all Indians in every matter of life and property.

No more confiscation of Indian property.

Specifically, how can these solutions and suggestions of Mr. Collier, Mr. Grorud, and Governor Smith, along with dozens of others, be achieved? The answer is purely political. So we were informed over five decades ago by Helen Hunt Jackson, in her flaming *Century of Dishonor:*

> There is but one hope of righting this wrong. It lies in an appeal to the heart and conscience of the American people. What the people demand, Congress will do. It has been — to our shame be it spoken — at the demand of part of the people that all these wrongs have been committed, these treaties broken, these robberies done, by the Government.

Success is possible. The Indian Bureau is not invulnerable; it has been pierced on several instances, which, unfortunately, neither dislodged nor altered the "accursed system." Nevertheless, the battles of the past ten years have proven that reforms can be achieved. In 1926, for example, it was a tremendous victory to have secured title for the Indians to their twenty-two million acres of executive reservations. It was a hard-fought, well-earned victory to have temporarily preserved the life of twenty New Mexico Pueblos. It was a well-deserved victory to have defeated Cramton on his Indian record when he ran for reëlection in September, 1930; nevertheless, while in the last session of the Seventy-First Congress he successfully blocked constructive Indian legislation, and in the matter of appropriations he succeeded in stretching his dead hand as far into the future as 1932. It was a momentous victory to have so accumulated the indictment against Burke and Meritt that they were forced to retire as heads of the Indian Bureau, even though President Hoover replaced them with the men he did. And it is a victory that these successors are compelled at least to *claim* they have reversed the old order, when in practice they are for the most part floundering amid familiar yet disastrous crags.

Effort has paid. Future successes only await the energies of a Congress whose conscience has been stricken by indignant constituents.

XXXIII

MASSACRE

IT was late afternoon when I came upon Wounded Knee. I had been driving hard, and I approached the scene a trifle weary, but somewhat excited over the prospect of viewing that famous spot, so prominent as a final page in the sad history of the Sioux. I walked into the Wounded Knee General Store, sat down in an obscure corner, and recollected the history of that tragedy.

Short Bull, Scatters-Them, and Kicking Bear, three Indians of the old spirit school, journeyed into the Rockies of eastern Oregon some time in 1890, to commune with a messiah, who they believed was coming to lead the Indians out of their bondage, their starvation, and all their misery into a happy hunting ground on earth. When the three returned from their pilgrimage Chief Big Foot's band planned to hold the much revered Ghost Dance, so that all might commune with the spirit of the messiah. The white man, however, had decreed that the Indians could not congregate and stage their religious festival. Colonel Sumner set out to prevent Big Foot's sacred Ghost Dance, but the Chief's band evaded him, and left the Cheyenne Reservation. They escaped southward over the Bad Lands, with four battalions from the Seventh Cavalry in full pursuit. Inspired by an ancient religious zeal, that had been lying dormant for years, they managed to worm themselves through a pass, leave the desolate, barren Bad Lands, and come to camp at Wounded Knee. In the meanwhile General Forsythe and Major White, with all the battalions of the Seventh Cavalry, surrounded Big Foot's camp on the Wounded Knee Creek. The old Chief willingly surrendered. He was not seeking a battle; he was only trying to find some forgotten corner of the earth where his band might worship unmolested.

The soldiers of the Seventh were still celebrating Christmas when Big Foot surrendered. All battalions were encamped together, and there was much carousing between old army friends. Many became too drunk to walk. The morning of December 29, 1890, found them still boozing. One inebriated soul conceived the brilliant idea of calling on the ailing, sick-a-bed Big Foot. A dozen staggered to the old Chief's tent, and stood outside beckoning the infirm sage to come outside for a conference. In the meanwhile, battalion squads under the direction of officers had begun to search the tepees for weapons. Big Foot managed to stand and creep to the door of his tepee in answer to the drunken shouts of his captors. The moment he stepped outside 12 bullets entered his body, and he crumpled to the frozen ground with a sad, sick smile on his face.

This shooting immediately unloosened a torrent of army bullets from the neighboring hills. Soldiers stationed on those commanding summits heard that the Indians were attacking the battalions. Immediately their Gatling guns were pouring lead into the tepees below. The soldiers, detailed to search the Indians for weapons, were caught under their own unrelenting crossfire. The Indians were too surprised to respond, nor could they climb the steep summits and attack the spitting guns with tomahawks.

This " battle " continued for one hour and in that brief space the passion for killing completely possessed the soldiers on the surrounding hills. With an ever-increasing fury they shouted drunkenly, lustily as they rushed about their Gatling guns, shooting bullets into the milling mass of toppling tepees, screaming squaws, screeching children, and waving flanks of warriors and soldiers, all heaped below. Suddenly their slaughtering ceased. All was quiet, except for the panting of the exhausted slaughterers. No Indian stirred. Forty-five of them lay dead in one heap, and a hundred others were scattered about on the granite-like soil. Of the trapped soldiers, two officers were wounded, 25 privates were killed, and 33 wounded, of whom three died later. Only one soldier was killed at the hands of an Indian. Captain Wallace of Troop K, Ninth Cavalry, died with a tomahawk sprouting from his forehead. But one hundred and thirty Indians lay scattered on the frozen ground.

That night it snowed, and countless white flakes came down from above and covered the bodies of the slain Indians, men, women, and children, with a white, holy blanket. The heavens had rung down a celestial curtain upon the scene of the tragedy. . . .

As I sat in the Wounded Knee General Store, recalling this meager history, an old soldier tottered into the building. He introduced himself to Roy Thomas, the proprietor, as D. E. Babb of Red Oak, Iowa, " a soldier in the Seventh who was present at the battle." During the past forty years he had never returned to the scene, but he had come on that day. When asked if he were going to survey the battlefield, located behind the store, he answered in the negative, adding that he never would if he could help it. Instead, he had returned to tell tourists that " it was the dirtiest fighting I have ever seen."

After forty years his conscience became slightly eased, with that simple confession.

Accompanied by Edison Glenn, an intelligent Indian, I set out at sundown for the battlefield. As I walked I recalled the words of Frank Goings of Pine Ridge: " After the Battle of Wounded Knee all ambition was taken out of us. We have never since been able to regain a foothold, and so we haven't progressed in farming."

I saw the circle of ridges on which were stationed the Gatling guns. They completely commanded the small valley below.

" My father helped dig the grave and bury the Indians," Edison Glenn said, as we walked toward the small cemetery. " The soldiers refused to bury the dead, and the slain lay in the snow until January, four or five days later, until some Indians were found who would dig a grave. In the meanwhile the bodies froze stiff."

The Christmas spirit lingered on.

We stood together on the top of a knoll, before a large, cement-encased plot of earth. At one end a modest monument had been erected by Indian relatives, bearing the names of those who had fallen. Unconsciously I removed my hat. A silence deeper than the combined deaths of the one hundred and thirty buried there had settled upon the grave.

My mind wandered, and I wondered which action of the Government was more merciful — this one-hour massacre, in which the suffering and misery were brief, in which the weariness of living was quickly extinguished and all the pains of life were snuffed out. Or today's slow starving, heart-breaking existence, today's gradual dissolution through disease, poverty, and hopelessness. Today's slow, torturing massacre.

My Indian companion turned to me, and we stood facing one another at sundown, beside the one grave of the slain. As though he had read my thought, his lips spoke. " Yes," he said, quietly, " it is better to be killed."

Slowly, in the gathering twilight, we walked down the knoll. Suddenly my mind throbbed with the pregnant challenge: It is my duty as an American citizen — it is every citizen's duty — to launch myself into the positive struggle of placing the living Indian on the respectable, human plane of a self-sufficing, culture-effusing American.